Naming
Our Sins

Naming Our Sins

HOW RECOGNIZING THE SEVEN DEADLY VICES CAN RENEW THE SACRAMENT OF RECONCILIATION

JANA M. BENNETT AND DAVID CLOUTIER, EDITORS

The Catholic University of America Press
Washington, DC

Copyright © 2019
The Catholic University of America Press
All rights reserved
The paper used in this publication meets the minimum requirements of American National Standards for Information Science—Permanence of Paper for Printed Library Materials, ANSI Z39.48-1984.
∞

Library of Congress Cataloging-in-Publication Data available from the Library of Congress.

ISBN: 978-0-8132-3163-1

Table of Contents

Acknowledgments vii

1. Introduction
*The Sacrament of Reconciliation and the Challenge
of Naming Sins*
JANA M. BENNETT AND DAVID CLOUTIER 1

2. Gluttony
BETH HAILE 29

3. Lust
JASON KING 52

4. Greed
NICOLE M. FLORES 73

5. Sloth
JULIE HANLON RUBIO 89

6. Anger
WILLIAM C. MATTISON III 106

7. Envy
DANA L. DILLON 126

8. Pride
CHARLES C. CAMOSY 146

9. Confessions of a Priest
The Unused Potential of the Rite of Penance
FR. JAMES DONOHUE, CR 168

10. Reflections from a Priest
Reconciliation as Ruptured Relationships Restored
FR. SATISH JOSEPH 181

Bibliography 199
Contributors 211
Index 215

Acknowledgments

As with any work like this, so many people have provided help along the way. First and foremost, we want to thank our wonderful group of authors. When we sent out invitations to contribute to this collection, we were so fortunate that everyone we asked accepted with enthusiasm. All the authors have been great about working with us throughout the editing process. This has turned out better than we might have hoped, largely because they have all stepped up to the task so well. Many of the authors have been or are part of the academic group blog, catholicmoraltheology.com, which the two of us have been privileged to edit since its inception in 2011. The collegiality fostered there (and in other venues) has certainly seeped into this work!

We also want to thank others who have helped, especially John Martino at The Catholic University of America Press. John suggested the possibility of such a volume and then provided supportive feedback all along the way. And to give the highest compliment authors can give to editors, he's just been great to work with logistically! We also thank the anonymous peer reviewers for the Press, whose critiques and suggestions showed the value of the peer review process and improved the collection in numerous ways. Earlier versions of a few chapters, including our opening chapter contextualizing the problems we have in naming sins, were presented at a session of the 2016 College Theology Society annual conference, and we are grateful for the discussion there. We also want to thank our graduate assistants, Colleen Campbell, Tyler Campbell, Catherine Moon, and Melissa Wass, who helped with details. Finally, we've been grateful to each other for the friendship and collegiality that sustains projects like this one. The community of Iredell House is a gift that keeps on giving.

Jana M. Bennett and David Cloutier

Chapter 1

Introduction

The Sacrament of Reconciliation and the
Challenge of Naming Sins

JANA M. BENNETT & DAVID CLOUTIER

I N   P O P U L A R   M E D I A , you know you're dealing with Catholics
when you see a confessional. The typical scene is a movie or TV show
where a Catholic character is in some kind of trouble, or has some
nagging spiritual question. The response is to find a priest in a confessional
box and talk about the problem.

The confessional is an easy way to identify Catholics in part because
the sacraments, reconciliation included, are central to Catholic identity. In
popular culture, about the only thing more likely to indicate Catholicism
than an image of the sacraments is a priest in a collar or a nun in a habit.
But the sacraments' importance is not simply a scene-setter in popular
culture; it is clear in the authoritative teaching of the tradition. Vatican II
insisted on the importance of "full, conscious, and active participation" in
the liturgical life of the Church, centrally oriented around the sacraments.[1]
Catholics are urged to "with great eagerness have frequent recourse" to the
sacraments in order to "nourish the Christian life" and "build up the Body
of Christ."[2]

However, does the reality match the imagery and theology? Often it does
not. Above all, the omnipresence of the confessional in popular imagery is
in stark contrast to the plunge in the practice of the sacrament. For typical
American Catholics, regular participation in the sacrament of reconciliation is strikingly absent from peoples' lives, let alone featured in any person's
serious wrestling with problems. A 2008 authoritative survey from Georgetown University's Center for Applied Research in the Apostolate (CARA),

---

1. Vatican Council II, Dogmatic Constitution *Sacrosanctum Concilium* (December 4, 1963), 14.
2. *Sacrosanctum Concilium*, 59.

the premier group examining Catholic practices and attitudes, shows only 14% of Catholics who attend reconciliation more than once a year, and another 12% who report going only once a year. About three-quarters of Catholics go "less than once a year" or "never."[3] Further, these numbers are somewhat inflated by the 42% of Catholics who grew up before the Second Vatican Council and who have much more of a habit of attending reconciliation than younger Catholics. More pre-Vatican II Catholics report yearly or better attendance, but as the generations progress, the numbers are worse. So much for "active participation."

Why is reconciliation so neglected? When we look just at the doctrinal words that tell us what the sacrament is meant to be, it seems that reconciliation should be quite attractive to people. For example, we read, "The whole power of the sacrament of Penance consists in restoring us to God's grace and joining us with him in an intimate friendship."[4] Being face-to-face with God's gracious, befriending power might seem a positive point. In addition, the theme of mercy and forgiveness is one that tends to attract people to the Church. We can see the warm reception people have given to Pope Francis as evidence of this, for the pope has been focused intently on the need for mercy. Given that the sacrament of reconciliation is the central ritual for encountering mercy, why is reconciliation avoided? Why miss a chance to receive mercy through a tangible ritual?

One simple answer is that mercy isn't what people most often experience in the confessional, especially because the ritual requires their own reflection on and naming of their sins. While the Catechism notes the various names given to the sacrament—reconciliation, penance, forgiveness, which our authors use interchangeably—the still-common name "confession" is appropriate "since the disclosure or confession of sins to a priest is an essential element of this sacrament."[5] And "confession" may still indicate our biggest difficulty with the sacrament: how and why do we *name* our sins? In this essay, we will first talk about how people encountered the sacrament of reconciliation in the mid-twentieth century, up to the major church council known as the Second Vatican Council (1962–65). We will compare that mid-twentieth-century experience to peoples' present-day experiences of the sacrament. What we shall suggest is that a sense of mercy

---

3. The Center for Applied Research in the Apostolate (CARA), *Sacraments Today: Belief and Practice among U.S. Catholics Center for Applied Research in the Apostolate*, edited by Mark M. Gray and Paul M. Perl (Washington, DC: Georgetown University, April 2008), 57. See especially "The Sacrament of Reconciliation"; https://cara.georgetown.edu/reconciliation.pdf.

4. *The Catechism of the Catholic Church*, 2nd ed., (Citta del Vaticano: Libreria Editrice Vaticana, 2000), no. 1468. Hereafter *CCC* followed by the paragraph number.

5. *CCC*, no. 1424. Paragraph 1423 gives the names of the sacrament that precede the quotation.

was missing. Combined with that, however, there is now a somewhat desperate sense of not knowing what to say in the confessional. In order to receive mercy, a person needs to know what they've done wrong. But as we shall see, people report not knowing how to *name* their sins, even though they also report knowing that they do sinful things that separate them from the love of God.

Following our discussion of some of the history and background, we will reflect on Pope Francis and his emphasis on mercy. We especially look at the paradox of people loving Francis's message of mercy but failing to embrace his clear directive to go to confession. Perhaps it is because Francis criticizes those who approach Christian living as a matter of keeping or breaking rules. But if he criticizes that approach, what is one supposed to do in the confessional, where the code-breaking aspect of naming sins still seems the obvious if unattractive way to go about "making a confession"?

We will conclude this essay with some thoughts on what it would take to renew our ability to name our sins in a meaningful and pertinent way, as a prelude to the essays on sins that make up the rest of this book. Naming sins is a particularly important task for moral theologians, whom we've gathered as contributors for this collection. The discipline of Catholic moral theology has its roots in serving the sacrament of reconciliation. The first moral theologians were priests, pastors who wanted to help hurting people who showed up in their confessionals, and so the manuals they developed were meant to help other priests hear confessions accurately. Moral theologians today tend to be lay people, and thus address different questions: how to use Scripture to consider social problems like poverty, racism, and abortion; or how to help people reflect on use of money; or how to live the Church's teachings on sexuality. These contemporary questions are usually connected to questions about sin in some way, but they are disconnected from the cleric-driven, confession-focused manuals that moral theologians used for centuries prior to Vatican II. Sometimes lay moral theologians raise these issues in a way that makes clear their implications for a parish social justice committee (or the voting booth), but not their implications for the naming of sins in the sacrament of reconciliation. Thus, the overall point of this collection is to remake that connection: the moral theologian's task of helping people name individual sins needs to be restored, though in ways distinctive from dominant pre-Vatican II notions.

The Mid-Twentieth-Century Story about the Confessional

The Second Vatican Council can be a helpful dividing line for thinking about peoples' encounters with the sacrament of reconciliation. Although this sacrament has a long and varied history, the Catholic practice of confession was relatively stable in the West from the Council of Trent (1545–63) until Vatican II. In this "Tridentine" model, early and mid-twentieth century Catholics identified sins as particular actions. The revised Baltimore Catechism of 1941 states: "Actual sin is any wilful thought, word, deed, or omission contrary to the law of God."[6] Accordingly, in the confessional, the penitent would confess the proverbial laundry list of sins. Historian Jay Dolan writes "Sins, 'like a mountain lie heavy upon' people, and confession was necessary not only because it absolved one of sin, but also because it relieved that 'anxiety of mind' brought on by sin."[7] In the pre-Vatican II confessional, the sacrament would be linked especially to "sexual sins and God's judgement" on children of God. The priest, acting *in persona Christi*, was imaged as the judgmental (though ultimately compassionate) father of naughty children. The priest-penitent relationship was one of father-child, which was known directly in the language spoken to the penitent: "my child."[8] One author notes that young children being catechized pre-Vatican II "learned to list their venial sins in number and kind, and feared committing a mortal sin, which would cause God to turn away from them, even though clergy and catechists generally agreed that youngsters were virtually incapable of these types of transgressions. Nevertheless, most religious educators at that time agreed that children needed to understand the dire consequences of sin and get in the habit of practicing the sacrament so that they would partake of it when they did commit a serious transgression."[9] People asked to recount their experiences of confession in the pre-Vatican II period describe feeling "humiliated rather than cleansed," and no one volunteered a fond memory of their own confessions.[10] Power operated in the hands of priests, on behalf of a stern God-Most-High.

The contrasting story after the Second Vatican Council is that the priest/penitent relationship is meant to be more of a relationship between Christian brothers and sisters rather than the angry Father/scared child motif. For children who grew up without any knowledge or experience of

---

6. "Baltimore Catechism," Catholic News Agency, accessed May 31, 2016.

7. Jay Dolan, *The American Catholic Experience* (Notre Dame, IN: University of Notre Dame Press, 1993), 228–29.

8. David Coffey, *The Sacrament of Reconciliation* (Collegeville, MN: Liturgical Press, 2001), 96.

9. Susan B. Ridgely, "Decentering Sin: First Reconciliation and the Nurturing of Post-Vatican II Catholics," *Journal of Religion* 86, no. 4 (2006), 606–34, at 614. It should be noted that the language of "causing God to turn away" is misleading, insofar as such sins involve a turning away on the part of the sinner, not of God.

10. Ridgely, "Decentering Sin," 615–16.

a pre-Vatican II church, the encounter with both sin and the sacrament was very different than for their parents and grandparents. Post-Vatican II sacrament formation has heavily emphasized reconciliation in the parable of the Forgiving Father/Prodigal Son (Luke 15:11–32), [11] which in turn means an emphasis on the power of God to restore relationships and celebration of that reconciliation. This is an important and beneficial shift in emphasis on the whole, but it does also raise particular questions about the practice of the sacrament, including naming sins.

For example, Susan Ridgely describes a study she did of children receiving their first reconciliation and communion in the early 2000s. The children focused far less on sin—indeed, often did not really know what to say. One of Ridgely's study subjects observed, "It wasn't scary. You only have to say one bad thing [you've done] and three or four good things."[12] Others stated that they couldn't remember any sins or couldn't think of what to say. Interestingly, the lack of specificity was a reason they disliked confession: it seemed impossible to come up with a way to name their sins.

Children are not alone in not knowing what to say. Sacramental theologian David Coffey describes how Catholics often say "I don't go to confession anymore because I don't know what to say."[13] Coffey's own opinion is that this is in large part because Catholics do not often receive instruction in the sacrament after they've made their first reconciliation in second grade. That is, as people grow in their faith, they are not also taught to grow in their concepts of sin.

Coffey argues that the contemporary ritual for the sacrament focuses on spiritual maturity far more than did the pre-Vatican II rite because "sins are no longer items to be put on a list, but manifestations of a discerned relationship of this person to God."[14] The new rite emphasizes that confessor and penitent "are present to each other in a way that is normal for a human encounter"[15] though grilles are to be provided for those who desire it. God's power was once represented by a judgmental father-child relationship on the part of the priest and penitent, but the new rite reimages the relationship to brothers and sisters in Christ.

---

11. Numerous religious education programs make use of this central scripture, including Catechesis of the Good Shepherd. Regina Marie Fisher describes a celebration focused on the Forgiving Father in "First Reconciliation: Renewal of our Baptism" *Catechist* 32 (January 1999): 40–41, cited in Ridgely, "Decentering Sin," 607.

12. Ridgely, "Decentering Sin," 630.

13. Coffey, *Reconciliation*, 100.

14. Coffey, *Reconciliation*, 106.

15. Coffey, *Reconciliation*, 107. See also 95–100.

The changes in the sacrament reflect changes in how the Church understands sin, the sacrament, and the priest-penitent relationship. Yet in our visual imagination, especially in films and online platforms, it is still the old way of doing confession that provides our visual image of what should happen.[16] Given that the sacrament is often experienced as a private affair, many people have no recourse to other images. Thus, the view of the pre-Vatican II confessional remains, however much theologians and clergy alike might image something different. And while the understanding of the sacrament now encompasses the parable of the forgiving father and immense joy and celebration, that earlier view of the judgmental Father God still persists.

Can We Sin in Modern America? (Spoiler Alert: Yes)

This story of the incomplete internal shift in the Catholic understanding of the sacrament is part of what leaves people at a loss when naming sins. But it is not the whole story; a number of other changes in cultural context have intensified the difficulty with this aspect of the sacrament.

"Question authority" is a popular U.S. bumper sticker that originated in the 1960s. Catholics at that time, like other people, began to question all manner of authorities, including their Church. To some extent, it did not help that at the same time, the Catholic Church called a council of bishops (Vatican II) that seemed to the popular imagination to put everything in its history and tradition into question. The Council itself—with its recovery of understandings of the Church's fundamental structure as "People of God" or "communion" that sought to soften (though not replace) the previously hierarchical emphasis—encouraged a more "democratic" view of the Church. Instead of the (somewhat mythical) pre-Vatican II image of a pure, unchanging Church with unchanging moral rules handed down from on high, Catholics began to expect that the Church's teachings should reflect changing contemporary values.

One obvious change in contemporary values was the increasing gap between Church and culture on questions related to sex. From academic study—Alfred Kinsey's *Reports* on sexual behavior being published in 1948 and 1953—to popular culture—*Playboy* magazine being launched in 1953—to everyday activity, sexual norms had begun to change dramatically

---

16. Films like *The Fugitive* (with Henry Fonda), the 1990s *Runaway Bride* starring Julia Roberts, and the more recent *Daredevil*, along with television shows like "The Sopranos," offer some examples of how the confessional operates. The online platform Second Life often depicts churches with old-style confessionals and practices. See Jana M. Bennett, *Aquinas on the Web? Doing Theology in an Internet Age* (New York: Continuum, 2012), especially chapter 5.

in America and throughout the West. In particular, the cultural consensus condemning contraception had largely reversed, even among most Christian churches. In 1960, "the pill," the first safe and approved hormonal contraceptive, was promoted as an essential feminist practice, and it was also highly convenient and quickly popular among both married couples and unmarried sexual partners. When Pope Paul VI in 1968, contrary to expectations, re-affirmed the traditional teaching condemning artificial contraception within his encyclical letter *Humanae Vitae*, large swaths of Catholics, even clerics, began to take official Catholic teaching not as a word from God but as another (highly questionable) human opinion. Perhaps it wasn't the people who were sinning, but rather the Church that was mistaken in its understanding of sin.

Indeed, some might view the practice of clerical confession not only as mistaken or irrelevant but unjust. Lay people can wield power in declining to use the sacrament, in protest against a priestly power that they see as keeping lay people, especially women, in oppressive situations (for instance, by considering abortion as a particularly grave sin). Against the historical backdrop of the pre-Vatican II confession, where sin was a weighty, almost palpable presence, and a Father-child relationship was heightened, such oppression could make itself even more keenly felt. Such a critical view of corrupt clerical power still operates today, especially in relation to the sexual abuse scandals that continue to roil the church.

Even for those still inclined to approach an authority for confession, the focus on sexual sins in the pre-Vatican II confessional meant that, once people named the church's teachings on sex as impossible (or even undesirable) to follow, a void opened up. Why confess something if the sin wasn't there? This question of the reality of sin soon extended well beyond the bedroom. In fact, it was popular in the 1960s and 70s to wonder whether people could sin at all, in part because of the rise of psychoanalysis. Maybe feeling guilty itself was the only "sin," to be overcome not with confession and grace but with therapy and self-acceptance. As theologian Maria Morrow has discussed, psychology enabled people to forgive themselves in order to help themselves and (as a side effect) be more loving to others.[17] In some understandings of psychoanalysis, people focus on the hurts and wrongs done to them, articulate how to break out of that pattern, and thus progress forward. Sin, and the need to confess sin, simply disappears. Archbishop Fulton Sheen noted in one of his popular television broadcasts that on the psychoanalytic couch, sin could simply be analyzed away.[18]

17. For much more, see Morrow's excellent *Sin in the Sixties: Catholics and Confession, 1955–1975* (Washington, DC: The Catholic University of America Press, 2016).

18. Fulton Sheen, "Psychoanalytic Couch," *The Fulton Sheen Program*, original broadcast 1966; https://www.youtube.com/watch?v=o9c6rX3UQmo.

The 70s pop psychology that tried to do away with sin still lives today, though now, some philosophers have named it by the technical terms "smarm" or "bullshit." Tom Scocca's essay on smarm states:

> What is smarm, exactly? Smarm is a kind of performance—an assumption of the forms of seriousness, of virtue, of constructiveness, without the substance. Smarm is concerned with appropriateness and with tone. Smarm disapproves. Smarm would rather talk about anything other than smarm. Why, smarm asks, can't everyone just be nicer?[19]

As Scocca goes on to discuss, smarm doesn't really seek truth. Whether the smarmist's statements are true (in any sense of the word "true") matters little; what matters more is a surface tone, a question of whether we're being "civil." For example, he notes that "[m]arket reasoning is deeply, essentially smarmy. We live, it insists, in a world that is optimized by the invisible hand. The conditions under which we live have been created by rational needs and preferences, producing an economicist Panglossianism: What thrives deserves to thrive, be it Nike or sprawl or the finance industry or Upworthy; what fails deserves to have failed."

From this perspective, our human responsibility is to be open and tolerant and nice. As long as everyone smiles and gets along with each other, all will be well with the world. Yet if that is true, there is no need of forgiveness, mercy, or humility. In other words, we're all good people armed with the "right answers" and therefore will never sin. If a person hints otherwise—at the possibility of sin—well, that person is the *real* sinner! Smarm is a power structure, covered in niceness. It enables people at the top to stay at the top, because they must be virtuous and nice.

Initially, niceness sounds nice. Yet, as Scocca notes: "Sympathy begets sympathy, to the benefit of things that don't deserve to be sympathized with." He continues on to say, "A civilization that speaks in smarm is a civilization that has lost its ability to talk about purposes at all. It is a civilization that says 'Don't Be Evil,' rather than making sure it does not do evil." Sin gets omitted, except for the people who call the whole smarm power structure into question.

In one way, the inability to name sins is challenged by cultural developments that dissolve the whole idea of sinning. But there is also a paradoxical counter to this development: we face a culture full of public condemnations that strongly imply sin. These loud and aggressive arguments may lead to other forms of "confession" not done in relation to the sacrament; these forms notably do not display mercy or the kind of alternative power

---

19. Tom Scocca, "On Smarm," http://gawker.com/on-smarm-1476594977. Scocca's post builds on philosopher Harry Frankfurt's well-known essay, *On B---s---* (Princeton, NJ: Princeton University Press, 2005).

that Christ offers in the Gospel. While the sacrament has gone into dis-
use, its vestiges are experienced in numerous locations. That is, while the
rite itself may have slipped out of favor, the power of sin in peoples' lives,
the need for confession, and especially the need for reconciliation has not
disappeared. The language people use, though, is distorted, and frequently
does not provide room for mercy or forgiveness.

One obvious location where this goes on is in socio-political dis-
courses, in which it has never been so easy to find people proclaiming
a litany of large-scale ills plaguing our society. Many theologians write
explicitly about social issues in terms of social sin or structures of sin. That
said, people have difficulty naming systemic sins as "my own sins."

Take the example of the explosive issue of racism. To name it as a sin
and to try to describe its contours is to name a history of complicity, often
unintentional but still real, in slavery: the ways the Church perpetuated
racism in the ways that it practiced baptism and Eucharist, the ways that
a political system first undergirded slavery and then supported segrega-
tion was supported, and the ways that today the practices of the Church
can still perpetuate deep patterns of racial division.[20] A problem for white
Catholics as well as other white Christians has been to wonder how to
properly repent, apologize, and seek forgiveness for sins, especially when
some of those sins have been perpetrated in past generations. More particularly, how can one confess individual sins that are practices of racism?

Of course, there is a connection between individual sins and social sins.
The popes have been clear, too, that what must be named in the confessional is an individual's own sins, which are at the root of social sin. But in
so big a problem as racism, where and how to start naming individual sins
seems insurmountable, not least because any individual who gives thought
to this knows that one person's confession will seem puny in the face of the
mountain of systemic, social sin.

On the other hand, some people will experience a different kind of difficulty in naming such sins. They will simply protest, "that was not me. I did
not sin in this way." Hearing the history of slavery is less likely to make a
person introspective about his or her own individual sins today, and more
likely to think about slavery in terms of past wrongs done by other people.
One example has been in the reparations debate. Few people today would
deny that slavery was horrific, yet many people would deny that they bear
responsibility for the sins of their fathers and mothers going back generations.

---

20.   On this point, see Katie Grimes, "Breaking the Body of Christ: The Sacraments of Initiation in
the Habitat of White Supremacy," *Political Theology* 18, no. 1 (2017): 22–43. For a deeply theological
account of racism and the paths to overcome it within the church, see Willie Jennings, *The Christian
Imagination: Theology and the Origins of Race* (New Haven, CT: Yale University Press, 2010).

Thus, the ability to confess sins becomes truncated in different ways: for some, by the sheer enormity of the sin, for others, an inability to see how to name one's own complicity.

Racism is relatively out in the open as an acknowledged systemic sin, even though in terms of naming it there is much work to be done. Yet sin can be far more implicit, not quite named, but presumed, leaving mostly shame in its wake. As Beth Haile notes in her essay, overweight people often feel "sinful" when seeking medical care: shame on them for not following their diets, exerting self-control, exercising, and so forth. Fatness automatically makes a patient noncompliant, which is one of the ultimate sins in US health care. Confession happens in the doctor's office, the white medical coat supplanting priestly garb. And the physician's supposed "healing" for this presumed sin is to parrot, "Move more, eat less," pushing penance back on the patient and offering little relief from the continued weight of sin. No matter that there is a systemic nature to our patterns of obesity, that all people are curiously gaining weight even if they are at a "healthy size," and that BMI as a measurement of health isn't very helpful.[21] A fat person is often seen as a walking manifestation of one of the chief things wrong in the world—that is, a lack of personal responsibility and willpower. In the current state of affairs, none of the slim people suffer from gluttony (though Haile's chapter will explain how that's mistaken).

Confession, in these implicit kinds of sins, often goes online. Numerous chat rooms and discussion boards are filled with confessions. Here, too, power gets distorted, in similar ways to how people say they encountered Tridentine confession: as overbearing, humiliating, or shaming rather than reconciling or healing. The ones who think they have the right side—of medical surveys or the latest parenting surveys or the best technologies—win. Unfortunately, this is covertly a power grab that often benefits wealthier people.

The conflictual form of these online versions of confession are similar in form to the more gauche version known for decades on daytime TV: for their chance in the spotlight, "real people" serve up their "confessions" of bad behavior on Judge Judy or Maury Povich. People want to talk about their failures (or at least vicariously hear others talk about them), but these contexts are not context-oriented toward mercy. These alternate versions seep into the holes left by the removal of the sacrament of reconciliation (and perhaps its forms that existed in other Christian churches).

---

21. See for example Yoni Freedhoff, "Ugly, Ignorant, Fat-Shaming, American Academy of Pediatrics, Childhood Obesity Ads," *Weighty Matters* (June 25, 2014), http://www.weightymatters.ca/2014/06/ugly-ignorant-fat-shaming-american.html. Accessed June 13, 2017.

Sin and Confession Today: The Call of Pope Francis

Against the backdrop of these changing ideas of sin and changing interpretation of what it means to make a good confession, we now turn to questions of what to do. What can confessing sin mean for us today? How can we receive Pope Francis's call to receive the sacrament of reconciliation?

As we have noted, it is important to know that confessing sins has not disappeared. Perhaps despite our own misgivings, we are a culture that likes to confess things to other people. Only now, confession has taken different forms, and the kinds of sins confessed have also taken some different shapes. The effect of this movement of sin and sacrament out of the confessional has meant that power, too, has been displaced, often in quite detrimental ways.

We might begin to unpack this problem by recognizing the complexity of the challenge Pope Francis presents to the above cultural contexts. Pope Francis's papacy has been defined by his emphasis on mercy, which he sees as deeply connected to the sacrament of reconciliation. In one of his Wednesday general audiences, the pope reflected on the meaning of the sacrament of reconciliation. "The Sacrament of Reconciliation is a Sacrament of healing. When I go to confession it is [in] order to be healed, to heal my soul, to heal my heart and to be healed of some wrongdoing… forgiveness is not something we can give ourselves. Forgiveness is asked for, is asked of another, and in Confession we ask for forgiveness from Jesus."[22] The use of the metaphor of healing helps bring out the absolute necessity of naming and diagnosing the injury—that is, to name sin well. Just as with a physical injury, we need to be able to understand what is wrong, especially if we are to actively participate in the healing process and not just "take a pill." Thus, the pope goes on to exhort people to attend the sacrament of reconciliation, reassuring them that most priests are neither abusive nor controlling, but acknowledging that facing one's own shortcomings in front of another person is not easy. "Go, the priest will be good. Jesus is there and Jesus is more benevolent than priests, Jesus receives you, he receives you with so much love. Be courageous and go to Confession!" The pope concludes his general audience address by citing the Scripture story of the Forgiving Father—he too wants people to remember the Father's forgiveness.

The pope's call for more frequent confession has been met with no little astonishment.[23] This is in part because the pope himself has been very

---

22. Francis, *General Audience* (February 19, 2014), https://w2.vatican.va/content/francesco/en/audiences/2014.index.html.

23. For example, this review in the *Washington Post* rehearses almost exactly the stereotypes of the "old" confessional, noting it as "one of the creepier aspects" of Catholicism. Carlos Lozada, "Pope Francis

public about his own attendance at the sacrament of reconciliation. The pope's move to make his own confessions more visibly present, if not quite a public airing of sins, is certainly a way to mitigate some of that priestly power that historians have described. Here is the pope himself, Vicar of the Church of Christ, shepherd of souls, submitting to a power and authority in a very public way. By also emphasizing the necessity that priests should be compassionate and benevolent when they hear confessions, the pope has worked to overcome the impression that we mentioned earlier, that the sacrament is merely an exercise of clerical power lording it over the laypersons.

Still, part of people's response has been, "Really? You want me to do what?" It seems as though many welcome a message of mercy but not the specific practice of the sacrament. We think a key reason for this is the specific element of the sacrament that requires naming sins. The requirement that one must name one's sins seems to play to the kinds of Catholics Pope Francis has criticized.

We might see this if we juxtapose two other well-known comments from the Holy Father. First, in his *America* interview, when asked who he was, he replied simply, "I am a sinner."[24] Second, Francis has subjected to harsh criticism those he calls "doctors of the law," and has even pointed out that many forget that the law is not an end in itself.[25] For many, there is a certain dissonance here, evident in diverse reactions to Francis. On the one hand, some worry that Francis is "weak on sin," while on the other hand, some welcome his "forgiving" attitude as a desirable change from a Church focused on accusation.

But neither reaction takes with full seriousness *both* of these remarks. The first approach cannot accept Francis's criticism of "doctors of the law" as anything other than "being weak on sin" … because the *only* way they know how to name sin is in relation to laws. The second approach, on the other hand, lacks resources for understanding how to cultivate a humble and genuine sense of sinfulness reflected in Francis's confession of his identity as a sinner. Another way to put this is that neither can really make sense of Francis's wholehearted recommendation of the sacrament of reconciliation, because for the first, he is weakening the whole point of

---

wants to hear your confession," *Washington Post*, January 12, 2016, https://www.washingtonpost.com/news/book-party/wp/2016/01/12/pope-francis-wants-to-hear-your-confession/?utm_term=.e78ff2675fb8.

24. Antonio Spadaro, SJ, "A Big Heart Open to God," *America*, September 30, 2015, http://americamagazine.org/pope-interview.

25. The pope frequently uses this image of "doctors of the law." For example, see Francis, Daily meditation *Those Who Take Away the Keys* (October 15, 2015); https://w2.vatican.va/content/francesco/en/cotidie/2015.index.html.

going, and for the other, he is recommending a kind of preemptive stance that makes the sacrament (particularly in the form of individual confession of sin) unnecessary.

Notice how both of these positions implicitly rely on a very fixed understanding of sin—an understanding that is particularly stuck on the way the Church taught about sin in the time prior to the Council. One side thinks the Council "overturned" that understanding, while the other says it did not. We think part of the problem is the need to recognize that the Church does develop in its understanding over time in dialogue with the wider culture, which is why we look so much to recent popes and moral theology and not merely the Bible or the ancient Christian writers in determining what to do. At the same time, this "dialogue" does not mean that the Church simply accepts whatever a culture accepts or blesses. The Church—leaders and lay people—need to learn more not only from the surrounding views of good people, but from itself—that is, by retrieving parts of its history that answer contemporary needs. This, indeed, was a big part of what the Second Vatican Council was actually for. And hence, we think looking to the older tradition of vices—filtered through modern moral theology and in conversation with contemporary society—can make confession vibrant again.

Naming Sins: Beyond Code Violations

What approach would be necessary to appropriate the full range of Francis's witness? It seems the task is to reclaim the naming of sins from those "doctors of the law," while not dissolving the *necessity* of this task in a sea of generic mercy. A key first move is disentangling the tendency to identify "sins" from the idea of code violations. Not infrequently, one encounters guides for examining conscience based on the Ten Commandments. Code violations—or moral rules—are a fair place to start developmentally for understanding what is right and wrong, and we continue to need them in our lives. But we are certainly called to go beyond them in order to understand more deeply what it means to do good. Take a sports analogy: early on, a young player may have to think a lot about following the rules of the sport, lest they constantly blunder into fouls or penalties. But as one develops as a player, worrying about the rules becomes less and less relevant. A player doesn't evaluate a bad day based on the number of rules broken but rather on the various aspects of play that did not live up to the best performance he or she could have given. Similarly, a musician must learn about musical notes, keys, time signatures, and tempos—the "rules" of what it means to be able to start to play music. An aspiring baker needs to know about measurements and how to follow the rules written in a recipe. Yet knowing these beginning sets of rules only helps one to become a good musician or baker; while these rules continue to guide musicians and bakers, the one who wants to become truly adept will have to learn things like how to improvise, how to put emotion into a piece, or why a particular loaf of bread tastes more awesome than another in order to go beyond the steps of following musical notes or baking recipes—things that can't be legislated in code, but which can nevertheless be learned.

Catholicism has helped many people name specific failures that violate the rules. Yet the Church has often done a poor job in helping people name ways in which we are playing the "game" of the Gospel badly. We can critique "legalism" all we want, but we won't make real progress unless an alternative paradigm for identifying failures is offered—preferably a paradigm which is compatible with the form of how we celebrate the sacrament of reconciliation.[26]

The project we are undertaking in this book suggests the alternative way of naming sins is to turn to the classic tradition of the vices. This is only the flip side of learning to describe goodness not as "following the rules," but as having positive virtues like generosity and integrity, not to mention prudence and justice or faith, hope, and love. Today, the word "vice" often implies a bad habit of indulgence; but in the early Church, the idea of thinking about sin in terms of vices went far beyond habits of indulgence. Vices indicated any habitual inclination to sin. Early monks compiled reflections on the struggle of living a holy life in terms of the vices. And the preference for vices, rather than just rules, is captured especially in Jesus's criticism of food laws. Speaking to his disciples, he says: "Do you not realize that everything that goes into a person from the outside cannot defile? . . . But what comes out of a person, that is what defiles. From within people, from their hearts, come evil thoughts, unchastity, theft, murder, adultery, greed, malice, deceit, licentiousness, envy, blasphemy, arrogance, folly" (Mark 7:18, 20–22).

Yet talking about pride and greed in general terms isn't enough to satisfy what the sacrament demands: the naming of specific sins. (Even Jesus's list above seems to contain a few specific actions!) It's all well and good if a batter can say, "Well, I didn't have a good day at the plate today because I was angry at the umpire." The batter needs to understand more precisely what he did poorly as a result of that anger, as well as what choices he made in responding poorly to whatever the umpire did to make him angry. As

---

26. We will say a bit more later about what might be considered the most prominent alternative, a "relational" account of sin—definitely a step forward, but still in need of certain further clarifications.

mentioned earlier, if we are to participate in the healing of sin, we need to
be able to name what went wrong, how we got an injury and what it is doing
to us. If we truly desire health, we shouldn't just take a (mercy!) pill and
move on unaware of how we injured ourselves. But why not? Because
it is crucial to the Christian understanding of sin that we recognize (a)
we bear at least some responsibilities for injuries, and (b) God wants
us to participate in the process of healing and conversion. Neither the
sin itself nor the healing simply comes from somewhere else; the task
of naming sins enlists us as mature, growing disciples. Naming sin is
meant to be empowering—empowering in that we take real responsibility for the past and we can participate in the process of doing better
in the future.

The Vices: "Contrary to Nature"

In order to gain this self-knowledge and take on this responsibility, we need
to understand the relationship between vices and individual sins. The great
medieval theologian Thomas Aquinas begins his section on sin by making
exactly this distinction. He calls sin "properly speaking" an "inordinate act,"
by which he means that the action is somehow not properly ordained to
the end—that is, the act misses the target we should be shooting for in our
lives. He also explains that a vice is a thing "not being disposed in a way
befitting its nature,"[27] and for human beings, this is specified in terms of
being "contrary to man's nature, in so far as it is contrary to the order of
reason."[28] While in one sense a vice is not as bad as a "vicious act" (a sin),
because "a habit stands midway between power and act," nevertheless in
general (though accidentally) "habit is more lasting than act" and both are
"found in a nature such that it cannot always be in action."[29]

This technical terminology can be off-putting and confusing, but it is
worth sticking with it because it leads us beyond the code violation
approach to sin. The key point to focus on the essence of a vice is to be
disposed "contrary to nature." This is the alternative: sin is contrary to
what it means for us to be fully human; not simply contrary to laws and
codes of conduct. A vice, we might say, is an *unnatural* disposition which
tends toward *inordinate* acts (sins). To call an act "inordinate" means that
it somehow lacks a proper ordering toward its goal. So, to go back to our

27. Thomas Aquinas, *Summa Theologiae* I-II, q. 71, a. 1.

28. ST I-II, q. 71, a. 2.

29. ST I-II, q. 71, a. 3. While, following Augustine, Aquinas does define sin as "a word, deed, or desire
contrary to the eternal law," (ST I-II, q. 71, a. 6) the eternal law "is God's reason" rather than a written
code (ST I-II, q. 93, a. 1).

batter example, he is able to name exactly what he did wrong because he understands what the goals of batting are. The vice is the disposition that tends to disrupt the ordering, and so it is "unnatural" for a baseball player to be in this kind of a state of anger with an umpire.

Thinking about what is natural and unnatural is a challenging exercise. We need to give up the idea that when we talk about our human "nature," we're talking about anything like animal "instinct" or about what "inevitably" happens. We're not talking about things that happen automatically. In the above example, when we say that it's "unnatural" for a baseball player to be that angry with an umpire, we don't mean it's rare. Rather, it's detrimental to being the best baseball player one can be.

Philosopher R.G. Collingwood also helps us by contrasting two ways of speaking about "nature." The more recent is based on thinking of the universe like a machine, designed and run by God. This view of nature seems at odds with our human freedom ... and in fact, it is. But when older philosophers and theologians spoke about "nature," they didn't make an analogy with a machine, but instead with an "intelligent organism."[30] That is, they saw the universe as a living thing, and to speak about something's nature was to speak about the *inner* source of its activity. Nature for Aristotle, writes philosopher Julia Annas, is "the source of a thing's inner development," as opposed to external forces.[31] What is natural for a human being is *contrasted with* what he or she might be forced to do—notice how different this is from a machine model of nature, where nature itself seems to "force" us to act in certain ways mechanically.

So what is the source of inner development for *human* nature? As we noted above, Aquinas says what is natural for human beings is to act according to "the order of reason." But we shouldn't rush on and reduce "the order of reason" to a code. What more does it mean? To use the baseball example, "unreasonable" is understood as somehow contrary to the *real meaning* of being a baseball player, the *reasons* that the game exists at all. And so when we talk about a disposition being "unnatural" to us just as a human being, we mean the same thing: it's contrary to the *real meaning* of being a human being.

So we could summarize to this point by saying that naming vice is about how we are disposed contrary to the real meaning of our lives. Obviously, the next question is: what is that "real meaning"? We can at this point turn to four elements of the Catholic tradition that help us name actions that are contrary to the real meaning of our lives.

---

30. R.G. Collingwood, *The Idea of Nature* (London: Oxford University Press, 1978), 8.

31. Julia Annas, *The Morality of Happiness* (New York: Oxford University Press, 1993), 148.

Obviously, first and foremost, we need some sense that there _is_ a "real meaning" to our lives! This meaning is something that we are called to realize through our actions. Our lives have potential, and it is up to us to realize that potential through our actions. For a batter stepping to the plate, _all_ at-bats are meaningful (though not equally meaningful), thus all are good or bad, because all happen in light of the goals of baseball. Similarly, all human acts are in fact moral acts, acts where we perform well or badly in relation to the meaning of our lives. Our modern tendency is to view morality as something "added to" actions ... and only to some actions. But we aren't only acting on morality when we decide whether to cheat on a test or not; we also act morally in making choices about how to prepare for it, making choices about which classes to take, even making choices about being in school at all. All human acts are moral because they are for ends, and the basic moral question in every action is about how these proximate (nearby) ends relate to "the general end of human life."[32] Any claims about virtue and vice depend on an account of "what sorts of being humans are."[33] That is to say, it depends on recognizing that all our acts aim at some real meaning of our lives that, at least in part, we discover as rooted in our nature as beings called "human."

Besides attending to a general end for life as a whole, a second key to naming sins as contrary to nature is a definite account of what Catholic moral theology has called _natural inclinations_. Catholic moral thought depends on a very broad and general account of the overall human end, which is then understood and connected to "basic human inclinations." Another way to put this is that the real meaning of our lives, the point of everything, isn't an alien imposition, but rather something that "fits" us, something for which we are made. An account of natural inclinations serves "to bring order and coherence" to everyday experiences, as well as enabling distinctions between "true and false" and "better and worse" inclination.[34] Again, these are not to be understood as raw instincts, because importantly, the nature of humans as rational allows for the _intelligibility_ of these inclinations—that is, our ability to name and know these inclinations means they can serve the purposes of distinguishing and ordering specific acts.[35]

---

32. Charles Pinches, _Theology and Action_ (Grand Rapids, MI: Eerdmans, 2002), 93. This is the term Pinches uses to distinguish the difference between doing bad art as an artist and doing bad art _as a sin_—that is, as something that departs from the _general_ end of human life.

33. Pinches, _Theology and Action_, 107.

34. Jean Porter, _Nature as Reason: A Thomistic Theory of the Natural Law_ (Grand Rapids, MI: Eerdmans, 2005), 80.

35. Another fine example of the central use of natural inclinations is the statement of the Vatican's International Theological Commission, _In Search of a Universal Ethic: A New Look at the Natural Law_, 2009, paragraphs 45–51; http://www.vatican.va/roman_curia/congregations/cfaith/cti_documents/rc_cti_index-doc-pubbl_en.html

What are these natural inclinations? A typical example of their content is Swiss theologian Servais Pinckaers's specification of five.[36] At the most basic level, we are inclined to do what we see as good and avoid what we see as evil, and we are inclined to preserve life—to go on living. These aren't difficult to understand; in fact, we typically suggest medical help if someone is inclined to inflict self-harm or cannot make basic moral distinctions between right and wrong. The other three inclinations are a bit more content-laden. We are inclined to reproduce, and Pinckaers suggests that this inclination is to what we call marriage, given especially the needs of the human development of children over a very long period of years. American theologian Jean Porter agrees, noting that despite the obvious variety of marriage customs in different cultures, the inclination to reproduce must mean more than just "making babies" because of the "relative weakness" of human children and their inclination to a "fundamentally social ways of life." Thus, "adultery" is seen as wrong because "it transgresses and undermines the structures of marriage and kinship necessary for the formation of children into fully functioning adults."[37] We are inclined to know the truth—that is, we are learners, and when we learn, we want to learn what is actually the case. And we are inclined to live in community—that is, we both need and want other human beings in our lives in order to achieve whatever end we seek.

A general end and some basic inclinations do not constitute a code, and there are only very general rules that might be derived from them.[38] Think about this: inclinations don't tell us exactly what sort of relationships to have with others, what to eat and drink, what exactly we need to learn, or whom or when to marry. However, they do provide a kind of orientation that starts to indicate to us what dispositions might be "contrary to nature," in the sense of disrupting our ability to follow our natural inclinations. Many of the natural inclinations, for example, require us to forge appropriate relationships with others; vices such as pride, envy, and greed clearly make it more difficult to achieve those relationships. Once we put together the inclination (community with others) and the vice (envy), we may be in a good position to name more specific sins in our own lives. Bad actions toward a coworker who has just received a deserved promotion, for example, might then be the sin we need to name

A couple further elements enable us to start thinking in richer ways about how to name specific actions in our own lives that defeat human

36. See Servais Pinckaers, OP, *Morality: The Catholic View* (South Bend, IN: St. Augustine's Press, 2001).

37. Porter, *Nature as Reason*, 75.

38. See ST I-II, q. 94, a. 2.

life's real meaning. One is some sort of distinction between "well-being" and "happiness," in order to distinguish between a *minimal* level of a life in accord with nature ("well-being") versus "a more specific and morally rich" idea ("happiness").[39] Researchers working on measuring levels of human happiness often distinguish between these by identifying the first with "How satisfied are you with your life as a whole?" and the second with "How *worthwhile* is your life as a whole?" So, for example, we might consider the difference between a form of life that fulfills the natural inclination of humans to sociality and communion (a lonely person is not likely to report high life satisfaction) and better and worse forms of such a communion (marriages and other long-term community commitments are often filled with frustration, but are often seen as the most worthwhile aspects of one's life). Since, in Christianity, our general end is understood as *maximal*, we gain further insight into actions that are contrary to such an end by being able to specify such differences, evaluating how we develop vices that lead us to make weaker choices than we should.

This may seem a little hard to grasp at first, but there are various ways to get more insight into this difference. Our language might distinguish between surviving and thriving, for example. We might say that we are "made for more." We might talk about "being the best that you can be." The point here is to get our enterprise of naming sins "off the ground," to recognize that by nature we strive to get more than a D- in life, and that when we get a C, we're still doing things that qualify as sin.

Of course, this example shows that the task of naming sins will differ for different people at different times. For some people, getting a C is a great accomplishment and an improvement. Recent popes have talked about the importance of "gradualism" in the moral life, what St. John Paul II calls "step-by-step advance."[40] While Pope Francis has affirmed that the objective truths of Catholic morality apply universally, he affirms "a gradualness in the prudential exercise of free acts on the part of subjects who are not in a position to understand, appreciate, or fully carry out the objective demands. . . ."[41] Part of Pope Francis's message is that we should stop paying attention to other people who might be getting C's (or F's!),when we have our own set of problems! After all, Jesus warns quite clearly that from those who are given much, much is expected (Mt 25:29). Perhaps the lazy B student has much more to worry about than the student working hard to get the C. But wherever we are in our own journey, it is important

---

39. Porter, *Nature as Reason*, 142–45, at 145.

40. John Paul II, Apostolic Exhortation *Familiaris Consortio* (November 22, 1981), 34.

41. Francis, Apostolic Exhortation *Amoris Laetitia* (March 19, 2016), 295.

to recognize what counts as acting contrary to where we are going. The imperative is to make progress; to sin, correspondingly, is to refuse opportunities to progress further.

What kind of language do we use to grasp this needed continual progress to become better? Philosopher Charles Taylor calls it the language of "strong evaluation," of actions having a certain "nobility," which he claims is necessary for moral agency. This is often most easily seen in the figures a society holds up for particular admiration. For example, when we think about acting for racial justice in our society, we hold up Martin Luther King, Jr. Why single out these people? It is often because what they have accomplished is particularly worthwhile—we call them "role models" for a reason—and we implicitly urge others to "be like them."[42] In the case of King, we recognize the particular nobility of his actions and character because he didn't only avoid being racist and practice basic fairness; he also took action on behalf of others who were suffering, and also did that in an intentionally nonviolent way. His willingness to suffer for others and his unwillingness to resort to violence even in the face of violence are "better" than just being fair on a day-to-day basis.

Here again, we should head off a couple misunderstandings. We don't mean that somehow only "famous" people are truly good. In fact, what we should admire in famous people is that they have developed some set of qualities—which moral theologians would call "virtues." But it is true that languages of strong evaluation suggest some people are "better" than others—and that may feel bothersome. Isn't everyone equal? Certainly, people are equal in potential. But to lose languages of "strong evaluation" is, unfortunately, to be a culture that can't distinguish between reality-TV "celebrities" and genuine heroes. In fact, we do want to make this distinction.

This point may seem more distant from our topic of naming sins, but in fact, it may have a great deal of relevance for us "non-notorious sinners." The act-centeredness of the confessional makes it a potent and powerful experience for those who are conscious of specific, gravely wrong actions for which they are seeking mercy. If you are plagued by a guilty conscience for a single, horrible thing you've done, you probably will not have difficulty knowing what to say when you enter the confessional! In many cases, these penitents may be cognizant of rejecting very basic things or

---

42. Taylor, like Porter, makes a key contrast between utilitarian approaches and more substantive account. See "What is Human Agency?" in *Human Agency and Language: Philosophical Papers I* (New York: Cambridge University Press, 1985), 15–44. Porter (*Nature as Reason*, 148–52) questions whether the commonly-used capabilities approach, developed especially by philosopher Martha Nussbaum in order to measure happiness in public policy interventions, can really get us to happiness. She shows how impossible it is to give any real account of capabilities without some stronger evaluations sneaking in.

even directly rejecting God, for example. But for many of us, this is not the ordinary situation of sin we face. Theologian Jim Keenan famously named sin as "a failure to bother to love," a failure to care, and unpacking the complexity of what it means to care for others around us is clearly an exercise of strong evaluation.[43] The failure to care may not take the form of an outright rejection of responsibility ("I just don't care"), but instead *an inattentiveness to what matters*, a prioritization of lesser goods over the greater good of care.

To use another example, it is often considerably more difficult to name what is "wrong" with a paper that is a B as opposed to D. Yet, especially for a college professor (and a student!), the ability to understand the B may be very important for their full development and flourishing. Of course, this example also makes clear that the task of "naming sins" needs to respect where people are at in the moral life. But here again, notice how a one-size-fits-all approach to naming sins—in terms of a code—is so limited.

As we said, recognizing and using language of strong evaluation, whereby we distinguish between surviving and thriving, is more complex than our first two points. And it has more individual variation. But if we recognize that our nature is to thrive, we may start being able to name the sins that are blocking that thriving. To recall the importance of the parable of the Loving Father, the elder son, who manifests ongoing good behavior in a way that his younger brother did not, may not suddenly become irresponsible. His sin, instead, may be a matter of refusing the invitation to celebrate the forgiveness and mercy extended to his brother.

A final point—one that all our later chapters will particularly exemplify—is getting right the role of language and description that "surrounds" us—in other words, when we name our actions, including our sins, we need to recognize that we think in terms from the cultures we swim in—and those languages may themselves be afflicted with sin. We tend to forget that correctly describing our acts typically involves selecting from pieces of language that we inherit from our social context, and that at different times and in different places, different descriptions are made more "available" to us than others. For example, can you really "bend a rule"? We know what we mean by this metaphor, but we also know that it can be abused. We "know what we are doing" because we find language that seems to fit, but how we judge the "fit" is related to what our social context tells us.

Think about this as a deepening of the prior point. Let's say we agree that it is noble to live life bravely, with fortitude, dealing directly with our

---

43. James Keenan, SJ, *Moral Wisdom: Lessons and Texts from the Catholic Tradition* (Lanham, MD: Rowman & Littlefield, 2004), 57.

fears and not letting them get in the way of our goals. This may lead us to consider actions in our lives when we haven't shown the bravery we should. But once we start doing that, we'll recognize that describing our actions correctly and accurately is itself challenging. It usually takes some fortitude to name wrongdoing in an office, for example. But is doing that an example of "whistleblowing"? (Sounds brave!) Or an example of "snitching"? (Sounds cowardly!) To take a more controversial example, is a person who leaves a difficult marriage "standing up for themselves"? (Brave!) Or are they "giving up"? (Cowardly!)

Theologian Charles Pinches talks about this in terms of act descriptions where we must acknowledge the reality of the world around us, that our actions have a context we can't create out of nothing. Pinches notes that, in this context, "the world" is "not merely the 'natural' or physical world, but the intentional, human world in which it takes place."[44] And a key part of this is receiving and appropriating language from our culture to understand what we are doing—and such descriptions should be not be understood as opposed to (language-less? Culture-less?) "natural" descriptions. Pinches quotes Oliver O'Donovan on this—O'Donovan states that Catholic moral theology often failed "to provide a developed account of *the field* of moral action, that is to say, of the created world with all its infinite variety of human goods and ends."[45] Because of this, our imagined models of action—and thus of sin—tend toward either a reduction to subjective expression of an inner intention or to "an instrumental technique, manipulating the world to some end." Or, to put it more simply, sin is bad if we feel bad or sin is bad because it has bad outcomes. Each of these imagined models corresponds to a way of thinking about sin: the first as a kind of inauthenticity of action, where we sin when we are not true to ourselves, and the second in terms actions which produce bad results, especially if they seem to harm others.

But notice that how you feel or what results you achieved don't really get at the action—at what you actually did. Think back to our example of whistleblowing versus snitching. A person trying to be brave may experience conflicting feelings and a person may well do the right thing and not get good results. Instead, we need to pay direct attention to the descriptions of what we are doing and drill down to understand and accurately grasp the proximate end of our action.

It's true that this final point is more subtle and difficult than the first three. In Pinches's treatment of act description, he focuses in particular .

---

44. Pinches, *Theology and Action*, 120.

45. Oliver O'Donovan, "A Summons to Reality," in *Considering Veritatis Splendor*, ed. John Wilkins (Cleveland, OH: The Pilgrim Press, 1994), 43–44, cited in Pinches, *Theology and Action*, 79. Italics added.

on Aquinas's notion that some (though not all) acts take their morality from their "species," or the kind of action it is. Aquinas's examples here—adultery, giving alms, theft—seem to him to be natural kinds. Pinches emphasizes that while virtue and vice descriptions are important for a rich identification of acts, they are not sufficient—he gives the example of a courageous act, which of course could be courageous almsgiving or "courageous" adultery. Pinches's point is to resist the tendency to make all morality dependent upon subjective intention or precise circumstances. "Whistleblowing" and "snitching" could be seen as distinct acts, arising from distinct dispositions toward the real meaning of our lives, and what we need are better act descriptions, so we can tell the difference between the two. If we can't tell the difference, then we fall prey to a sense that our actions are infinitely malleable, that they mean whatever we want them to mean—it is, in fact, a dissolving of nature.

However, attention even to Aquinas's modest examples should alert us to the fact that these descriptions simply aren't available in some a-cultural language. The sense that there are in fact actions called adultery and theft which are characteristic of the (unnatural) human condition does not mean that we have access to some Platonic ideal of these acts. These are words in a language, and the words matter. It's also important to note that Aquinas's account of acts that are "morally indifferent according to the species" is so modest. The examples of picking up straw or walking through a field are almost "physicalist" in their modesty—that is, they name merely external physical motions without any account of the reason a subject might be performing them. Are "writing a conference paper" or "playing with one's children" more like picking up straw ... or more like giving alms? The latter, right? That is to say, our store of morally weighted species descriptions may be considerably larger than a short list of intrinsically evil acts. And we have no choice but to avail ourselves of that "store" via the cultural descriptions available to us.

To tie this back to the workplace dilemma with which we started, we can say we are insufficiently attentive to how much our self-understanding of actions, in terms of how we grasp "what we are doing," depends on *descriptions* we inherit—but not passively—from a social context. Naming our *sins* is partly a matter of examining how we name our *actions* in the first place. In a situation of pluralism, where there is widespread moral disagreement, this is especially challenging. We live in a situation where there are multiple social configurations of practical reason (reasoning about how to act) available; these often are compatible in certain ways, but conflict in others. For example, the configuration of cultural ideas about money and possessions lies in a complicated relationship to Catholic social teaching; one of the difficulties is that the cultural configurations often polarize around the stances of the competing political parties, neither of which matches up well with the whole range of Catholic social teaching. Descriptions like "treat yourself" and "I deserve a break today" can cover over sins better named by "extravagance" and "waste." But wait, you might say, can't I "treat myself" once in a while? Sure. But we need to be honest about these descriptions, as well as the cultural forces of consumerism (condemned by all the popes of the last fifty years) that push us toward believing the innocent descriptions instead of the guilt-ridden ones. In short, this aspect of naming sins shows how demanding the context of cultural pluralism is. It makes unavoidable a level of reflection that might not be as necessary is contexts where cultural scripts are relatively mono-lithic and are simply to be followed or rejected.

The language of the vices, it seems to us, provides a space for the moral examination of these descriptions. For example, thinking carefully about what is indicated by lust, in conversation with the descriptions—or as Jason King calls them in his essay, the "sexual scripts"—generated by our culture, helps us become more careful in the sexual act descriptions we appropriate for ourselves. As mentioned earlier in our essay, current cultural understandings of sexuality can be very dismissive of the traditional "code violations" identified by the Catholic tradition; however, the culture also has "normative scripts" that imply what is right or wrong sexually. Thus, even if we don't approach our sexual sins as though a nun is about to hit our knuckles with a ruler, it's hard to argue that people never 'miss the mark' with their sexuality. In calling our attention to these scripts, King helps us recognize how the tradition itself can go beyond legalism and yield a much richer description of the sexual sins that tempt us. The aim, always, is that we become more discerning—in the language of the virtues, we become more prudent. The prudent person is like the baseball player who has a full command of the potential descriptions of his performance (good or bad), knowing when and how to apply them, in order for him to achieve his "general end" of excellence in baseball.

Describing actions in terms of arising from vices which are contrary to nature, as we can see, is more difficult than just thinking in terms of code violations; on the other hand, it's not at all a matter of being a rocket scientist. It's the kind of logic we use every day when we consider our actions as a parent or a student, a friend or a worker—just like our batter, we constantly see ourselves acting in accord with or contrary to "nature," and what it means to grow up is to be able to understand these roles more richly. Sin is a violation not simply of any particular role, but of our overall role, the real meaning of our lives.

Challenges: Sins, Relationships, and Social Structures

We have offered a way of thinking about naming sin, indebted to the tradition of the virtues and the vices, that relies on a careful understanding of what it means for actions to be "contrary to nature." Other ways of naming sin should be addressed before we move on to thinking through specific vices.

Many Catholic thinkers have suggested thinking of sin not as violating a code, but as harming *relationships*. This move is helpful—surely, when Jesus summarizes the law in terms of love of God and neighbor, he is saying that relationships are what human life (and divine life) are all about. They are its "real meaning"!

But referring to relationships, while correct, isn't a full answer; rather, it pushes us toward further questions. Yes, we are made for relationships, but what sorts of relationships are good or bad? How do we name the appropriate dynamics? Suddenly, we are back with our batter, and we've returned to the question of what is "contrary to nature," but by another route. Relationships are all quite different, and we gain a sense of the complexity of understanding how to navigate them. Consider the complex questions that arise from incidents of anger, which William Mattison's chapter will explore in more detail. For example, professors sometimes get angry with students; we usually feel guilty in the wake of such (rare) encounters, since we take seriously the need to maintain good mentoring relationships with students. Yet of course, sometimes such anger may very well *not* be sinful. And in fact, especially with students, we know well, we've had experiences of them coming back and saying, "You were right to be angry, I've learned from this." So, navigating good and bad, or naming sin in relationships, turns out to require much of the same sort of discernment we are suggesting above.

A further challenge is that a focus on relationships can sometimes turn into a focus on *outcomes*. We can feel guilty of sin because the student with whom we got angry *didn't* come back, and now they are blowing our class off. But just because the relationship didn't get fixed, was the initial action actually a sin? The *Catechism of the Catholic Church* is quite astute on this issue. It suggests that sin often "injures human solidarity" (as well as "wounding nature"). But this breaking of human relationships is a *result* of sin. It's not what sin is. The *Catechism* instead defines sin as an "offense against reason, truth, and right conscience."[46] We often cannot control the results of actions—and this is especially true when it comes to the reactions

---

46. *CCC*, no. 1849. It also says it is "a failure of genuine love of God and neighbor"—but here again, the defining of "genuine love" will drive us back to questions about nature.

of other people. However, we can control the actions themselves—to put it in terms of our discussion above, we can name the *aims* (or "ends") of the action, offer a description of what we are doing, even if we can't be assured of the *results*. It is for these aims that God holds us "responsible"; therefore, it is here, in terms of naming the action itself, where we need to focus when naming sin. Thus, as Nichole Flores's essay on greed particularly explains many of the social sins of injustice that happen in our economy are traceable back to our inordinate desires for particular material objects at a particular price (so that, presumably, we can acquire even further material objects). So of course, relationships are crucial; every one of the sins we will describe in this book involve distorting the relationships God wants us to have with others (and with the earth, as Pope Francis has recently reminded us in his encyclical *Laudato Si'*). But this is because of a deeper failing in the choosing itself, not simply in the outcomes.

A second objection calls into question this whole project of individuals naming their sins by pressing the category of "social sin." Perhaps the whole enterprise of naming the sinful actions of individuals is itself part of the problem? But we think, rather than abandoning the traditional model of naming individual sins, we need *better ways of understanding how social structures shape our dispositions and intentionality*, so we can really see how they distort a person specifically. In particular, recognizing the inevitability of social scripting means that we really need to do two things—both identify how all our sinful actions relate to sinful social structures, while at the same time, distinguishing this inevitable formation from "duress" which would genuinely mitigate responsibility.

Put another way, displacing sin onto social structures makes it too easy to take our daily actions off the hook. As with the point about relationships, we're not denying that there are sinful structures. But what we need to do is find them in our own lives, name the ways in which they are distorting our understanding of the *real meaning* of our lives. In particular, we think the task of paying careful attention to act description—to the ways we appropriate competing languages from our cultural settings—builds a bridge between individual sins and sinful social structures. It helps us own how these structures are "in" our everyday actions, thus helping us confess them more accurately (rather than just feel generally guilty), and then struggle to change, with the help of grace.

Conclusion: Toward Using the Vices to Name Sins

In this introduction, we've tried to outline where we've been and where we might go as Catholics with the sacrament of reconciliation. We especially think the task of naming sin—but in a nonlegalistic way—is a key barrier to the sacrament, and we've offered some ideas about a different way to think about the basic tools we have (other than codes) for naming sin.

We've contended that the vices are the hinge on which this task must turn, because they are the places where we confront our tendency to distort the meaning of our lives, to distort our nature. The specific vices we discuss in this book are the ones traditionally known as the "seven deadly sins": gluttony, lust, greed, sloth, anger, envy, and pride. They are "deadly" because they have the potential to distort our relationships with God and others and that they bring about death to those relationships, the kind of death that can be bodily, or spiritual, or both.

Bodily sins (especially those of gluttony, lust, greed, and sloth) often show their effects in our bodies. These sins connect our bodily senses to our desires for food, sex, things, and pleasure. As Beth Haile will describe in more detail in her chapter on gluttony, bodily sins relate most to our sensitive appetites—that is, our sensory responses to our world. What we name as more spiritual sins (anger, envy, and pride), however, link more to our rational appetite, or our intellectual responses to our world. It is not the case that anger or pride never impacts our bodies, or that lust isn't also related to our rationality. Yet bodily sins, by themselves (and not, say, intricately connected also to pride or anger), can be simpler, more fleetingly connected to physical stimuli. Spiritual sins are often more deeply felt, more integrally related to our whole person and thus to our whole way of relating to our world. So Dante's famous poem *Inferno* described lust as further away from the depths of hell than anger, which can seep into all our relationships in ways that lust might not. But again, lust might be intertwined with anger sometimes, so that the way our sins are felt and impact others can vary quite widely.

In this collection, we've chosen to begin with the sins traditionally understood as "bodily," and then move "deeper and deeper" into more seriously spiritual vices, ending with the vice traditionally understood as the deepest: pride. In part, this is a gesture toward the stereotype that the confessional is a place where people name sexual sins, and that those always are the most pressing and concerning of sins. It is also because, we think, sins get more and more difficult to name in this way of progressing. Yet certainly, the reader could dive into the collection at any point.

Through being given the language of the vices to see the distortions and deadliness, we gain lenses to be able to drill down to the level of our actions, naming the actual sins we commit, both so we can receive forgiveness and so we can "go and from now on do not sin anymore" (John 8:11).

Does using the tradition of the seven deadly vices work for the confessional? The proof of the pudding, as they say, is in the tasting. There's no other way to see if it does than to explain the vices themselves and see what fruit it bears.

Chapter 2

Gluttony

BETH HAILE

EVERAL YEARS AGO, a friend and I decided to have dinner at an all-you-can-eat buffet that advertised itself with the tantalizing slogan "Help yourself to happiness." The experience was anything but happy. We watched as our fellow diners rushed through the buffet lines, piling plates high with eclectic mixtures of rich foods: barbecue ribs and pot roast, butterfly shrimp and fried chicken, spaghetti, French fries, and steak. For myself, I remember getting a plate from the salad bar, which did not taste particularly good but did fill me up, yet feeling a strong desire to go back to the buffet line to ensure that I got my money's worth. As we left, feeling overly-full but far from satisfied, my friend joked, "If that was gluttony, give me temperance!"

In many ways, the all-you-can-eat buffet is a symbol of gluttony, so much so that some restaurants have started using the label "All You Care to Eat" buffets in order to avoid the impression that they are encouraging people to over-consume. But does this experience of a buffet gorge adequately describe the sin of gluttony? When people speak of gluttony today, it is usually in the context of overeating. To be sure, overeating is a significant problem in the United States, but if we restrict the word gluttony to mere overconsumption, we miss the potency of this sin and also its rich moral history. This chapter will turn to historical accounts of gluttony in order to draw our attention to the often-unexpected ways—apart from just overeating—that the sin of gluttony manifests itself in our actions today.

First, I will describe in more detail some of the troubling ways we think about food and morality. Then I will draw on a rich philosophical and theoretical history, particularly the work of St. Thomas Aquinas, to argue that gluttony pertains more to the experiences of desire and pleasure than it does to the food itself. I argue that gluttony is best understood as inordinate or disproportionate pleasure in relation to the food consumed, which stands in contrast with much contemporary understanding. I then develop three different modes or occurrences of gluttony: overconsumption (the gluttony of excess), pickiness (the gluttony of delicacy), and sloppiness (the gluttony of consumption). In my conclusion, I will nod toward the many other, nonfood ways that we might indulge in gluttony.

In this chapter, I draw heavily on Aquinas's writing on gluttony. As we shall see, his ancient worldview enables rethinking, in hopefully helpful ways, some of our contemporary quandaries about gluttony and eating. When it comes to food, a Thomistic approach allows us to focus less on *what* is eaten and more on the *why* and *how* of the eating. Such an approach allows us to move beyond the idea that certain *foods* are bad to focus instead on how certain *ways* and *reasons* for eating are what actually matter.

Describing Gluttony in Contemporary America

In America, we moralize eating in very strong ways. In an episode of the popular television show *Portlandia* entitled "Winter in Portland," Peter's pasta addiction leads him and Nance to forego eating pasta for the entire winter. He eventually starts ogling pasta online like pornography and covetously watching other people eat pasta before finally bingeing on raw spaghetti and almost committing "carbicide" alone in a motel room. This episode humorously illustrates how much eating can become a moral matter in at least two ways.

First, one of the problems is the tendency to name food itself as either good or bad (i.e., protein is good, carbs are bad; organic is good, processed is bad). This fear-mongering about carbs or gluten or sugar is actually unhelpful and often counterproductive in making good food choices, as the above *Portlandia* sketch illustrates, in part because such reasoning often leads people to act unreasonably and unhealthily. Peter's complete abstinence, all-or-nothing approach to the whole food group of "carbs" leads to bingeing, which doesn't enable a truly reflective or healthy attitude toward eating pasta.

Although there has been a certain amount of backlash against such ads from different eating disorder advocacy groups, advertisers and companies persist in labeling food as good or bad, and therefore as a key aspect of making a moral choice. Trader Joe's, for example, has a "Reduced Guilt" line of foods. One of the crucial difficulties about such moralizing is that what counts as "good" or "bad" often seems arbitrary and contradictory, with some eschewing fat and calories, and others identifying sugar or even gluten as the primary culprit.

Second and related, we consider one's self good or bad in relation to what a person has eaten. I regularly hear people (usually women) claim that they were "good" because they hadn't eaten any junk food in x amount of time, or conversely, that they were "bad" because they had indulged in some birthday cake or chocolate. Psychologist Paul Rozin speculates that the reason for this is that Americans have inherited Puritan values that contribute to the belief that "anything that is extremely pleasurable, and that includes sex and sweetness, must be bad." Advertisers regularly appeal to these impulses. A couple of years ago, a yogurt company ran an ad with a woman agonizing over her desire for a slice of cheesecake, reminding herself about how "good" she had been and how long it would take to work off the calories of the slice.

A particular view of choice and the use of willpower is at the center of contemporary food moralizing. For example, there is a strong tendency to place blame on those who seem to physically manifest the sin of gluttony—the overweight and the obese—and especially to name overweight and obese people as severely lacking in willpower. Francine Prose, a novelist and food writer, equates gluttony, overeating, and obesity. In fact, she claims gluttony is the only sin which carries visible effects on the body. She links gluttony, obesity, and use of free will: "But now that we are more likely to believe in some form of free will, we are paradoxically more willing to believe that eating or not eating is a response to something that happens outside of ourselves, something that was done to us, and that we must struggle to overcome."[1]

In Prose's view, good use of our freely made choices about foods (and choosing "good" foods) is the key to changing our habits, to eating better, and to weighing less. Moreover, how lucky it is that we live in today's era when we recognize we can make free choices about food. We've come a long way, Prose says approvingly, "from the image of the devil tempting the sinner with pies and cakes, plying the glutton with the joys of the table as a substitute for—a dangerous distraction from—the more profound rewards of the spirit."[2]

Yet, I suggest, it is Prose and others who exclusively emphasize willpower in relation to eating who operate from troubling moralizing beliefs about food and eaters. A focus on willpower (or the more popularly put phrase "eat less, move more") neglects the impact of immense changes that have occurred regarding eating in the twenty-first century, including the rise of industrially processed foods, the rise of food deserts in the United States, the increase in weight-loss programs claiming miracle cures for weight gain, and the shifts in body image. Such complexities in the modern

---

1. Francine Prose, *Gluttony* (New York: Oxford University Press, 2003), 61.
2. Prose, *Gluttony*, 60.

eating environment need to be reflected in our considerations of gluttony. The "eat less, move more" mantra, to be done by sheer dint of willpower, comes across as tone-deaf about how easy it is to do "good" eating. The so-called "good" diets of our day—the gluten-free, plant-based diets—to be orchestrated carefully with a good bout of exercise at the gym are luxuries for many. These particular forms of diet and exercise require access, time, and money, which mitigates the kinds of choices people are able to make.

Not only that, but some scientific studies' conclusions about the use of willpower suggest that the picture of the "devil tempting sinners with pies and cakes" may not be too far off the mark. One recent study suggests that people who experience fewer temptations are the ones best able to exercise their willpower; the greater the number of temptations (being faced by many more opportunities to eat the cake, for example), the less effective any one person's willpower was.[3] In other words, exercising willpower isn't the same as exercising muscle: it is not the case that the more one uses it, the better one's willpower becomes. As one key example, many processed snack foods are hyperpalatable, heavy in salt, fat, and sugar. A concept known as "sensory-specific satiety" names how foods like Doritos and Dr. Pepper have complex formulas that pique the taste buds. Yet the complexity of their formulas means they don't have a single overriding flavor that signals the brain to stop eating; people never get satiated and indeed, "no one can eat just one!" Willpower doesn't work in such instances.[4] In addition, many scholars have noted the stark rise in overweight and obesity since the 1980s, but there is no corresponding study that suggests a massive, culture-wide decrease in willpower.[5]

Perhaps we can even say, along with religious studies professor Alan Levinovitz, that the moralizing language attributed to certain "bad" foods like gluten, sugar, and fat have more in common with quasi-religious beliefs than scientific evidence. "Fiction, not food, is the real demon," writes Levinovitz.[6] Prose limits the idea of gluttony to freewill choices about

3. See W. Hoffman, et. al., "Everyday Temptations: An Experience Sampling Study of Desire, Conflict, and Self-Control," *Journal of Personality and Social Psychology* 102, no. 6 (2012): 1318–35.

4. For some of the scientific data surrounding food, hyperpalatability, and the limits of willpower, see David Kessler, *The End of Overeating: Taking Control of the Insatiable American Appetite* (New York: Rodale, 2009), 44. The book's title belies the nuance and concern of Kessler's book, and Kessler develops some discussion of communal habits that might enable, form, and shape better views of food.

5. For some of the scientific discussion of willpower and its use in the dieting industry, see Darya Pino Rose, *Foodist: Using Real Food and Real Science to Lose Weight Without Dieting* (New York: Harper-Collins, 2013). On the connections between the obesity crisis, fat shaming, and willpower, see Dr. Yoni Freedhoff's blog Weighty Matters (http://www.weightymatters.ca/).

6. Alan Levinovitz, *The Gluten Lie: And Other Myths About What You Eat* (New York: Regan Arts, 2015).

whichever food *du jour* is the "evil" food of the day. She also limits the possibility of the sin of gluttony to obese people who seem most especially prone to eating such "evil" foods. Yet recall that, as I suggested above, societal understandings about what foods are "good" and "evil" are prone to being mistaken, and even unhealthy or utterly wrong. Following the current social norms about what constitutes gluttony will not make for healthier people and will not correctly help us identify sins.

What we need, instead, is a way of thinking about gluttony that does involve willpower when appropriate, but that also enables us to broaden our vision of gluttony and to think more intently about what it means to broaden our vision of, use our reason in relation to, gluttony.

Aquinas's Account of Gluttony

Historical accounts of gluttony offer a different and broader view for our consideration. Historically, people have assessed gluttony in quite serious ways. In Deuteronomy 21:18–21 which addresses how to deal with a disobedient child, the punishment for gluttony is death: "His father and mother shall take hold of him and bring him out to the elders at the gate of his home city, where they shall say to the elders of the city, 'This son of ours is a stubborn and rebellious fellow who will not listen to us; he is a glutton and a drunkard.' Then all his fellow citizens shall stone him to death. Thus shall you purge the evil from your midst. " Gluttony here demands an extreme punishment precisely because it threatens the stability of the community. As philosopher Susan Hill writes, "Uncontrolled, gluttonous behavior represents an impure malignancy in the cultural body that must be excised for the community to be healthy."[7]

Therefore, the accusation of gluttony could be applied to anyone who transgressed social norms of food and drink, regardless of amount eaten or drunk. In Matthew and Luke, Jesus is called a glutton and a drunkard, which seems to just be a general insult that his eating violates social norms and expectations. John Cassian, an early-fifth-century monk and theologian, argues that Eve's sin in the Garden was gluttony that bore the consequence of "ruin and death" to the human race.[8] Even nonreligious sources like Plato associate gluttony with what is worst in human nature: irrationality, animality, and impurity. Theological sources historically have also seen gluttony as serious because it paved the way to other, graver sins. For St. John Chrysostom, for example, gluttony becomes a pathway to greed and

7. Susan E. Hill, *Eating to Excess: The Meaning of Gluttony and the Fat Body in the Ancient World* (Santa Barbara, CA: Praeger, 2011), 35.

8. John Cassian, *Conferences*, trans. Colm Luibheid (Mahwah, NJ: Paulist Press, 1985).

neglect of the poor. He compares gluttony to a flooding ocean that "when it passes its bounds, does not work so many evils as the belly does to our body, together with our soul."[9]

One of the chief lessons from history is that the concern was not one of fatness and the ways gluttony is embodied, (Prose's own concern) but rather of *preoccupation*. In the works of writers like Aristotle who see in gluttony what is worst in the human soul, we see an absence of any discussion of fatness. Gluttony isn't bad because of its effect on the body as much as its effect on the soul. To return to Levinovitz, the religious studies scholar quoted above:

Without fear, not only will eating be more pleasurable, it may also be more healthful. As Paul Rozin likes to remind people, 'Worrying about food is not good for you.' He suggests that the cause of expanding waistlines and exploding hearts in America isn't necessarily what we eat but how we eat—anxiously, obsessed with nutrition, counting calories, scanning food labels, eliminating foods and then bingeing on them.[10]

Our preoccupations—both social and individual—are concerns when considering gluttony.

Compared to these historical accounts, Thomas Aquinas actually takes a relatively lenient view of gluttony. In terms of sinfulness, we name degrees of seriousness partly in terms of "venial" and "mortal" sins, where venial sins are less-serious sins that do not imply a total separation from God and mortal sins are grave sins that do imply a total separation from God.

Aquinas says that gluttony can be both. Gluttony can be a mortal sin when a person is so attached to the pleasure of food that she is willing to forsake God and God's commandments in order to obtain these pleasures.[11] An example might be ignoring the Church's requirements to fast on Ash Wednesday and Good Friday if one did so knowingly, willingly, and completely voluntarily. Aquinas specifies that the sin of gluttony is diminished both by its matter, which is food, and by the person who sins both because "of the necessity of taking food and on account of the proper discretion and moderation in such matters."[12] In other words, because we need to eat and because it is easy to err in something we do so frequently, most instances of the sin of gluttony would be venial.

9. Quoted in Hill, *Eating to Excess*, 116.

10. Levinovitz, *Gluten Lie*.

11. Thomas Aquinas, *Summa Theologiae* II-II, q. 148, a. 2.

12. ST II-II, q. 148, a. 3.

From Aquinas's point of view, a proper moral discussion about food ought not to focus on the food itself but on the person doing the eating and the human action of eating. A human action, according to Catholic moral thought, aims at a particular end or purpose, and it is according to this end that the action of eating might be judged. Here we see the great advantage of a Thomistic approach to talking about eating and gluttony. Aquinas tells us that gluttony is not just immoderate consumption of food, but rather an inappropriate *appetite* towards food:

Gluttony denotes, not any desire of eating and drinking, but an inordinate desire. Now desire is said to be inordinate through leaving the order of reason, wherein the good of moral virtue consists: and a thing is said to be a sin through being contrary to virtue.[13]

Aquinas's definition needs further explanation. In his worldview, every created being has an "appetite" or internal motion corresponding to its proper nature, and this internal "inclining" is what Aquinas calls "appetite." He distinguishes three levels of appetite: natural, sensitive, and rational. The first two types of appetite are what concern us here.

The *natural appetite* is the part of our soul that shares its powers both with animals and plants. It is the inclination of a living organism to do things in accord with its nature. It includes reproduction, nourishment, and growth. Aquinas says that the vegetal soul is not under the power of reason, which means that it does things without consent of the will or guidance from the intellect. No amount of intentionality or learning will induce the vegetal soul to cause the body to grow faster. In like manner, no amount of intentionality or learning will stop the soul from experiencing hunger. Hunger, or more generally, the need to eat, is beyond the control of human rational powers. It is simply natural to need to eat and to feel hungry in response to that biological need.

The second level of appetite is called the *sensitive appetite*. Human and other creatures that can respond to external stimuli received by the senses have this kind of appetite. The operations of the sensitive appetite need guidance from our intellect lest they become destructive. In other words, we can use reason to practice virtues (good habits) that help us control our sensory responses to the world. The sensory pleasure of taste and touch that we might associate with eating is called the concupiscible appetite; the virtue we can use in response is temperance (sometimes also called moderation). We might say that temperance disposes a person to experience pleasure well, in a way befitting a rational creature. On the other hand, we can attribute sin to the concupiscible appetite when we are no longer using reason: this is the sin

13. ST II-II, q. 148, a. 1.

of gluttony. We might say that gluttony occurs when a person experiences the pleasures associated with food in a way not befitting a rational creature.

The language of "not befitting" might be unfamiliar but the experience Aquinas is describing is not. For example, I am eight months pregnant and becoming very, very hungry. My experience of hunger is due to my natural appetite that is producing the sensation of hunger in response to the needs of my body to eat. I can't help feeling hungry right now. But I am also writing this fascinating description of the appetites with my *Summa Theologiae* spread out in front of me. I know I should get up and make a healthy lunch with a sufficient balance of healthy veggies and proteins— that would be eating "befitting of a rational creature." But instead, I am eating goldfish crackers that my son left in a bowl next to my computer. They are delicious, and though I know they aren't the nutritious meal that my growing baby and I need, I am still eating them because they taste good and because I would rather write about the appetites than get up and make myself a better meal. My desire for the goldfish and the subsequent pleasure I experience while eating them is due to my concupiscible appetite, which has arguably transgressed the dictates of reason by seeking to satisfy my desire for food in such a wholly inadequate lunch.

It is as Aquinas says: the desire of my sensitive appetite is where the vice of gluttony exists. "Hence," he says, "the first movement of gluttony denotes inordinateness in the sensitive appetite, and this is not without sin."[14] What he means is that I can be held responsible not for the experience of hunger, but rather for my experience of pleasure in the satisfaction of my hunger. If my pleasure is <u>inordinate</u>, which simply means inappropriate, or more specifically <u>disproportionate</u>, my action "is not without sin."

Aquinas identifies two general ways that the pleasure of food can be inordinate: first, regarding the food consumed (both the type and quantity of food), and second, with regards to the actual consumption of the food or the manner of eating. In the first way, our experience of pleasure might be disproportionate by requiring (1) too much food (gluttony of excess) or (2) food that is too rich or fine (gluttony of delicacy). For the sake of clarity, these ought to be treated separately. Regarding the actual consumption of food, a person might experience pleasure by eating in ways that are unbefitting a human (gluttony of consumption).[15]

Some of Aquinas' thoughts on gluttony will seem familiar by comparison to the twenty-first century narrative I sketched above. Some, however, are unfamiliar to us, yet help deepen our vision. We will turn now to three

---

14. ST II-II, q. 148, a. 1.
15. ST II-II, q. 148, a. 4.

different modes or types of gluttony which I call the gluttony of excess (overconsumption), the gluttony of delicacy (pickiness), and the gluttony of consumption (sloppiness). In all three areas, we will focus on this central point that gluttony pertains more to pleasure of eating than the food itself, and that its consequences on the soul are more relevant than those we see on the body.

Gluttony of Excess

In some of my online reading on gluttony, I happened across a message board where Catholics debate whether or not different actions were sins and needed to be confessed. A self-described "overly scrupulous" individual posted a question asking if a recent incident constituted "gluttony." He described how he had been eating out and midway through the meal, started feeling full. He didn't want to waste food and apparently it was quite inconvenient to ask for the remainder of his food to go, so he chose to finish the meal. He described the uncomfortable feeling of fullness afterwards and asked if he needed to confess to the sin of gluttony.

Here is a perfect example of how people tend to conflate overeating and gluttony. It is clear that this individual overate, and it is also clear that the consequences of doing so were unpleasant. But gluttony is not simply about overeating, but rather about the disorder of the appetite, such that it pursues pleasures disproportionate to the food consumed. This individual did not eat to excess because of the pleasure he experienced. Indeed, he apparently felt the opposite of pleasure as he continued to eat but nevertheless persisted because of a strong sense of duty (to prevent waste and avoid the inconvenience of packing up the rest of the meal to go). A gluttonous action would be if the individual in question felt the sensation of fullness but reasoned that the meal was simply too delicious to leave unfinished.

I wish to note here that the experience of overeating is ubiquitous. All of us have had the experience of eating too much and regretting it. But how is it meaningful to talk about this experience as sinful, particularly when the involvement of freewill is questionable, for the reasons I noted above? Aquinas addresses this very issue, noting that if a person "exceed in quantity of food, not from desire of food but through deeming it necessary to him, this pertains not to gluttony but to some kind of inexperience. It is a case of gluttony only when a man knowingly exceeds the measure in eating, from a desire or the pleasures of the palate." In other words, for the sin of gluttony to be present, a person must not simply overeat, but overeat *because* it brings her pleasure to do so.

The question of gluttony of excess is further exacerbated by the fact that quantity is a relative concept. Aristotle, one of the greatest Greek philosophers at the origin of Western thought, famously argued that virtue was found in the mean between too much and too little, notes specifically the relative nature of the mean as it pertains to food. He says,

If ten pounds are too much for a particular person to eat and two too little, it does not follow that the trainer will order six pounds; for this also is perhaps too much for the person who is to take it or too little . . . Thus a master of any art avoids excess and defect but seeks the intermediate and chooses this—the intermediate not in the object but relatively to us.[16]

Aristotle compares virtuous eating here to an art, and he is not blind to the challenges of applying the doctrine of the mean to a question as complicated as food consumption. In his discussion of the mean in the *Nicomachean Ethics*, he says flat out: "Hence also it is no easy task to be good."

For in everything it is no easy task to find the middle, e.g. to find the middle of a circle is not for every one but for him who knows; so too any one can get angry—that is easy—or give or spend money; but to do this to the right person, to the right extent, at the right time, with the right aim, and in the right way, that is not for everyone, nor is it easy; that is why goodness is both rare and laudable and noble.[17]

With food it is especially difficult to find the middle. This is because the goal in eating is not at all to avoid the experience of pleasure, since food is, by nature, pleasurable, but rather, to feel the right amount of pleasure in response to right things. An additional difficulty is that appetite for food often persists even when the natural appetite has been satisfied. Thus, I may continue eating goldfish crackers (as I have done) long after they stopped satisfying my immediate hunger.

So how might we commit gluttony of excess? By intentionally overeating for the sake of the consequent pleasure. This is a common human experience that may be exacerbated by certain circumstances like an endless buffet as described in the beginning of this chapter. In such a situation, there may be so many choices of appetizing foods that it becomes easy to transgress the standards of rational quantity because we want to try one more thing.

It is not just all-you-can-eat buffets that provide such temptations. We Americans (or Westerners, and increasingly non-Westerners) live in an age of plenty where we often find ourselves in situations with an abundance of good food choices that tempt us to transgress the bounds of reason. The

---

16. Aristotle, *Nicomachean Ethics*, Book II, 1106b1–5.

17. *Nicomachean Ethics*, Book II, 1124–29b.

proliferation of brands and flavors of frozen pizzas and yogurts at the grocery store may encourage us to overconsume precisely because they all seem different. So too may menus that are constantly in a state of flux, as is the case at fast food restaurants. The more new sources of (supposed) pleasures we are exposed to, the less likely we are to judge the value of these pleasures rationally, because we desire the new pleasures.[18]

Other situations that encourage overeating are those in which food is always available. I used to have an office right across from the teachers' lounge, which was almost always stocked with coffee and some sort of treat like donuts or pumpkin bars or leftover Halloween candy, usually brought in by one of the faculty to share. It was easy to duck in several times a day (which I, along with many other faculty members, did) to grab a tasty snack, not because we were hungry but because the food was pleasurable and easy to get. Such actions might seem relatively inconsequential and definitely too trivial to label "sin," but remember that we are defining sin here as anything that transgresses the bounds of reason and detracts from human flourishing.

Researchers studying food consumption name "obesogenic environments" as a reason for a rising obesity epidemic, but also for the kind of mindlessness in eating that people describe about their own habits. The more food is available in an environment, the more we eat, regardless of the quality of food.[19] This is what Aristotle condemned so contemptuously as the self-indulgence characteristic of gluttony: "This is why we should describe as self-indulgent rather the man who without appetite or with but a slight appetite pursues the excesses of pleasure and avoids moderate pains, than the man who does so because of his strong appetites."[20]

The great advantage of employing an Aristotelian-Thomistic appraisal of gluttony here is that such a view allows us to reclaim control of such situations and claim that such "mindlessness" is unbefitting a rational creature. In other words, it is possible in such situations to act otherwise because we judge our actions to be inconsistent with our ultimate flourishing, which I judge that most people would say of overeating five-day-old popcorn!

18. Charlotte A. Hardman, Danielle Ferriday, Lesley Kyle, Peter J. Rogers, Jeffrey M. Brunstrom, "So Many Brands and Varieties to Choose From: Does This Compromise the Control of Food Intake in Humans?" PLoS ONE 10(4), e0125869, http://journals.plos.org/plosone/article?id=10.1371/journal.pone.0125869.

19. See, for example George Osei-Assibey, et al, "The Influence of the Food Environment on Overweight and Obesity in Young Children," British Medical Journal Open 2013, https://bmjopen.bmj.com/content/2/6/e001538; Amelia Lake and Tim Townsend, "Obesogenic Environments: Exploring the Built and Food Environments," The Journal for the Royal Society for the Promotion of Health 126, no. 6 (2006): 262–67.

20. Aristotle, Nicomachean Ethics, book VII, 1148a18–20.

Another great advantage of calling our attention to these seemingly harmless transgressions of overconsumption by identifying them under the sin of gluttony is that we potentially become aware of the larger inter-personal ramifications of disproportionate food consumption. On the environmental impacts of gluttony, Philip Cafaro writes,

> All else being equal, Americans' habit of consuming approximate-ly 25 percent more calories than necessary increases the amount of land needed to grow crops and graze animals by 25 percent. It increases the amount of pollutants dumped onto agricultural lands and running off into rivers and streams by 25 percent. Excess food consumption harms Americans' health; if we take ecosystem health to include clean rivers and streams and robust populations of our na-tive flora and fauna, we must conclude that excess food consumption also harms environmental health.[21]

In other words, we can see how gluttony is harmful not only to the flourishing of the glutton but to the larger ecological community.

There is another and perhaps more pressing way in which we transgress the bounds of reason in proportion to the quantity of pleasure we receive from food. This is the <u>attention</u> we give to food. St. Gregory the Great alludes to this in his *Moralia*. As theology professor Dennis Okholm notes, he talks about the way we commit gluttony by "anticipating eating with preoccupied, eager longing" and (referring to desert monks) "checking the angle of the sun every fifteen minutes."[22] What Gregory could not have predicted was the way in which technology facilitates this habitual over-attention we give to food. Entire television channels are now dedicated to food. Multiple mag-azines are dedicated exclusively to food and countless others devote large sections focused on recipes and/or dieting. Computer and cell phone apps allow us to constantly track what we consume, and social media allows us to give infinite attention to what we did or didn't eat.

Such hypervigilance might strike us as harmless or even beneficial, but the whole point I am trying to emphasize here about gluttony is that it is pri-marily a question of proportionality. Paying too much attention to food can be as irrational as mindless eating. When we spend too much time thinking about food, we neglect more important things that we ought to attend to. It is clear then why Gregory identifies "excessive attention" as a species of glut-tony—thinking about food distracts his monks from the most important thing they (and all of us Christians) should be thinking about: God.

21. Philip Cafaro, "Gluttony, Arrogance, Greed, and Apathy: An Exploration of an Environmental Vice" in *Environmental Virtue Ethics*, ed. Ronald Sandler and Philip Cafaro (Lanham, MD: Rowman & Littlefield, 2005) 135–58, at 141–42.

22. Dennis Okholm, "Gluttony: Thought for Food," *The American Benedictine Review* 49, no. 1 (1998): 33–59.

I discussed above our tendency to equate fatness with gluttony and some of the problems with this tendency. Here, we can see more clearly how thinness can be implicated in gluttony. It is impossible to provide an adequate account of eating disorders and their moral implications in the scope of this chapter, but it is worth noting that many scholars on eating disorders from many different disciplines have noted the role of the relentless pursuit of thinness in the motivations of women with disordered eating and body image. In her award-winning book, *Fasting Girls: The History of Anorexia Nervosa*, Joan Jacob Brumberg argues that the "modern anorectic strives for perfection in terms of society's ideal of physical, rather than spiritual beauty."[23] This view is tragic precisely because it distracts us from what is important by, as Michelle Lelwica puts it, "reduc[ing] the scope of our decision-making to how we look and how many calories we consume. When body size becomes the grounds for proving our virtue, we lose sight of the pursuits that truly have meaning for us—pursuits that require us to care about something greater than the numbers on a scale."[24]

A proper appreciation of the gluttony of excess therefore should make us skeptical of the kinds of food- and people-moralizing I discussed above, and it further broaden our view of gluttony.

Gluttony of Delicacy

We have already examined how gluttony occurs when the relationship between pleasure and quantity are disproportionate. Now we will turn to the ways that gluttony occurs when pleasure and *quality* of food are disproportionately related. One of the best descriptions of this form of gluttony is found in C. S. Lewis's *Screwtape Letters*. Screwtape writes to Wormwood:

> One of the great achievements of the last hundred years has been to deaden the human conscience on that subject, so that by now you will hardly find a sermon preached or a conscience troubled about it in the whole length and breadth of Europe. This has largely been effected by concentrating all our efforts on gluttony of Delicacy, not gluttony of Excess. Your patient's mother, as I learn from the dossier and you might have learned from Glubose, is a good example. She would be astonished—one day, I hope, will be—to learn that her whole life is enslaved to this kind of sensuality, which is quite concealed from her by the fact that the quantities involved are small. But what do quantities matter, provided we can use a human belly and palate to produce

23. Joan Jacob Brumberg, *Fasting Girls: The History of Anorexia Nervosa* (Cambridge, MA: Harvard University Press, 2000), 48.

24. Michelle M. Lelwica, *The Religion of Thinness: Satisfying the Spiritual Hungers Behind Women's Obsession with Food and Weight* (Carlsbad, CA: Gurze Books, 2010), 166–67.

querulousness, impatience, uncharitableness, and self-concern? Glu-
bose has this old woman well in hand . . . She is always turning from
what has been offered her to say with a demure little sigh and a smile
'Oh please, please . . . all I want is a cup of tea, weak but not too weak,
and the teeniest weeniest bit of really crisp toast.' You see? Because
what she wants is smaller and less costly than what has been set before
her, she never recognizes as gluttony her determination to get what she
wants, however troublesome it may be to others.[25]

This species of gluttony, what we might call gluttony of delicacy, is related to gluttony of excess in that is often accompanied by excessive attention.
The person who thinks constantly about food is often also the same person
who is overly-discriminating in her food choices.

Lewis is right in his claim that we tend to dismiss this as gluttony. For
example, food critic Jeffrey Steingarten is explicit in resisting the label of
glutton for the gourmand:

A person who eats ten bags of potato chips or SnackWell's cookies in an
afternoon has an impulse-control problem. But a person like me, who
spends the afternoon—or a week of afternoons—planning the perfect
dinner of barbecued ribs or braised foie gras, has clearly mastered his
impulses. We passionate eaters elevate, we ennoble the bestial impulse
to feed into a sublime activity, into an art, into the art of eating.[26]

There is something attractive about the image of eating that Steingarten lays
out, more attractive than the mindlessness and seemingly sloppiness of the
gluttony of excess. So what is precisely sinful in the actions of the gourmand?

The gourmand is a glutton because he loves such pleasures more than they
are worth. A couple of years ago, a scathing article against so-called "foodies"
lambasted their tendency to elevate eating to a religious act. B. R. Myers writes,

References to cooks as "gods," to restaurants as "temples," to biting into
"heaven," etc., used to be meant as jokes, even if the compulsive recourse to
religious language always betrayed a certain guilt about the stomach-driven
life. Now the equation of eating with worship is often made with a straight
face. The mood at a dinner table depends on the quality of food served;
if culinary perfection is achieved, the meal becomes downright holy—as
we learned from Pollan's *The Omnivore's Dilemma* (2006), in which a pork
dinner is described as feeling "like a ceremony ... a secular seder."[27]

25. C.S. Lewis, *The Screwtape Letters* (New York: HarperCollins, 1942), chapter 17.

26. Jeffrey Steingarten, *It Must Have Been Something I Ate: The Return of the Man Who Ate Everything* (New York: Vintage Books, 2002), 27.

27. B.R. Myers, "The Moral Crusade Against Foodies," *The Atlantic* 307, no. 2 (March 2011): 81, http://www.theatlantic.com/magazine/archive/2011/03.

Myers clearly sees in the contemporary foodie something akin to those St. Paul condemned in his letter to the Philippians as the "enemies of the cross of Christ" whose god is their belly (Phil 3:18–19). It is not wrong to experience pleasure in eating, nor is it wrong to try to make food more pleasurable by cooking a recipe well or using good ingredients. What is problematic, indeed *gluttonous*, is elevating the pleasure of food above other considerations that rightfully deserve a higher place.

The one who commits the gluttony of delicacy is also too concerned with the pleasures of the body to the neglect of other rational considerations, which may include financial stability and the good of the community. In his *Institutes*, for example, Cassian argues that the gluttony of delicacy threatens the well-being of the monastic community. He writes that

> [w]e should then choose for our food, not only that which moderates the heat of burning lust, and avoids kindling it; but what is easily got ready, and what is recommended by its cheapness, and is suitable to the life of the brethren and their common use. . . [A] monk ought not to ask for foods which are not customary for others, lest his mode of life should be exposed publicly to all and rendered vain and idle and so be destroyed by the disease of vanity.[28]

While Cassian is writing for monks, his point is that gluttony of delicacy makes the individual too concerned with one's self and own preferences, thus threatening the communal nature of the meal and the very community itself. But how is this true of the gluttony of delicacy today? In what way can we meaningfully say that the gourmand directly threatens the good of the community? There are several ways.

First, gluttony of delicacy is a direct threat to <u>hospitality</u>. Food is inherently relational, and hospitality is a practice that calls us to a conscious recognition of that inherent relationality. The practice of hospitality teaches us both to give and to receive food well. As L. Shannon Jung writes, "Hospitality is a way of being in the world, an orientation to others and to life itself. It is a means of grace, a way of both receiving God's grace and being in tune with the gracious life of the world."[29] A gluttony of delicacy threatens hospitality on the receiving end by placing excessive demands on the host or by rejecting what the host has to offer.

Cassian addresses this concern specifically, arguing that the monk shows gluttony "if we are kept to dine by one of the brethren we are not content to eat our food with the relish which he has prepared and offers to us, but take the unpardonable liberty of asking to have something else poured over it

---

28. John Cassian, *Institutes*, trans. Boniface Ramsey (Mahwah, NJ: The Newman Press, 2000), 5.23.

29. Shannon Jung, *Sharing Food: Christian Practices for Enjoyment* (Minneapolis: Fortress Press, 2006), 51.

or added to it."[30] Cassian's reasons include that we might be exposing our host's poverty, or even simply that we are annoying to our host and their guests.[31] It is customary today to ask guests what their food preferences are and to cater to those accordingly. But the pressing need to cater to *every* demand of the guest puts a significant burden on the host and makes it difficult, if not impossible, to practice hospitality spontaneously.

Second, the gluttony of delicacy allocates a disproportionate amount of wealth to the pleasures of food. St. John Chrysostom makes a direct connection between gluttony and luxury: "Let us seek meats to nourish, not things to ruin us . . . seek food which has comfort, not luxury which is full of discomfort: the one is luxury, the other mischief; the one is pleasure, the other pain"[32] and "why do you thus gorge your own body with excess, and waste that of the poor with want?"[33] B. R. Myers today writes scornfully about the elitism and moral impoverishment of foodies who "talk of flying to Paris to buy cheese, to Vietnam to sample pho" and "are notorious for $100 lunches as great value for money."[34]

It is easy to see how spending hundreds of dollars on the pleasure of a meal is disproportionate, but we ought not to succumb to the temptation to caricature this species of gluttony. The gluttony of delicacy occurs whenever the pleasures of food are placed higher than other more important considerations. We might say that the person who opens the kitchen cupboard and sees an abundance of adequate but wholly boring foods and just prefers to "go out for dinner" or the individual who sneers at home-brewed coffee but pays top dollar for a cup at a high-end coffee shop is committing this form gluttony. While there is not a direct correlation between luxury consumption and global hunger, there is something to the utilitarian argument that the moral value of eating luxury foods ought to be weighed against the obligation of providing basic nutrition for the poor.[35] As Paul B. Thompson writes, "Such reasoning might reasonably be applied to upper middle-class people who pay more for foods at boutique supermarkets. If

30. Cassian, *Institutes*, 5.23.

31. Cassian, *Institutes*, 5.23.

32. Hill, *Eating to Excess*, 118.

33. Quoted in Hill, *Eating to Excess*, 117.

34. Myers, "Moral Crusade."

35. While it is simplistic to assume that changes in quantity or quality of the food I eat will have a direct impact on global hunger, it is the case that securing the world's future food security demands significant changes to agricultural practices and subsequently dietary habits. In North America, only 40% of cropland is devoted to growing food for human consumption while the remainder is dedicated to feeding animals. If, as some estimate, global food production will need to double by 2050 to feed the global population, such environmental practices will simply become unsustainable. Jonathan Foley et al. "Solutions for a Cultivated Planet, *Nature* 478 (October 20, 2011), 337–42.

we see our dietary choices as needing to contribute to an optimal amount of good in the world, we will see many of our meals imposing moral costs on the poor that simply cannot be justified."[36]

Readers therefore should consider how high they are prioritizing food over other concerns. Not all high-end shopping might fit into a category of gluttony of delicacy, for example. Choosing to spend more money at places that pay a living wage would not be a gluttony of delicacy, precisely because the person involved is not placing food at a higher premium than the person.

This is not to say that we should never overspend on a meal or should feel obligated to always apply a rigid utilitarian calculus to the food we buy, carefully measuring whether the cost spent is proportionate to the good gained. Hospitality, for example, demands a certain liberality with food and drink. Yet an awareness of the dangers of a gluttony of delicacy can help distinguish between the liberality proper to hospitality and habitual wasteful extravagance. The rhythm of the liturgical year—fasting during Lent, feasting at Easter—provides a useful balance, particularly when fasting is matched with almsgiving. This helps us caution against an excess of feasting at the expense of our duties to the poor.

Finally, and on a related note, a gluttony of delicacy has direct ecological and environmental implications.[37] There is a strange contradiction in the moral logic of a gourmand who rejects factory-farmed meat and highly processed snacks yet relishes such sustainable but arguably cruel dietary pleasures like veal and foie gras. Meyers points to the extreme version of this:

Not too long ago MSNBC.com put out an article titled "Some Bravery as a Side Dish." It listed "7 foods for the fearless stomach," one of which was ortolan, the endangered songbirds fattened in dark boxes. The more lives sacrificed for a dinner, the more impressive the eater. Dana Good-year: "Thirty duck hearts in curry … The ethos of this kind of cooking is undeniably macho." Amorality as ethos, callousness as bravery, queenly self-absorption as machismo: no small perversion of language is needed to spin heroism out of an evening spent in a chair.[38]

Such a concern is not only for the gourmand. For example, we might consider that Americans eat more meat per person than consumers of almost any nation on earth, on average about 150 pounds per day, which has been fueled even further in recent years by the rise of high-protein,

36. Paul B. Thompson, *From Field to Fork: Food Ethics for Everyone* (New York: Oxford University Press, 2015), 32.

37. I do want to note that an increased attention to food can be good—as in our increased awareness of the benefits of organic produce, or allowing WIC and food stamp recipients to use their funds at farmers markets.

38. Myers, "Moral Crusade."

low-carb diets. While there are no fixed rules for what constitutes "excess" with regards to gluttony, the data on meat consumption raises the question: Is a third of a pound of meat per person per day excessive?

We can address this question by considering our desire for meat compared to the direct environmental impact of raising animals for food. According to one study, 89–97% of gross energy contained in animal feed is not converted to edible protein and fat and "total mass of cereal and leguminous grain eaten annually by animals is . . . roughly a third of the global harvest of these crops, and it contains enough energy to feed more than three billion people."[39] So-called "sustainable" farming practices may look less bleak, but some suggest that the environmental impact of grass-fed and pastured animals is actually worse. Grass-fed cows produce considerable more methane than grain-fed, with one study showing a 500% increase in greenhouse gas emissions from grass-fed cattle, 35% more water use, and 30% more land use.[40]

A more reasonable alternative is eating less meat. In the above-cited study, the authors speculate a realistic alternative to current agricultural practice is to "assume that the area now devoted to feed crops would be planted to a mixture of food crops, and only their milling residues would be used for feeding: this adjustment would mean that roughly an additional one billion people could be sustained on predominantly vegetarian diets containing small, but adequate amount of animal protein."[41]

Historically, abstinence from meat has been one of the most commonly practiced methods of resisting the temptations of the gluttony of delicacy and concentrating the efforts of the soul on higher matters. The Catholic Church has historically stipulated certain days (i.e., Fridays) as days of abstinence during which no meat was to be eaten. Regular abstinence from meat may also help to shield the desire to eat more ethically from the apparent elitism of the meat-eating gourmands, about which Meyer is so critical: "Even if gourmets' rejection of factory farms and fast food is largely motivated by their traditional elitism, it has left them, for the first time in the history of their community, feeling more moral, spiritual even, than the man on the street."[42] This is a healthy reminder that even the desire to be moral can lead us into single-mindedness and sin.

---

39. V. Smil, "Worldwide Transformation of Diets, Burdens of Meat Productions, and Opportunities for Novel Food Proteins," *Enzyme and Microbial Technology* 30 (2002): 305–11.

40. Studies cited in John Comerford, "Telling the Grass-Fed Beef Story," Penn State Animal Science Blogs, October 7, 2010; https://sites.psu.edu/tetherton/2010/10/07.

41. Smil, "Worldwide Transformation."

42. Myers, "Moral Crusade."

Gluttony of Consumption

The final form of gluttony we need to address is that which Aquinas describes as inordinance in the actual consumption of food, "either because one forestalls the proper time for eating, which is to eat 'hastily,' or one fails to observe the due manner of eating, by eating 'greedily.'"[43] Rather than attending to the food we eat (either in terms of its quantity or quality), gluttony of consumption means we are concerned more with the circumstances of the eating itself. The gluttony of consumption identifies those times when the pleasure of eating itself is disproportionate to other pleasures available at a particular time. Again, we see an overlap with this type of gluttony and the previous two we have examined. The one who eats to excess is often the one who scarfs down his food with little awareness, or perhaps little care, about signals of satiety and propriety. And even the gourmand is not immune from improper displays of manners at table as Todd Kliman describes:

> I watched tears streak down a friend's face as he popped expertly cleavered bites of chicken into his mouth ... He was red-eyed and breathing fast. 'It hurts, it hurts, but it's so good, but it hurts, and I can't stop eating!' He slammed a fist down on the table. The beer in his glass sloshed over the sides. 'Jesus Christ, I've got to stop!'"[44]

But we must be clear as to why the gluttony of consumption is its own species of gluttony apart from concerns of excess and gormandizing. Remember that gluttony is essentially about a lack of harmony between the movements of the appetite both in the experience of desire and pleasure and the dictates of reason. The goal is for our eating to befit a rational creature and to properly balance all the relevant concerns necessary in promoting the good of the individual eater (psychosomatic, communal and spiritual) and the community in which that person is situated.

We already have some sense of what is good here. Proper attention to manners makes us aware of the community around us. We wait before eating and before partaking of seconds to make sure others have a fair share. We avoid eating quickly in order to gauge for feelings of satiety and to avoid embarrassing situations of appearing sloppy. We avoid eating with our mouths open so that we do not disgust our tablemates with the appearance of our mastication and so that we leave a space for others to contribute to the conversation while we are forced to listen. To neglect any of these means to put our own desires—for more food, for the pleasure of food, for the pleasure of conversation—above other higher goods.

43. ST II-II, a. 148, a. 4.

44. Todd Kliman, "The Perfect Chef" in *Cornbread Nation 7: The Best of Southern Food Writing*, ed. Francis Lam, 55–70 (Athens, GA: University of Georgia Press, 2014), 61.

There are other aspects to the gluttony of consumption to consider. Aquinas, drawing on Gregory the Great, mentions specifically the tendency to "forestall the proper time of eating," or more generally, to eat at the wrong times. For St. Gregory, who is concerned with the monastic community, this means eating apart from communal meals, what we might refer to today as "snacking." It would be foolhardy to condemn snacking outright. Snacking is often a necessity in light of busy schedules and is sometimes even considered a healthier way of eating, as opposed to sitting down to three square meals. Habitual snacking can, however, threaten certain dimensions of communal life by putting too much attention on eating under the wrong circumstances. A key insight here from Aquinas is that we ought to make sure circumstances justify the eating, or that we avoid eating at the wrong place or the wrong time.

I remember one Christmas when I was very young, my father took me to see *The Nutcracker*. It was the first ballet he had ever attended, and he made a big deal about what a special occasion it was. His experience was unfortunately sullied by the fact that concession snacks were sold both at the beginning of the ballet and at the intermission, and he could not get over the sound of crinkling Doritos bags and slurping straws that drowned out the orchestra. While many social occasions are enhanced by food, snacking can begin to look like this third form of gluttony when it undermines communal practices or elevates the pleasure of eating above other pleasures. It is gluttonous if the experience of watching a movie or a play requires food to be pleasurable because such a view assigns a disproportionate weight to the pleasures of food above the pleasures of the occasion itself. By avoiding snacking in so many of the situations in which this has become commonplace, we might better attend to other goods these circumstances have to offer. It seems obvious to propose that one appreciates a ballet more when one is not distracted by the contents of a chip bag. Even time in the car might be enhanced by avoiding snacking and instead directing our efforts and attention to talking with passengers, singing, listening to audiobooks, or even praying.

Snacking can also become a problem when it threatens the community-building effects of a shared meal. Take for example Lauren Campbell.

The 28-year-old Atlanta accountant fuels up every few hours on small servings of instant oatmeal, sliced chicken or microwavable brown rice. If she meets friends at a restaurant for dinner, she skips the entree. Ms. Campbell munches instead on snow peas stashed in her purse.[45]

45. Mike Esterl, "Forget Dinner. It's Always Snacktime in America," *Wall Street Journal* (July 2, 2014), accessed June 17, 2016, https://www.wsj.com/articles/forget-dinner-its-always-snack-time-1404240759.

Campbell's snacking is problematic because it allows the pleasure of eating to become an exclusively private rather than a communal affair. Her eating has arguably become "gluttonous" not because she eats too much or even too pickily, but rather because she does not properly balance the relevant concerns—the food and the community. More specifically, her eating choices are problematic because she puts a disproportionate emphasis on her own individual pleasure (her desires to eat at certain times) and not the shared experience of those pleasures.

Contrast Campbell's experience with one which virtually every parent of young children can identify with: snack time. Young children often do not play with other children but rather engage in parallel play where each child does his or her own thing. This can be frustrating for parents who orchestrate playdates so children can learn to socialize. Snack time, however, is a time when children talk to each other and learn critical social skills as they share their raisins and graham crackers, conversing pleasantly about the quality of the snack and their general food preferences.

The focus on this third form of gluttony reminds us that the pleasure of eating is inextricably connected with the sharing of food. We are relational creatures and our eating practices can be judged in part by how they enhance or damage our relationships with others.

Conclusion

This chapter has had a sweeping scope in its approach to the sin of gluttony, from its global ecological ramifications and potential for threatening global food security, to the relatively mundane concern of licking one's fingers and snacking on popcorn during *Schindler's List*. What unites these various issues is the underlying concern over the proportionality of the appetite for food with other rational considerations. When the desire for food becomes disproportionate, meaning that other more important concerns are neglected, the sin of gluttony is present.

At its core then, gluttony is about thinking of self-indulgence, and that can help us to identify when we have sinned. We can be said to commit a form of gluttony anytime we allow our desire for any pleasure, even not connected to food, to overcome us. This is applicable especially to drink, which is likewise linked to gluttony, though I have not focused on it here. With drunkenness as with gluttony, the problem is not so much the quantity or quality of drink, but rather the *appetite* for alcohol.[46] A person who

---

46. Although drunkenness can also involve other dangers that food does not, chiefly "knowingly depriving oneself of the use of reason," which Aquinas considers a deadly sin. See ST II-II, q. 150, a. 2.

thinks about alcohol constantly, who plans far in advance for the next drink, might be a "drunkard" even without overindulging. The same reasoning can be applied to many pleasures, like the pleasures of shopping or technology (i.e., social media, television and film, music).

As such, the sin of gluttony is particularly the fruit of consumerism, which Pope John Paul II critiqued as "conspir[ing] to give free reign to the instincts of self-interest."[47] Consumerism not only encourages us to develop an insatiable appetite, but it also provides readily available opportunities to act on those appetites and to ignore more pressing moral concerns. Monsignor Charles Murphy draws a helpful comparison between the rich man and Lazarus and the danger of consumerism: "Enclosed in his world of wealth and self-sufficiency that wealth brings, he simply failed to notice Lazarus begging at his gate, much less help him."[48] The critique of consumerism is not so much a critique of wealth, but as with gluttony, of misplaced appetite and excessive attention to the pleasures of all sorts of material (and digital) consumption.

Consumerism turns us in on ourselves and blinds us to the needs of others. It elevates our own desires and appetites but ultimately distracts us from the good life, a life that is marked by moderation, proportionality, and balance. Pope Francis exhorts us to recognize that "Less is more."

A constant flood of new consumer goods can baffle the heart and prevent us from cherishing each thing and each moment. To be serenely present to each reality, however small it may be, opens us to much greater horizons of understanding and personal fulfilment. Christian spirituality proposes a growth marked by moderation and the capacity to be happy with little. It is a return to that simplicity which allows us to stop and appreciate the small things, to be grateful for the opportunities which life affords us, to be spiritually detached from what we possess, and not to succumb to sadness for what we lack. This implies avoiding the dynamic of dominion and the mere accumulation of pleasures.[49]

The sin of gluttony can even apply to the highest pleasures, that is, those associated with prayer and worship. St. John of the Cross warns against what he calls "spiritual gluttony" which is found in many who "lured by the delight and satisfaction procured in their religious practices, strive

---

47. John Paul II, Homily *Holy Mass at Yankee Stadium*, New York (October 2, 1979), https://w2.vatican .va/content/john-paul-ii/en/homilies/1979.index.html.

48. United States Conference of Catholic Bishops, "The Good Life from a Catholic Perspective: The Challenge of Consumption," http://www.usccb.org/issues-and-action/human-life-and-dignity/global -issues/the-good-life-from-a-catholic-perspective-challenge-of-consumption.cfm. Cf. Luke 16:19–31.

49. Francis, Encyclical Letter *Laudato Si'* (May 24, 2015), 222.

more for spiritual savor than for spiritual purity and discretion."[50] Even doing penance out of an appetite for the pleasures they afford is gluttony according to St. John of the Cross because the desire of the sensory appetite for satisfaction becomes disproportionate. For such "spiritual gluttons," a "dark night of the soul" is necessary in order to train them to achieve proper balance in the spiritual life.

The view of gluttony we have presented here ought to illustrate that gluttony is a common sin that all of us likely commit on a pretty regular basis. One the one hand, the ubiquity of gluttony might take some of the "teeth" out of calling it a sin. On the other hand, the fact that gluttony is so common ought to alert us to the larger social dimensions of the sin: we live in a society whose structures and practices encourage gluttonous acts. Rather than excusing us from guilt, this recognition ought to encourage us to promote certain structural changes that will better promote the total flourishing of all members of our society. These changes begin with "practices of resistance" like reviving family meals, cooking together, and saying grace but must also include critical changes on multiple levels, from food marketing to agricultural reform. In the end, however, the goal of our discussion of gluttony is not to provoke guilt but rather to encourage readers to find ways that they might recover a "good appetite" in their own approach to food and eating.

---

50. John of the Cross, *Dark Night of the Soul*, trans. E. Allison Peers (Westminster, MD: Newman Press, 1953), Book I, chapter 6.

Chapter 3

Lust

JASON KING

IN HIS *INFERNO*, Dante finds those being punished for lust almost immediately after entering hell. These souls are being tossed around by winds, perpetually out of control. In the midst of these gales, Dante sees lovers looking at and unable to turn away from each other. As in life so in death, their lust for each other traps them so that no other good, not even God, can deter their gaze or stop the passionate chaos. Dante sees Paris and Helen there, and Francesca justifies her infidelity with Paolo by appealing to the story of Lancelot and Guinevere. They seem to be lovers driven to madness by their mutual longing. Their fate leads to tears, grief, and pity.

On the surface, Dante may seem to depict irrational lust overcoming reason, but instead he is exploring a different kind of passionate logic. The lust that leads to hell is where sexual pleasure is valued and pursued regardless of its impact on people and relationships. It breeds chaos not in the person's mind—which remains resolutely focused—but in the world around them. War seems like a reasonable cost for Paris and Helen's lust. Francesca's betrayal of her husband is justified, just as Lancelot and Guinevere's affair was even though it brought down Camelot. Far from being erratic and irrational, lust is a narrow logic that excludes concern for other people so that sexual satisfaction can be pursued.

This essence of lust is captured in *New York Times* reporter Kate Taylor's story about a college student:

> She had been making out with a guy at his house, not sure how far she wanted to go, when he stood up and told her, "Get down on your knees." At first she froze. "I was really taken aback, because I was like, no one has ever said that to me before," she said. Then he said something like, "'I think that's fair,'" she recalled. When she still hesitated, he pushed her down. "It was at that point that I was like, 'I'll just do it,'" she said. "I was like, 'It will be over soon enough.'"[1]

1. Kate Taylor, "Sex on Campus: She Can Play That Game, Too," *New York Times*, July 12, 2013, http://www.nytimes.com/2013/07/14/fashion/sex-on-campus-she-can-play-that-game-too.html.

The logic of Dante's lust that turns people against spouses, cities, and humanity is clearly seen by this man who orders the woman on her knees, believes he is owed it, and physically pushes her down when she hesitates. The problem is not irrational desire but rather a focused logic of sexual desire that values individual satisfaction over and against concern for other people. It is pleasure detached from compassion.

In this essay, I build on this understanding of lust as sexual desire directed in opposition to people and relationships. I begin by setting out Thomas Aquinas's understanding of lust as a passion that focuses our reasoning rather than a passion that overpowers it. The result is that lust turns our sexual desire against people. Building off this insight, the second part of this paper names three ways lust turns pleasure against people: dominating lust that finds pleasure in violating human dignity, dissipating lust where pleasure wanes from neglecting relationships, and truncating lust that cuts off concerns for anything other than sexual satisfaction with a partner. All are problematic not because of the overwhelming strength of the sexual desire but because they move the mind and will in ways that are at odds with the love called for in Christian discipleship.

Aquinas on Lust

One strain within the Catholic tradition understands the problem of lust as an excessive desire that overpowers reason. It was thought to be a "chaotic power"[2] that hindered "the best working of the mind"[3] and "was a disruptive force in mankind's present state."[4] It diminished reason—the essence of human beings—so acting upon it was "to outrage nature."[5] The *New Catholic Encyclopedia* provides an example of this understanding of lust. "Lust always indicates an excessive, that is, irrational, attachment to venereal pleasure."[6] The entry continues by noting that lust is destructive because it subjects humanity's "sexual activity not to it its proper ends recognized by reason . . . . but instead to mere bodily pleasure."[7] According to this perspective, the main problem of lust is that it makes people irrational.

---

2. Margaret Farley, *Just Love: A Framework for Christian Sexual Ethics* (New York: Continuum International Publishing Group, 2006), 22.

3. Farley, *Just Love*, 44.

4. Shaji George Kochuthara, *The Concept of Sexual Pleasure in the Catholic Moral Tradition* (Rome: Gregorian and Biblical Press, 2007), 167.

5. Kochuthara, *The Concept of Sexual Pleasure*, 144.

6. "Lust" in *The New Catholic Encyclopedia*, 2nd ed. Detroit: Thomson/Gale; Washington, DC: Catholic University of America Press, 2002.

7. "Lust," *The New Catholic Encyclopedia*.

Aquinas stands against this line of thought. He does not operate with a sense that the passions are erratic movements that work against reason.[8] Rather, the passions respond to the good and move people toward it.[9] They do this not only for immediate sensible goods but also for difficult and challenging goods.[10] In fact, for Aquinas, one of the greatest delights is acquiring intellectual knowledge.[11] Because the passions have an orientation toward the good, their movements help the intellect grasp not just a thing but the goodness of a thing. Thus, the intellect does not control the passions so much as build upon them to discern what the good is and how to pursue it.

However, with the fall of humanity, the passions do not reliably indicate what is truly good. The passion can narrow one's focus on a single aspect of something good while neglect its other attributes.[12] The passions can pit one good against another, hindering the intellect's ability to effectively prioritize competing goods.[13] Passions can also become so focused on a particular good that they hinder the intellect from considering any other good.[14] In each of these instances however, it is not that the passions have abandoned their pursuit of the good and hence become erratic and irrational. Instead, the logic and direction of the passions have narrowed to focus on a specific good and pursuing it while obscuring other goods that demand attention and need to be considered.

Aquinas's analysis of lust is a specific instance of the passions. Sexual desire is, at root, good.[15] God made it pleasurable, but its logic was not a pleasure divorced from human beings, but rather a desire that moved one toward loving relationships.[16] With almost every turn of his discussion of lust, Aquinas finds lust sinful because it drives people to think and act in ways that lack concern for other human beings. It is a logic "discordant with right reason in relation to other persons."[17] He sees lust as pursuing sex in a way that would neglect the "upbringing and

---

8. Diana Fritz Cates, *Aquinas on the Emotions: A Religious-Ethical Inquiry* (Washington, DC: Georgetown University Press, 2009).

9. ST I-II, q. 22, 2.

10. ST I-II, q. 23, a. 1.

11. ST I-II, q. 31, a. 4.

12. ST I-II, q. 77, a. 1.

13. ST I-II, q. 77, a. 2.

14. ST I-II, q. 77, a. 3.

15. ST I-II, q. 24, a. 2.

16. John Milhaven, "Thomas Aquinas on Sexual Pleasure," *Journal of Religious Ethics* 5, no. 2 (1977): 157–81.

17. ST II-II, q. 154, a. 1.

advancement of the child" that might emerge from the sexual union.[18] In his discussion of seduction and rape, he notes its violation against woman stemming from the man's willingness to exercise deception and violence for the goal of pleasure.[19] It is not an overwhelming sense of irrational pleasure that is the problem in these sins, but the fact that the narrow desire for pleasure has displaced other, more important goods. While his discussion makes problematic assumptions about the status and passivity of women, the more fundamental point is that lust rationalizes violence for achieving its satisfaction as it excludes care of others. Against children and spouses, lust is opposed to marriage and so "the common good of the whole human race."[20] Thus, Aquinas categorizes lust as a mortal sin because it is a passion whose logic is sexual pleasure pursued "directly against human life."[21]

This Thomistic background helps us to see more clearly the logic of Dante's depiction of lust. It is not so much an irrational desire that creates chaos within a person, but rather the logic of lust focuses on the good of sexual satisfaction and obscures or devalues the surrounding chaos caused by one's lack of compassion for other human beings. Aquinas's view also helps us to understand that the man who pushed the woman down on her knees was not devoid of reason. He knew he wanted sexual satisfaction and so employed reason and will to obtain it. He just did so lacking any concern for the good of the woman, and this lack of concern is the corruption lust causes.

Thus, lust is not so much an excessiveness of desire or a force opposed to reason. As Aquinas indicated, feelings have a logic that orients people in the world. Pitting them against reason is to misunderstand them and their role in the moral life. Feelings are not irrational and chaotic but direct the way people think, act, and thus, live. Lust is a vice because it is a logic that moves people to satisfy their sexual desires in opposition to people. It hinders people from considering any good greater than sexual pleasure and moves them to act accordingly. To effectively name the vice, however, we need to specify its logic of sexual satisfaction that excludes consideration of care and compassion for others. In what follows, I name three ways lust sets sexual desire against people: dominating lust, dissipating lust, and truncating lust.

18. ST II-II, q. 154, a. 1.
19. ST II-II, q. 154, a. 4–5.
20. ST II-II, q. 154, a. 2.
21. ST II-II, a. 154, a. 2.

Dominating Lust

John Cavadini, a professor of theology at the University of Notre Dame, argues that, for St. Augustine, lust was ultimately a desire to dominate others, sexual pleasure derived from the control over or manipulation of others, which he named *libido dominandi*.[22] Augustine saw this lust deep within humanity. In politics, this lust was expressed in the stories—what Augustine called their myths—that empires used to justify their existence and expansion.

> There is no imperial history without the myth because there is no true rationale for any particular empire; each is actually motivated by the desire to dominate [*libido dominandi*] and, even more importantly, each is completely a function of the desire to dominate, since the earthly city is the one that, even in its domination, is itself dominated by the lust for domination.[23]

Empires tell myths about their greatness and destiny, but, according to Augustine, these are just means for masking the lust for domination. Empires seek only their own perpetuation and expansion. They seek ever greater control over people and land. To do so, they tell some story, a "myth of empire," that justifies their rule and masks the truth that there is no true reason behind their dominance other than the raw drive for control. Thus, empire is "intrinsically pornographic" because it relishes power over others.[24] From Augustine, Christians came to understand the problem of lust as a pleasure in domination.

In Cavadini's reading of Augustine, Christianity provides an anti-myth, a true story of history. This story undermines violence at the heart of creation and speaks to peace. It speaks to emotions "rightly ordered" so that they seek not domination of others but love and mutuality. Cavadini makes this point when he presents Augustine's view of sex without lust, sex without domination. In contrast to the "rape of the newly married wife" normalized by religions of empire, Augustine imaged "something more gentle, something in fact so completely free of violence that it would not injure the woman in the least."[25] In paradise, sexual pleasure would not

---

22. John Cavadini, "Feeling Right: Augustine on the Passions and Sexual Desire," *Augustinian Studies* 36, no. 1 (2005): 195–217.

23. John Cavadini, "Spousal Vision: A Study of Text and History in the Theology of Saint Augustine," *Augustinian Studies* 43, no. 1 (2012): 133.

24. Cavadini, "Spousal Vision," 134.

25. Barbara Hilkert Andolsen, "Whose Sexuality? Whose Tradition? Women, Experience, and Roman Catholic Sexual Ethics," in *Readings in Moral Theology No. 9: Feminist Ethics and the Catholic Moral Tradition*, ed. Charles Curran, Margaret Farley, and Richard McCormick, SJ (Mahway, NJ: Paulist Press, 1996), 207–39, at 208–09.

be tainted by violence or dominance but be part of "joyful fellowship of noble, transparent love."[26]

In her classic essay "Whose Sexuality? Whose Tradition? Women, Experience, and Roman Catholic Sexual Ethics," Barbara Andolsen, a professor of theology at Fordham University, noted that the lust for domination was so pervasive in the ancient world that responses to it often led, not to greater gentleness and love, but to further domination. Using Tertullian as a representative, Andolsen noted how women were counseled against "cosmetics and alluring cloths."[27] They should avoid anything that "heightened sexual attractiveness" and "disguise even naturally attractive bodily features."[28] Women were to do so not only to restrain their own sexual desires but also those of men.[29] Thus, as Andolsen's perspective implied, the angle of the attack against the lust for domination was an attempt to suppress it, and this often took the form of men attempting to control women and their sexuality. Instead of overcoming the lust of domination with sexual desire rooted in "joyful fellowship," the solution became an attempt to dominate the domination, of using the *libido dominandi* to overcome the *libido dominandi*. These solutions merely repeated the "myth of empire."

The lust of domination discussed by Cavadini and Andolsen helps to name a type of lust that still plagues the contemporary world. According to the Center for Disease Control, 1 in 5 women became victims of completed or attempted rape sometime in their lives, 1 in 59 men were raped, 12.5% of women and 5.8% of men have been sexually coerced, and 27.3% of women and 10.8% of men have experienced unwanted sexual contact. [30] The National Sexual Violence Resource Center reports that "46.4% lesbians, 74.9% bisexual women and 43.3% heterosexual women reported sexual violence other than rape during their lifetimes, while 40.2% gay men, 47.4% bisexual men and 20.8% heterosexual men reported sexual violence other than rape during their lifetimes."[31] Thus, it is no wonder that, after the 2017 revelation

26. Andolsen, "Whose Sexuality? Whose Tradition?" 209–10.

27. Andolsen, "Whose Sexuality? Whose Tradition?" 211.

28. Andolsen, "Whose Sexuality? Whose Tradition?" 211.

29. Andolsen, "Whose Sexuality? Whose Tradition?" 212.

30. Center for Disease Control and Prevention, "National Data on Intimate Partner Violence, Sexual Violence, and Stalking," https://www.cdc.gov/violenceprevention/pdf/nisvs-fact-sheet-2014.pdf; Center for Disease Control and Prevention, "Sexual Violence Surveillance: Uniform Definitions and Recommended Data Elements," https://www.cdc.gov/violenceprevention/pdf/sv_surveillance _definitionsl-2009-a.pdf.

31. National Sexual Violence Resource, "Statistics About Sexual Violence," http://www.nsvrc.org/sites /default/files/publications_nsvrc_factsheet_media-packet_statistics-about-sexual-violence_0.pdf.

of Harvey Weinstein's sexual harassment of women, numerous other offenders were quickly exposed.[32]

The situation on college campuses is similar. There, 20% of women in college experience completed or attempted rape. 80% of these women know their assailants, the most being friends or acquaintances (50%) but some being intimate partners (24%).[33] When assaults occur, victims and perpetrators struggle to recognize it as such.[34] Even when victims do recognize it, they rarely come forward, reporting it to the police only 5% of the time.[35] In part this is because, even if they do report it, they are often ignored or disparaged.[36] Even though these sexual assault numbers have been practically unchanged since 2007, colleges and universities have only recently started to wrestle with them, and then only after the Department of Education began investigating several institutions of higher education for Title IX violations in early 2014.

While not the cause of sexual assault—which is more related to beliefs about alcohol, gender, and rape[37]—pornography provides another clear depiction of dominating lust.

> Pornography would suggest that men are socialized to find both male power and female powerlessness sexually arousing. In pornography, domination of women by men is portrayed as sexy. It is the power of the man or men to make the woman do what she does not want to do—to make her do something humiliating, degrading, or antithetical to her character—that creates the sexual tension and excitement . . . . In pornography, women are raped tied up, beaten, humiliated—*and* are portrayed as initially resisting and ultimately enjoying their degradation.[38]

32. Sarah Almukhtar, Larry Buchanan, and Michael Gold, "After Weinstein: 71 Men Accused of Sexual Misconduct and Their Fall from Power," *The New York Times*, February 8, 2018, https://www.nytimes.com/interactive/2017/11/10/us/men-accused-sexual-misconduct-weinstein.html.

33. US Department of Justice, "Rape and Sexual Assault Victimization among College-Age Females, 1995–2013," https://www.bjs.gov/content/pub/pdf/rsavcaf9513.pdf.

34. See Arnold S. Kahn, "What College Women Do and Do Not Experience as Rape," *Psychology of Women Quarterly* 28, no. 1 (2004): 9–15 and Ruth Mann and Clive Hollin, "Sexual Offenders' Explanations for Their Offending," *Journal of Sexual Aggression* 13, no. 1 (2007): 3–9.

35. Antonia Abbey, "Alcohol-Related Sexual Assault: A Common Problem among College Students," *Journal of Studies on Alcohol, Supplement* 14 (2002): 118–28, at 118–19.

36. Abbey, "Alcohol-Related Sexual Assault," 118–19.

37. See Matthew Hogben, Donn Byrne, Merle E. Hamburger, and Julie Osland, "Legitimized Aggression and Sexual Coercion: Individual Differences in Cultural Spillover," *Aggressive Behavior* 27, no. 1 (2001): 26–43; Laina Y. Bay-Cheng and Rebecca K. Eliseo-Arras, "The Making of Unwanted Sex: Gendered and Neoliberal Norms in College Women's Unwanted Sexual Experiences," *Journal of Sex Research* 45, no. 4 (2008): 386–97; Sarah R. Edwards and David L. Vogel, "Young Men's Likelihood Ratings to Be Sexually Aggressive as a Function of Norms and Perceived Sexual Interest," *Psychology of Men and Masculinity* 16, no. 1 (2015): 88–96.

38. Karen Lebacqz, "Love Your Enemy: Sex, Power, and Christian Ethics," *Annual of the Society of Christian Ethics* 10, no. 1 (2006): 8.

This description of pornography provides a contemporary "myth of empire." Pornography assumes a world where men enjoy dominating and women enjoy being dominated. Men can force themselves on women because, even if women say "no" or resist or are incapacitated, they will find it acceptable because they enjoy it. Thus, it is no wonder that typical pornography depicts male dominance as pleasurable—with 88% of pornography containing physical aggression and 49% verbal aggression—and women as compliant with the aggression.[39] Given that 70% of 18–24 year-old males visit porn sites at least monthly,[40] pornographic ways of thinking and acting are widely available and so provide a clear expression of how dominating lust is seen as good.

This pornographic world, this myth of empire, is a world where human dignity is violated, where human relationships in general and sexual relationships in particular are rooted in dominance and submission, control and compliance. It is why Reinhard Hütter, professor of theology at the Catholic University of America, argued in "Pornography and Acedia" that pornography "does not inflame but rather freezes the soul and the heart in a cold indifference to the human dignity of others and of oneself."[41] Best-selling author Nancy Jo Sales argues in *American Girls: Social Media and the Secret Lives of Teenagers* that, in the sexual activity of teenagers, males dominate females. [42] Pleasing boys is the goal; whatever girls desire or want (or even who they are) is irrelevant.

These perspectives help to name the sin of dominating lust. First, it is sexual desire that finds *pleasure in the dominance and control* over another person. Second, it *values this pleasure over the dignity of another person*, violating the demands of simple justice—of rendering the basic respect due another—and defacing the image and likeness of God in another, the *imago dei*. Finally, it *moves people to coerce others* into sexual acts against their own desires and wants.

At its worst, dominating lust manifests in such acts as rape and assault. Human freedom, which is at the heart of human dignity,[43] is ignored in the perpetrators' pursuit of pleasure. Similar to rape is seduction. It also finds

39. A. J. Bridges, R. Wosnitzer, E. Scharrer, S. Chyng, and R. Liberman, "Aggression and Sexual Behavior in Best Selling Pornography Videos: A Content Analysis Update," *Violence Against Women* 16, no. 10 (2010): 1065–85, at 1065.

40. Pamela Paul, *Pornified: How Pornography is Damaging Our Lives, Our Relationships, and Our Families* (New York: Times Books, 2005).

41. Reinhard Hütter, "Pornography and Acedia," *First Things*, April 2012; http://www.firstthings.com /article/2012/04/pornography-and-acedia.

42. Nancy Jo Sales, *American Girls: Social Media and the Secret Lives of Teenagers* (New York: Knopf, 2016).

43. *Catechism of the Catholic Church*, no. 1705.

pleasure in dominance and compromising another's freedom, but it does so by substituting manipulation for physical force. Sexual harassment has this same structure of demeaning another person but does so through a persistence of unwanted sexual comments or advances.

In relationships, dominating lust can express as persistent whining or begging for sex, forcing submission despite another's lack of sexual interest. It can also occur when one person feels like sex is acceptable as long as the other person does not "forcefully resist."[44] While these actions do not entail physical violence, they are still coercive, with the offender seeking sexual pleasure against the wishes or desires of others. If dominating lust permeates a whole environment, harassment, seduction, and even rape can become normalized, generating what some call a "rape culture"[45] and what Catholics would categorize as a social sin.

This understanding of dominating lust also helps to explain the actions of those victimized by it. In situations where dominating lust is pervasive, resistance is difficult. Some might resist it but this usually comes with at a cost. College students who do not participate in this hookup culture often suffer from a kind of "social suicide."[46] Moreover, the most at-risk group for murder by a sexual partner are women at the time they are trying to leave an abusive relationship.[47] Given the high cost for resistance, many feel that they have no choice but to cooperate with the dominant perspective. When they do, those in vulnerable positions often employ methods of "supplication" or "manipulation" in order to secure their safety, status, or dignity.[48] In sexual relationships, those in weak positions emphasize their sexuality as a way to control the person in the strong position and so secure their safety and, at times, their existence. It is one of the few ways for those in vulnerable positions to hold on to their dignity.[49] In these situations,

44. See Kahn, "What College Women Do and Do Not Experience as Rape," 13 for how people do not think of verbal pressure as coercive.

45. See Emilie Buchwald, Pamela Fletch, and Martha Roth, eds., *Transforming a Rape Culture* (Minneapolis: Milkweed Editions, 1993).

46. Donna Freitas, *The End of Sex: How Hookup Culture is Leaving a Generation Unhappy, Sexually Unfulfilled and Confused About Intimacy* (New York: Basic Books, 2013), 70–73.

47. Lori Heise and Claudia Garcia-Moreno, "Violence by Intimate Partners," in *World Report on Violence and Health*, ed. Etienne Krug, Linda Dahlberg, James Mercy, Anthony Zwi, and Rafael Lozano, (Geneva, Switzerland: World Health Organization, 2002), 87–121, at 96. http://www.who.int/whr/2002/en/.

48. Judith Howard, Philip Blumstein, and Pepper Schwartz, "Sex, Power, and Influence Tactics in Intimate Relationships," *Journal of Personality and Social Psychology* 51, no. 1 (1986): 102–09.

49. Elaine Richardson, "Developing Critical Hip Hop Feminist Literacies: Centrality and Subversion of Sexuality in the Lives of Black Girls," *Equity and Excellence in Education* 46, no. 3 (2013): 327–41; Debbie Weekes, "Get Your Freak On: How Black Girls Sexualize Identity," *Sex Education* 2, no. 3 (2002): 251–62; Ina Skafte and Margrethe Silberschmidt, "Female Gratification, Sexual Power and Safer Sex: Female Sexuality as an Empowering Resource among Women in Rwanda," *Culture, Health, and Sexuality* 16, no. 1 (2014): 1–13.

those who are vulnerable might be sexually active and explicit, but only to protect their dignity against those who threaten it. In other words, what they are engaged in are not acts of lust but acts of self-protection.

Dissipating Lust

While pornography often portrays dominating lust that finds pleasure in denigrating another person, the consumption of pornography can have a different effect. In her *Time* magazine essay "Porn and the Threat to Virility," Belinda Luscombe describes Noah:

> When he was 9, he found naked pictures on the Internet. He learned how to download explicit videos. When he was 15, streaming videos arrived, and he watched those. Often. . . . . In his senior year of high school, he had an opportunity to have actual sex, with a real partner. He was attracted to her and she to him, as demonstrated by the fact that she was naked in her bedroom in front of him. But his body didn't seem to be interested. "There was a disconnect between what I wanted in my mind and how my body reacted," he says. He simply couldn't get the necessary hydraulics going. He put it down to first-timers' nerves, but six years went by, and no matter which woman he was with, his body was no more cooperative. It responded only to the sight of porn.[50]

Luscombe's story of Noah is part of her argument that the first generation of men who have grown up with the widespread availability of internet pornography have found themselves unable to be aroused by actual people, only responding to the visuals of pornography. The result is a sexual desire divorced from other people. It is so widespread that Luscombe contends it should be viewed as a health crisis regardless of people's moral evaluation of pornography. Her argument is built around the view of Gary Wilson's *Your Brain on Porn: Internet Pornography and the Emerging Science of Addiction*.[51] In this book, Wilson argues that pornography conditions the pleasure centers of the brain to only enjoy pornography and, as a result, not actual physical relationships with other people.

Outside of the United States, Japan has seen the rise of "herbivore" men who forgo romantic relationships.[52] These individuals are typically young men who are timid and shy. They are "herbivores" who dislike the "meat" and "flesh" of human interactions and prefer digital reality.

50. Belinda Luscombe, "Porn and the Threat to Virility," *Time*, April 11, 2016, 41–47, at 42.

51. Gary Wilson, *Your Brain on Porn: Internet Pornography and the Emerging Science of Addiction* (N.p.: Commonwealth Publishing, 2014): 39–41.

52. Mashahiro Morioka, "A Phenomenological Study of 'Herbivore Men,'" *The Review of Life Studies* 4 (September 2013): 1–20.

Causes for their rise have been said to be either a backlash against the violence of World War II or the lack of economic prospects for young men in Japan's economy. Whatever it might be, the result is that increasing numbers of Japanese men tend to be uninterested in or averse to sex with flesh and blood people.[53]

These two examples point to the reality that sexual desire wanes when it becomes detached from people and relationships. As Helen Fisher explains in "Lust, Attraction, Attachment," human beings typically link their three primary emotion systems for mating and reproduction: desires for sex, attraction to a particular partner, and emotional union.[54] While it is not too surprising that these desires can and do become detached from one another, Fisher argues that such decoupling is problematic. When one's sex drive is separated from the desire for a particular person and emotional union, the sex drive can lead to problems, including depression and the rejection of love.

Sexual desire declines not only when it is separated from people but also when people neglect or are inattentive to existing relationships. A lack of intimacy or an inequality of power in a relationship diminishes and hampers sexual desire, causing some to become more aggressive and others to lose interest.[55] Sexual desires often wane in relationships where there is an unresolved discrepancy in sexual expectations.[56] The dissipation can be seen in those neglecting the romantic and interpersonal aspects of their relationships.[57] In all of these cases, the key aspect is a sexual desire that weakens because of a problem in a relationship, where one or both partners disregard the desires of the other.

Hooking up provides a paradigmatic example of the waning of sexual satisfaction resulting from its detachment from relationships. A hookup is usually defined as a sexual encounter without the expectations of a relationship. While the emphasis is usually placed on the sexual activity itself, it should actually be placed on this activity being divorced from any hoped

---

53. Yuri Tomikawa, "No Sex, Please, We're Young Japanese Men," *The Wall Street Journal*, January 13, 2011, http://blogs.wsj.com/japanrealtime/2011/01/13/no-sex-please-were-young-japanese-men/.

54. Helen Fisher, "Lust, Attraction, Attachment: Biology and Evolution of the Three Primary Emotion Systems for Mating, Reproduction, and Parenting," *Journal of Sex Education and Therapy* 25, no. 1 (2000): 96–104.

55. Carl Ridley, et al., "The Ebb and Flow of Marital Lust: A Relational Approach," *The Journal of Sex Research* 43, no. 2 (2006): 144–53.

56. Kristen Mark, "The Impact of Daily Sexual Desire and Daily Sexual Desire Discrepancy on the Quality of the Sexual Experience in Couples," *Canadian Journal of Human Sexuality* 23, no. 1 (2014): 27–33; Sara Bridges and Sharon Horne, "Sexual Satisfaction and Desire Discrepancy in Same Sex Women's Relationships," *Journal of Sex & Marriage Therapy* 33, no. 1 (2007): 41–53.

57. Kristin Mitchell, Kaye Wellings, and Cynthia Graham, "How Do Men and Women Define Sexual Desire and Sexual Arousal?" *Journal of Sex & Marital Therapy* 40, no. 1 (2014): 17–32.

for or real relationships. Not only can a hookup entail different kinds of sexual activities—it can mean anything from kissing to intercourse—but it is also intentionally ambiguous.[58] Some people even use the ambiguity so that they do *not* have to have meaningless sex but can still appear to be participating in hookup culture and so avoid "social suicide." Instead, the emphasis in hooking up should be placed on having "no expectations of a relationship" after sexual activity. The goal is to not feel, not care, and not get involved beyond the hookup. As Donna Freitas explains in *The End of Sex*, "emotional entanglement is not only not part of the deal, it is verboten, going against the very nature of a hookup. Men and women learn to shut down emotionally in order to 'safely' turn on physically."[59]

Even though no relationships are expected from hooking up, it goes against what most people want. In "Sexual Hookup Culture," Justin Garcia and his fellow authors surveyed research on hookup culture and found that "65% of women and 45% of men reported that they hoped their hookup encounter would become a committed relationship."[60] Moreover, 51% of women and 42% of men explicitly talked about the possibility of starting a relationship after hooking up.[61] The potential to form a relationship is one of the main reasons given for hooking up.[62] Despite the fact that sexual desire is often oriented toward relationships and most people desire relationships, hooking up still assumes no expectations of a relationship.

The result of this situation is not just a thwarting of what students desire but also the loss of pleasure. Because hookup culture is based on "a stereotypically male construction of pleasure and women's subservience," women's pleasure is grossly neglected.[63] Women tend to have less pleasure in hooking up than in relationships and only have orgasms about a third of the time that men do.[64] This bias toward male pleasure does not mean

58. Jason King, *Faith with Benefits: Hookup Culture on Catholic Campuses* (New York: Oxford University Press, 2017), 84–87.

59. Freitas, *End of Sex*, 30.

60. Justin Garcia, Chris Reiber, Sean G. Massey, and Ann M. Merriwether, "Sexual Hookup Culture: A Review," *Review of General Psychology* 16, no. 2 (2012): 161–76, at 167–68.

61. Garcia, Reiber, Massey, and Merriewether, "Sexual Hookup Culture," 167–68.

62. Caroline Heldman and Lisa Wade, "Hook-Up Culture: Setting a New Research Agenda," *Sexual Research and Social Policy* 7, no. 4 (2010): 323–33, at 325. See also M. Lynne Cooper and Cheryl M. Shapiro, "Motivations for Sex and Risky Sexual Behavior Among Adolescents and Young Adults: A Functional Perspective," *Journal of Personality and Social Psychology* 73, no. 6 (1998): 1528–58 and Emily J. Ozer, M. Margaret Dolcini, and Gary W. Harper, "Adolescents' Reasons for Having Sex: Gender Differences," *Journal of Adolescent Health* 33, no. 5 (2003): 317–19.

63. Freitas, *The End of Sex*, 113.

64. Heldman and Wade, "Hook-Up Culture," 325. See also Elizabeth Armstrong, Paula England, and Alison Fogarty, "Accounting for Women's Orgasm and Sexual Enjoyment in College Hookups and Relationships," *American Sociological Review* 77, no. 3 (2012): 435–62.

men enjoy it though. While men do seem more open to hooking up, most do not like it, with one study indicated that was the case for 75% of men.[65]

These examples help us name dissipating lust. It has three elements. First, dissipating lust is *the fading of pleasure resulting from neglecting relationships with people*. It might seem strange to name the weakening of sexual desire as a type of lust, but the strength of the desire is not what defines lust. It is its logic, and the logic of dissipating lust is its ordering of sexual desire away from relationships with people.

Second, this logic results in *a failure to grasp the good in one's relationship with another person*. This aspect can be seen in the loss of pleasure in hookups that suppress emotional attachment and relationships. It can also be found in couples who fail to attend to a partner's sexual desire or do not consistently reciprocate sexual pleasure. Leaving conflicts unresolved also causes each person in a relationship to pull away from the other and, thus, sexual activity with each other. All of these are examples of dissipating lust that sabotages relationships and so undermines pleasure.

The third and final aspect of dissipating lust is that people *seek pleasure apart from relationships* because of the fading pleasure within the relationship. Unlike dominating lust's pleasure in violating another's dignity, like the man who felt that the woman should serve him on her knees as "only fair," dissipating lust moves people like Noah to find sexual pleasure, not with real women, but only with their images offered up through pornography. It is exemplified by masturbation when it is a substitute for or, in the case of herbivore men, preferred to sex within a relationship.

Sexual desire is not supposed to function in this way. It is supposed to arise out of and be oriented back toward relationships.[66] That sexual pleasure moves one toward relationships was the point in Eilee Zurbriggen and Megan Yost's "Power, Desire, and Pleasure in Sexual Fantasy."

65.   Marina Epstein, J. P. Calzo, Andrew Smiler, and L. Monique Ward, "'Anything from Making Out to Having Sex': Men's Negotiations of Hooking Up and Friends with Benefits Scripts," *Journal of Sex Research* 46, no. 5 (2009): 414–24, at 415; See also Owen, Rhoades, Stanley, and Fincham, "'Hooking up' Among College Students," 660.

66.   Carl Ridley, Brian Ogolsky, Pamela Payne, Casey Totenhagen, and Rodney Cate, "Sexual Expression: Its Emotional Context in Heterosexual, Gay, and Lesbian Couples," *Journal of Sex Research* 45, no. 3 (2008): 305–14; Marita McCabe and Denisa Goldhammer, "Demographic and Psychological Factors Related to Sexual Desire Among Heterosexual Women in Relationship," *Journal of Sex Research* 49, no. 1 (2012): 78–81; Sarah Murray, Olga Sutherland, and Robin Milhausen, "Young Women's Descriptions of Sexual Desire in Long-Term Relationships," *Sexual and Relationship Therapy* 27, no. 1 (2012): 3–16; John DeLamater and Morgan Sill, "Sexual Desire in Later Life," *The Journal of Sex Research* 42, no. 2 (2005): 138–49; Alison Huang, et al., "Sexual Function and Aging in Racially and Ethnically Diverse Women," *Journal of the American Geriatrics Society* 57, no. 8 (2009): 1362–68; E. Sandra Byers, "Relationship Satisfaction and Sexual Satisfaction: A Longitudinal Study of Individuals in Long-Term Relationships," *The Journal of Sex Research* 42, no. 2 (2005): 113–18.

In their survey of 162 21–45 year olds, they found sexual desire to be relational and reciprocal for both males and females.[67] While men were expected to be dominant pleasure seekers, they fantasized about pleasing women. While women were supposed to be thinking of pleasing the other, they fantasized about receiving pleasure. Ultimately, in both cases, pleasure was found in the mutual giving and receiving of it. Likewise, in "Why Humans Have Sex," Cindy Meston and David Buss noted the main reasons people have sex included valuing a partner and feeling valued, giving and receiving pleasure, nurturing and caring for a partner, and procreating.[68] In all, almost all of the top reasons for having sex were relational and almost half of them were explicitly focused on the partner. Finally, in "Sexual Expression," Carol Ridley et al. write, "It is not surprising that when partners indicate love and positivity toward each other, and define the relationship in positive terms (e.g., satisfied, intimate, and committed), they are more open to sexual experiences and more likely to report sexual involvement."[69]

The link between sexual desire and relationships is not just a psychological claim but also a theological one. David Gallagher argues in "Thomas Aquinas on Self-Love as the Basis for Love of Others" that attention to the self is the basis for loving others and God.[70] The self properly loved fosters relationships with others. So, something like sexual desire need not be a focus on pleasure that makes one forget others but can alert one to care and concern for oneself and, thereby, others.

Julie Hanlon Rubio makes an even stronger case for pleasure being relational rather than solipsistic. In her "The Practice of Sex in Christian Marriage," she writes, "Self-giving entails vulnerability, the willingness to

67. Eileen Zurbriggen and Megan Yost, "Power, Desire, and Pleasure in Sexual Fantasies," *The Journal of Sex Research* 41, no. 3 (2004): 288–300. While there does seem to be some differences in men and women—namely that men are more open to casual sex and women less open to it—both still find sexual desires oriented toward relationships. See Diane Holmberg and Karen Blair, "Sexual Desire, Communication, Satisfaction, and Preferences of Men and Women in Same-Sex Versus Mixed-Sex Relationships," *Journal of Sex Research* 46, no. 1 (2009): 57–66; Kristen Mark, Justin Garcia, and Helen Fisher, "Perceived Emotional and Sexual Satisfaction Across Sexual Relationship Contexts: Gender and Sexual Orientation Differences and Similarities," *The Canadian Journal of Human Sexuality* 24, no. 2 (2015): 120–30. Kirstin Mitchell, Kaye Wellings, and Cynthia Graham, "How Do Men and Women Define Sexual Desire and Sexual Arousal?" *Journal of Sex & Marital Therapy* 40, no. 1 (2014): 17–32; Roy Baumeister, Kathleen Catanese, and Kathleen Vohs, "Is There a Gender Difference in Strength of Sex Drive? Theoretical Views, Conceptual Distinctions, and a Review of Relevant Evidence," *Personality and Social Psychology Review* 5, no. 3 (2001): 242–73.

68. Cindy Meston and David Buss, "Why Humans Have Sex," *Archives of Sexual Behavior* 36, no. 4 (2007): 477–507.

69. Ridley et. al, "Sexual Expression," 305–14.

70. David Gallagher, "Thomas Aquinas on Self-Love as the Basis for Love of Others," *Acta Philosophica* 8, no. 1 (1999): 23–44.

risk bringing one's true self and one's desires to another person."[71] Rubio
continues that this is not a selfish desire. It is an opening up of the self to
another. It is so people can "free themselves of self-centeredness in order
to enter more fully into the reality of their union."[72] Thus, sexual desire is
not narcissism but part of the longing for relationships. "Seeking pleasure
for oneself gives pleasure to one's partner and experiencing the pleasure
of one's partner cannot easily be separated from one's own physical pleasure."[73] This desire is a reminder of humanity's "neediness and interconnection" as well as the joy in belonging.[74]

Truncating Lust

There is a third kind of lust that neither moves people to dominate others
nor detaches their sex drive from others. Like the lust of Paris and Helen
and Francesca and Paolo, it is a lust that values a person to such a degree that
anything beyond this concern is abandoned. Take the example of former
South Carolina Governor Mark Sanford. Considered a potential Republi-
can presidential candidate for 2012, Sanford's political career was upended
in 2009 when he disappeared from June 18 to 24, 2009, cutting off contact
with not only other government officials but also his staff and his family.
No one knew where he was; eventually the staff claimed he was hiking the
Appalachian Trail.[75] In fact, he soon admitted that he had jetted to Argentina to see the woman with whom he was having an affair.[76] After years of
casual encounters with women that fell short of sexual relations, he had
met a woman he called his "soul mate."[77] Because of this affair, Sanford
neglected a number of responsibilities, including those to spouse, children
(on Father's Day weekend), friends, police, colleagues at work, and the state
of South Carolina. While there are other failures in the midst of Sanford's
affair, these are enough to name this as truncating lust: sexual desire for

71. Julie Hanlon Rubio, "The Practice of Sex in Christian Marriage," in *Leaving and Coming Home:
New Wineskins for Catholic Sexual Ethics*, ed. David Cloutier, 226–49 (Eugene, OR: Cascade Books,
2010), 233. For a slightly different argument that prioritizes pleasure as the norm for evaluating sexual
relationships, see Christine Gudorf, *Body, Sex, and Pleasure: Reconstructing Christian Sexual Ethics*
(Cleveland, OH: The Pilgrim Press, 1994).

72. Rubio, "The Practice of Sex in Christian Marriage," 235.

73. Rubio, "The Practice of Sex in Christian Marriage," 243.

74. Rubio, "The Practice of Sex in Christian Marriage," 238.

75. Jim Davenport, The Associated Press, "SC Governor to Return to Work after Mystery Trip," *The
San Diego Union-Tribune*, June 23, 2009.

76. Gina Smith, "Sanford Met in Atlanta after Returning from South America," *The State*, June 24,
2009.

77. "'Soul mate' was Unlike Others," *The Augusta Chronicle*, July 1, 2009, http://www.augustachronicle.
com/stories/2009/07/01/met_529459.shtml.

another that cuts off one's obligations beyond the relationship. Truncating lust does not lead to greater love and generosity toward others but to a truncated existence where one's sexual relationship is the highest value in one's life.

David Cloutier and William Mattison highlight this same danger of elevating sexual pleasure to an ultimate good in their critique of John Paul II's *Theology of the Body*. In their "Bodies Poured Out in Christ," Cloutier and Mattison argue that, despite the many positives of his sexual ethics, John Paul II's approach ultimately makes sex the pinnacle of married life. As Cloutier and Mattison write, "holding up a model of intense private intimacy shortchanges the real miracle of graced marriage by focusing the attention of spouses to ecstatic, transcendent moments as paradigmatic of their marriage."[78] If sex is the key to marital love, all other ordinary moments of living together are devalued. The focus becomes having these "intense and private ecstatic moments" and, by extension, one's purity between and in preparation for these moments. The result, Mattison and Cloutier conclude, is that the Theology of the Body can encourage a view of marriage as a purely private endeavor if it causes spouses to focus Christian marriage on "sex or wedding vows," instead of a loving relationship between people who are of "service to each other."[79] While not as flashy and obviously sinful as the Sanford affair, the focus on marital ecstasy will similarly cut off a couple from other obligations of love.

This focus on sexual satisfaction as a good over and against other goods has long been a concern. In "Passionate Attachments in the West in Historical Perspective," Lawrence Stone argues that, for much of its history, western culture viewed romantic feelings as inadequate grounds for marriage. Stone writes,

> In the sixteenth century marriage was thought to be best arranged by parents, who could be relied upon to choose socially and economically suitable partners who would enhance the prestige and importance of the kin group as a whole.[80]

The overriding concern was that romance caused couples to neglect social aspects of marriage—like money, status, and family—that were important for the success of marriage.

---

78. David Cloutier and William Mattison III, "Bodies Poured Out in Christ: Marriage Beyond the Theology of the Body," *Leaving and Coming Home: New Wineskins for Catholic Sexual Ethics*, ed. David Cloutier (Eugene, OR: Cascade Books, 2010), 206–25, at 221.

79. Cloutier and Mattison, "Bodies Poured Out in Christ," 219–20.

80. Lawrence Stone, "Passionate Attachments in the West in Historical Perspective," in *Perspective on Marriage: A Reader*, ed. Kieran Scott and Michael Warren, 176–85 (New York: Oxford University Press, 2007), 178.

Sanford's "hiking the Appalachian trail," Cloutier and Mattison's critique of "intense and private ecstatic moments," and Stone's point about the place of "romance and lust" each indicate a myopic tendency of sexual desire. While it takes seriously the value of sexual desire for a person, it does so in a way that hinders people from considering goods beyond the person. Sanford focuses on his "soul mate" and so abandons family, colleagues, and citizens. Couples prioritize themselves and their relationships in ways that neglect daily, concrete acts of love. Romance can cut a couple off from friends and family, money and security. Truncating lust stops people from attending to the aspects of love that expand beyond a couple toward neighbors and strangers.

Truncating lust prevents the kind of marital love that John Paul II called for in *On the Family (Familiaris Consortio)*. In this apostolic exhortation, the Pope emphasized that the love at the heart of the family was a "reflection of and a real sharing in God's love for humanity and the love of Christ the Lord for the Church" and, as such, meant that families were not meant to be closed in on themselves. They were to be engaged in four general tasks: "1) forming a community of persons; 2) serving life; 3) participating in the development of society; and 4) sharing in the life and mission of the Church."[81] All of these tasks called the couple to reach out beyond themselves. Perhaps this is most clearly expressed in the third familial task of advancing the development of society. In *Familiaris Consortio*, no. 46, John Paul II indicates that families are to work for suitable housing, religious freedom, "physical, social, political and economic security" for the poor, wholesome recreation, and the right to immigrate. Care for broader society, a care beyond the home, is crucial to the pope's vision of the family.

The kind of marital love John Paul II calls for can also be found in David McCarthy's *Sex and Love in the Home*. McCarthy describes two types of households, an open household and a closed household. The closed household is what is typically held up as the ideal in our society. "The closed family understands its health and well-being in terms of emotional and financial independence."[82] People seek to find jobs that provide a kind of sufficiency where they do not have to depend upon others. Work in and for the family—child care, lawn care, maintenance work, house work—is contracted out. The family does not need to depend upon grandparents, aunts and uncles, friends, or neighbors. Interactions with these people are thus leisure activities and not necessary ones. Children are optional. They are merely one way in which a couple can invest their time and money and emotions.

---

81. *Familiaris Consortio*, no. 17.

82. David Matzko McCarthy, *Sex and Love in the Home: A Theology of the Household* (London: SCM Press, 2001), 93.

In contrast, McCarthy proposes an open household. An open household is one that depends for its well being upon family, friends, neighbors and kin and operates, in part, through a gift economy. McCarthy provides an example of one of his neighbors using his snow blower after a winter storm. The neighbor used the machine to clear everyone's sidewalks. This created a situation where nobody quite knew how to respond. When a lighter snow came, another neighbor used his leaf blower to clear the sidewalks. When another light snow came, one family sent their kids out to shovel everyone's drive. Another family made cookies for the snow-blower neighbor. There was no one way to respond, yet these responses were key, according to McCarthy,

> ... to a basic pattern of household exchange between kinfolk, friends, and neighbors. No one responded to our good neighbor by writing him a check or by dashing out of the house to help him. In either case, he rightfully would be offended. If he were obviously struggling with a shovel, that would be a different matter. Given his mastery of his task, our duty as neighbors was to accept and appreciate his kindness. ... in one sense, his benevolent use of his snow blower will always be understood as a gift; yet in another, it would become part of a pattern of reciprocity, part of the neighborhood equilibrium whereby we sustain a certain status among others and exchange benefits.[83]

Julie Hanlon Rubio provides a final example of the kind of marital love to which Christians are called. In her essay "The Dual Vocation of Christian Parents," Rubio contends that parents have a "dual vocation."[84] Part of parents' vocation is a public one, one outside of the home. Rubio notes that early Christians were somewhat suspicious of families because families often looked after their own and neglected neighbors and strangers. Thus, early Christians were exhorted to leave the family behind for the sake of the kingdom. This call was not, Rubio writes, a dismissing of the importance of the family and parenting but realizing that the Christian call requires people to love and work for the good beyond the family. Rubio states, "[O]ne cannot, I would argue, fully realize the demands of discipleship to Jesus of Nazareth unless one also has a public vocation."[85] This public vocation entails the work the parents do outside of the home.

This work, though, is not at odds with parenting but rather part of its dual vocation. The work relates to the rearing of children in two ways.

---

83. McCarthy, Sex and Love in the Home, 102–03.

84. See Julie Hanlon Rubio, "The Dual Vocation of Christian Parents," in A Christian Theology of Marriage and Family, 89–110 (New York: Paulist Press, 2003). This chapter is a slightly revised version of an essay of the same name published in Theological Studies 63, no. 4 (2002): 786–812. My references are to the chapter in the book.

85. Rubio, Theology of Marriage, 99.

First, being a parent and loving a child call one to love other children. As Rubio states, "[b]eing a parent does not lead [one] to abandon the world; it inspires [one] to change it."[86] It is the love that one lives and learns in the family that leads one outside of the home to work for the good of others. Yet, this assistance is not just one directional of the family opening outward to serve. Thus, second, the work of the parents outside the home is brought in so that the family learns love of others. Rubio gives an example of how her father discussing his legal work at the dinner table shaped both the children's commitment to justice in the world and their understanding of what it meant to be Christian.

John Paul II, McCarthy, and Rubio provide a vision of a couple oriented beyond fascination with a "soul mate" and ecstatic and isolated moments. It is a marriage that is oriented toward the development of society in the case of John Paul II, a home that is open to the neighbor in the case of McCarthy, and an understanding of parenting that engages in and opens children up to service of others in the case of Rubio. Sexual desire nourishes and builds up healthy marriages by apprehending the value of the spouse and the relationship and moving people to act on this good. While sexual desire should nourish and build up marriages, this sexual desire should not lead couples to turn in on their selves and make sexual fulfillment the peak of their marital life. Instead, sexual desire should nurture and support a good marriage that can open up to others, in whatever form this service might take.

Truncating lust is the name of the lust that stops this expansion of love. First, truncating lust begins with *sexual pleasure as part of a relationship*. In fact, truncating lust implies a couple's mutual attention and care. It is just that truncating lust stops with the sexual value of a relationship, failing to grasp anything more important than sexual satisfaction. Accordingly, second, truncating lust orients people to a life where *the good of sexual desire becomes primary*. It apprehends few goods beyond the relationship or beyond "ecstatic" sex. As a result, it prevents people from being of loving service to others and, thus, thwarts the expansive nature of love called for by Christian discipleship. Truncated lust manifests Cloutier and Mattison's and Stone's concern that romance or ecstatic sex stops with the good of the couples and so fails to go beyond to the kinds of goods suggested by Rubio, McCarthy, and John Paul II. It is a lust that thwarts one's care for family, friends, work, and community because one so prioritizes a sexual relationship. Consequently and finally, truncating lust moves one *to act almost exclusively for the sexual satisfaction found in a relationship*.

---

86. Rubio, *Theology of Marriage*, 108.

Truncating lust is exemplified by adultery, a far too common reality, where one feels that an extra-marital encounter will bring satisfaction despite the harm to one's spouse and family.[87] But truncating lust rarely looks as extreme as Mark Sanford in daily life, nor need it involve actual adulterous choices. More typically, it happens when we find ourselves neglecting our friends and family for our sexual relationships, as when the excitement of a new relationship causes people to stop hanging out with their friends or when a couple's decision to cohabitate puts them at odds with their families. The whole idea of a "soul-mate" can be an expression of truncated lust when it is used to justify abandoning friends, family, or an established relationship in pursuit of sexual satisfaction with another. Truncating lust can be also seen in choices that sever the essential relationship between sex and procreation, like couples who intentionally chose not to have children so that they may maintain their sex life.[88] Even neglecting one's relationship to neighbors or the larger community can be examples of truncating lust as when a couples' sexual relationship makes welcoming people into the home, caring for children, or volunteering to help with school, youth sports, scouts, or music recitals tertiary concerns.

Conclusion: Recognizing the Logic of Lust

When naming sins of lust, then, we should recognize all these types of lust as variations on the initial theme: lust is not irrational but has a logic. Naming the sin is naming the distortions in its logic. I have named three types of lust that direct sexual desire over and against people and relationships, moving people to value and act in ways that contrast with a Christ like love. As in the case of the man who verbally and physically forces the woman on her knees, dominating lust leads one to find pleasure in damaging another's dignity. As with Noah who preferred pornography to people, dissipating lust neglects people and, in so doing, leads to the loss of sexual pleasure. Finally, as when Mark Sanford left his family and job as governor to visit his mistress in Argentina, truncating lust values sexual pleasure with a person to such a degree that it cuts off one's concerns for anyone outside of that pleasure and relationship. Naming these three types of lust exposes the different ways in which people's sexual desires can become oriented over and against people.

87. Adrian Blow and Kelly Harnett, "Infidelity in Committed Relationships II: A Substantive Review," *Journal of Marital & Family Therapy* 31, no. 2 (2005): 217–33.

88. Lauren Sandler, "Having It All Without Having Children," *Time*, August 12, 2013, http://time.com/241/having-it-all-without-having-children/.

As I have been setting out lust's distorted logic, I have also been suggesting the role sexual desire should have in the life of Christians. Like all desires, sexual desire grasps a good and moves people toward it. For sexual desire to orient people into a life of Christian discipleship, it should move people to pursue sexual pleasure in three ways. In contrast to dominating lust, sexual desire should find pleasure in the dignity of the other person. Whatever actions are taken should respect the demands of justice and honor the image of God found in the other person. In contrast to dissipating lust that fails to value relationships, sexual desire should apprehend the good of another and the joy of being in relationship with that person. It should call couples to attend to and prioritize each other and their relationship. These actions will foster pleasure because it will foster the love between the couple. Finally, in contrast to truncating lust that values little beyond sexual satisfaction within a relationship, sexual desire will nourish a relationship that expands beyond the couple to love of their neighbor and to a love of God with their whole mind, heart, and strength.

Chapter 4

Greed

NICHOLE M. FLORES

"Whoever has the power to project a vision of the good life and make it prevail has the most decisive power of all."[1]

Introduction: The Cathedral of Capitalism

Color. Glass. Light.

ISPLAYS BURST WITH VIBRANT color and intricate design. Images invoke the playfulness of childhood, the freshness of youth, the pleasure of bodies in motion, the exhilaration of power. Playful pop music pumps through mounted speakers, familiar chords inviting toes to tap, heads to bob, credit cards to swipe. Perfumes waft through the promenade, scents of rose petals, lavender, and sandalwood mingle with those of fries and funnel cakes. Blouses fan out on display tables, strutting an enticing range of colors. Clean, angular paths cut between racks and shelves, laying out a labyrinth leading to the most attractive apparel, beckoning one to reach out and touch fine surfaces cooled by artificial air.

These are not merely external forces; they seek to get inside of us, shaping our imaginations of what we desire. Processing through the cathedral of capitalism, we easily feel the urge to commune with the brilliant colors, the gorgeous displays, the dioramas of lives cleaned, curated, and secured in ways that we dream for our own. Even as we yearn for consumer communion, we transgress against our prized possessions. We pine for stuff that we don't use. We break, discard, and forget the stuff that we sacrificed to buy. We atone for this neglectful behavior by buying new things, sent out from the store with a new resolve to honor and care for our latest purchase.[2] This picture of Any Mall USA indicates much about the state of American consumption culture—to shop has the façade of a transcendent, even salvific, end.

---

1. William Leach, *Land of Desire: Merchants, Power, and the Rise of a New American Culture* (New York: Random House, 1993), xiii.

2. See Vincent J. Miller, *Consuming Religion: Christian Faith and Practice in a Consumer Religion* (London: Continuum, 2005), 16.

This is the consumerist vision of the good life, one which is always just one purchase away from true happiness. It is easy to be enticed into the illusion of security and personal enjoyment rooted in wealth and material possession, but what does this consumerist vision of the good life have to do with the Christian vision, rooted in justice for all and shared pursuit of common goods? This chapter probes this consumerist vision, linking it with the vice of greed and structural injustice. While greed is often misconstrued as a strictly personal vice—or even reconstructed as a personal virtue—we will see that greed is a kind of "grasping" that harms both interpersonal relationships and the societal common good.[3] The Christian vision of the good life, on the contrary, requires resistance against the endless pursuit of wealth and material possessions in order to defend and honor the dignity of every human person, especially "the least" (Mt 25:40) whose safety and well-being are often sacrificed to the unyielding pursuit of money and possessions.

Greed is a pervasive sin, and yet we struggle to (1) name the sin precisely in both its personal and social dimensions and (2) reorient affections—our emotions or feelings—and practices—the things that we do—in ways that free individuals and society from its grip. This sin has taken hold in the hearts of Catholics much in the same way it has in the hearts of all society: by subtly accepting and living out of a vision of the good life through a consumption-driven culture. This chapter exposes the consumerist vision of the good life and its connection to greed before reasserting a Christian vision in which the good life is experienced in direct relationships with others and in larger social wholes. After outlining the consumerist vision, we will explore the meaning of greed, especially its often-overlooked social dimensions, in the writing of Thomas Aquinas. We will then identify the ways that structures of greed can be named as sin because they cause and perpetuate suffering of invisible others on the lowest rungs of the global economy—people victimized by human trafficking. Finally, we will explore several practices that resist the habits of greed, supplanting the consumerist vision of the good life with a Christian vision that acknowledges the necessity of a shared common good for personal flourishing.

Consumption and the Art of Desire

Delving deeper into the liturgy of consumption, or the way in which consumer activity structures our daily lives, we should recognize first how

---

3. David Cloutier, *The Vice of Luxury: Economic Excess in a Consumer Age* (Washington, DC: Georgetown University Press, 2015), 32–33.

seemingly innocent desires for comfort and security can calcify into the vice
of greed. The consumerist vision of the good life has been offered to us as a
defense against unhappiness and insecurity. Indulging our desires through
"retail therapy" is the cure for all that ails us. George W. Bush, in the wake of
the terrorist attacks on the World Trade Center and Pentagon on September 11, 2001, encouraged Americans to resist terrorism by going to Disney
World: "Take your families and enjoy life, the way we want it to be enjoyed."[4]
Spending money becomes a patriotic act, one that reaffirms the goodness
of conspicuous consumption in the face of fresh national wounds and a
realization of vulnerability. The Bush tax cuts sought to send the consumer into the hallowed halls of area malls. But this policy ended up
exacerbating national insecurity in the form of the 2007–08 financial crisis.
Historian Andrew Bacevich says it thusly: "So as the American soldier
fought, the American consumer binged, encouraged by American banks
offering easy credit."[5]

This sense of longing for the comfort and security of wealth—material
possessions and the status they bring—is ingrained in us from childhood
through our constant exposure to the arts of advertising and merchandising. Desire is the goal rather than an accident—of advertisement and
merchandising schemes; companies want us to want their products. They
do not simply offer wares that seek to address our already-existing needs;
rather, they seek to name our desires in terms of their products. And we
easily adopt those desires as our own. This is a common experience of
the twenty-first-century shopping mall previously described, which has
laboriously honed the craft of customer enticement. But as Leach argues,
today's advertising and merchandising practices were honed from the
1890s on, when the "arts of decoration and display" were perfected by
figures such as L. Frank Baum, author of *The Wonderful Wizard of Oz*,
and stores such as Woolworth's and Wanamakers's. They created attractive
displays meant to entice the senses, imaginary worlds adorned with glitter
and light. These images were intended to shape consumers' desire and not
simply to respond to it, encouraging them to long for the latest and greatest
offered by the department store.

Most contemporary consumers would not immediately name the
desire for wealth and possessions as greed. The love of wealth and money
seems a normal aspect of consumer life. "Greed is good" in a capital-
ist economy; desire for greater wealth drives many social interactions,

4. Andrew J. Bacevich, "He Told Us to Go Shopping. Now the Bill Is Due.," *The Washington Post*, October 5, 2008; http://www.washingtonpost.com/wp-dyn/content/article/2008/10/03/AR2008100301977.
html.

5. Bacevich, "He Told Us."

whether professional or personal.[6] Yet we don't see ourselves as greedy, per se. Greedy people, we like to think, live in gilded penthouses overlooking Manhattan. Obviously, we tell ourselves, human beings need to consume in order to live.[7] It is thus easy to imagine our love of wealth and material possessions as being natural, and therefore socially acceptable, and subsequently religiously permissible. Yet it is also easy for the satisfaction of basic needs to morph into accumulation of material possessions that we do not need.

Our rationalization for the accumulation of wealth and possessions reflects the initial objections to Aquinas's argument that greed is a sin. He notes that some say:

> ...it is not a sin to desire external goods: since man [sic.] desires them naturally, both because they are naturally subject to man, and because by their means man's life is sustained (for which reason they are spoken as his substance) ... In like manner neither is it apparently a sin against one's neighbor, since a man harms no one by keeping what is his own...Further, things that occur naturally are not sins.[8]

But Aquinas refutes the argument that the accumulation of wealth does no harm to one's neighbor. Instead, he insists that the desire to acquire or keep riches beyond one's need is *avaritia*, a vice opposed to liberality.[9] Today, as in the thirteenth century, we construct thin justifications for our inordinate love of riches. We like to think we need a television in every room, a new smartphone every year, a new dress for every season. These perceived needs grip us in subtle ways, shaping how we imagine the good and flourishing life. For this reason, greed can lurk in the shadows of seemingly-legitimate desires, masquerading as benign preference (a taste for "the finer things in life") or even positively virtuous behavior (wealth and extravagant possessions as a sign of personal discipline associated with success).

---

6. Oliver Stone, *Wall Street* (Twentieth Century Fox, 1987). The script was inspired by Ivan Boesky's 1986 commencement speech for the School of Business Administration at University of California, Berkeley: "Greed is all right, by the way. I want you to know that. I think greed is healthy. You can be greedy and still feel good about yourself." See Bob Greene, "Million Idea: Use Greed For Good," *Tribunedigital-Chicagotribune*, December 15, 1986, http://articles.chicagotribune.com/1986-12-15/features/8604030634_1_ivan-boeskys-greed-fund.

7. William T. Cavanaugh, *Being Consumed: Economics and Christian Desire* (Grand Rapids, MI: William B. Eerdmans, 2008), 53.

8. Thomas Aquinas, *Summa Theologiae* II-II, q. 118, a. 1.

9. ST II-II, q. 118, a. 1. The English Dominican translates *avaritia* here as "covetousness," but this might be misleading, since "coveting" can also be understood as not simply as an immoderate desire, but as a desire that specifically wants a material good that rightly belongs to someone else. For more on this distinction, see Rebecca Konyndyk DeYoung, *Glittering Vices* (Grand Rapids, MI: Brazos Press, 2009), 43.

Thus, we need to examine how our natural needs for material goods become transformed into the inordinate desires of the consumerist vision of the good life. Leach describes this vision:

> From the 1890s on, American corporate businesses, in league with key institutions, began the transformation of American society into a society preoccupied with consumption, with comfort and bodily well-being, with luxury, spending, and acquisition, with more goods this year than last, more next year than this.[10]

This transformation is veiled by economic perspectives that claim that markets merely reflect values but do not shape them. However, as Michael Sandel argues, "Economists often assume that markets are inert, that they do not affect the goods they exchange. But this is untrue. Markets leave their mark. Sometimes, market values crowd out nonmarket values worth caring about."[11] This crowding-out of more important goods is an important place to start when naming the sin. Markets are especially adept at crowding out the value of other humans, whether members of our families or neighbors. Habituation into this false vision of the good life can also crowd out the Church's account of flourishing, one which is concerned with both the spiritual and the material, both the personal and the social. This consumption-driven vision of the good life can only be overcome by recognizing the interpersonal implications of greed, identifying the ways in which greed can harm our communities—this recognition of higher values that are displaced by our consumption will help us name the ways we fall into the sin. Then, we can identify practices that change our habits of avarice into ones of sharing and promoting the good of all people.

In a global market driven by a vision of wealth, possession, security, and luxury as the good life, it is easy for one's desire for material goods to morph into one's highest love. Such an inordinate desire for money and things is certainly a sin with serious spiritual consequences for individuals, forging individualism and isolation that can sever ties with family and community.[12] Yet, as we will see, greed is a vice that also damages human relationships well beyond our own homes and local neighborhoods. Thomas Aquinas's understanding of greed can illuminate the wider social implications of inordinate love for silver and gold.

---

10. Leach, *Land of Desire*, xiii.

11. Michael J. Sandel, *What Money Can't Buy: The Moral Limits of Markets* (New York: Farrar, Straus and Giroux, 2012), 9.

12. William Schweiker, *Theological Ethics and Global Dynamics: In the Time of Many Worlds* (Oxford, UK: Blackwell Publishing, 2004), 49. Schweiker elaborates on the social isolation of greed: "Ironically, the life of the greedy person undercuts participation in the very social network that defines her or his desires. This is why the greedy person appears in books and films as isolated, friendless."

What is Greed?

If consumerist desire is rooted in greed, it is necessary to elaborate the specific meaning of this vice. On a basic level, greed is defined as the inordinate love of money and/or wealth. Similarly, Aquinas defines *avaritia* as immoderate love of possessing. He acknowledges the necessity of possessions for sustaining human life but rejects the claim that natural desire for possessions excuses greedy inclinations. While he does not reject the desire to secure material wealth in itself, he asserts the necessity of moderation in both material possession and desire for material possession.

Aquinas asserts that greed manifests in one's inordinate desire for material possessions, desiring to accumulate things for their own sake. This longing for wealth and possessions orients one's mind and appetite toward individual and material goods, becoming sinful by displacing the desire for transcendent and universal goods. "All things obey money," Aquinas says, "so that in this sense desire for riches is the root of all sin."[13] For this reason, greed is a special sin from which other sins emanate: "Accordingly, we must say that *avaritia*, as denoting a special sin, is called the root of all sins, in likeness to the root of a tree, in furnishing sustenance to the whole tree."[14] Aquinas's designation of greed as the root of all sin is partly rhetorical; he designates a set of capital vices—vainglory, envy, anger, sloth, covetousness, gluttony, and lust—as foundational to sin in general.[15] Still, it is clear that he views greed as particularly detrimental to living a good life, a life characterized by virtue and genuine human flourishing. When we come to cherish wealth as a means of fulfilling our deepest longings, we lose sight of our radical dependence on God's grace and mercy. Because of this turning away from our ultimate end, Aquinas designates the immoderate desire for possessions as a catalyst for the other death-dealing vices.

Interpreting greed within the larger context of the *Summa Theologica* exposes its deleterious implications for both individuals and communities. Specifically, greed poses a challenge to justice, defined as the flourishing of each of the community's individual parts. The social dimension of this vice emerges from Aquinas's concern for what he calls "particular justice," or justice among individuals.[16] A crucial dimension of greed is that it is a sin against one's neighbor. As Aquinas explains, this vice harms the neighbor through the unjust accumulation of money and wealth. Disproportionate

13. ST I-II, q. 84, a. 1.
14. ST I-II, q. 84, a. 1.
15. ST I-II, q. 84, a. 4.
16. ST II-II, q. 58, a. 7.

material accumulation can deprive the neighbor of her basic needs.[17] And while Aquinas enumerates theft among mortal sins, he teaches that holding more property than we need, in accord with natural law, is a sin against our neighbor in need. Holding more possessions than I need while other members of the human family are hungry, naked, and homeless is unjust and a sin against that neighbor. Indeed, Aquinas even leaves open the possibility that, in an emergency in which there is no other remedy, it is lawful for one to "succor his own need by means of another's property."[18] Greed, then, is a violation of particular justice, or justice among individuals and thus a violation of the common good.[19]

Injustice among individuals, however, is not greed's only harm. Aquinas's category of general or legal justice, the virtue which directs one's relationships toward the common good, is also helpful for identifying greed's social harms.[20] Aquinas maintains a distinction between the common good and the individual good as the difference between the whole and its parts.[21] Society is made up of human beings who are created in the image of God. Society, then, is really a "whole of wholes" in which the common good "flows back" to the members of society, showering the goods we share on each particular person.[22] While every part is ordained to the whole, the common good aims to produce and preserve happiness among its many parts. Greed violates the particular person by depriving her of what she needs from the common good to survive and thrive; often enough, our inordinate desires harm particular others because they are sins against what we owe to the common good. The sparkling displays that entice our desire may seem innocent because we don't seem to be directly "hurting anyone." But we may need to name this sin in terms of hurting everyone— that is, hurting the common good on which we all depend.

Thus, Aquinas's social vision involves a dynamic of mutual enrichment between individuals and society. This vision should chasten the greedy heart, reaffirming the ordination of persons and families to the common good: "And therefore, as the good of one man is not the last end, but is ordained to the common good; so too the good of one household is ordained to the good of a single state, which is a perfect community."[23]

17. ST II-II, q. 118, a. 1.

18. ST II-II, q. 66, a. 7.

19. ST II-II, q. 58, a. 7.

20. ST II-II, q. 58, a. 6.

21. ST II-II, q. 58, a. 7.

22. Jacques Maritain, *The Person and the Common Good* (Notre Dame, IN: University of Notre Dame Press, 1946), 55–56.

23. ST I-II, q. 90, a. 3.

Our proper orientation to the common good should be kept in mind as we examine our consciences for confession, acknowledging how greed undermines not only the dignity of particular human beings directly but also the efficacy of the common good. Read within the context of Aquinas's articulation of the common good, then, greed can be understood as eroding the good of the whole community resulting in the violation of particular neighbors.

Justice and the common good are indispensable aspects of Aquinas's vision of the good life, a cornerstone for Catholic social teaching and thought. Greed not only involves sins against the good of one's soul through pervasive and distorting desires for acquisition, but also sins against the neighbor and the larger community through unjust distribution of goods. As William Schweiker, professor of theological ethics at the University of Chicago, explains, "Greed is a passion, a human desire, to draw some socially defined material or ideal value (money, power, etc.) into the self and thereby to undercut the domain of social meaning. Greed works to isolate the self by breaking necessary bonds of human community."[24] Greed takes, and takes, and takes, weakening and eventually severing the ties that bind us together: our basic investments in the good of the neighbor. Endless accumulation leaves someone else without the means to survive and is thus a violation of justice. Aquinas's vision of the common good thus extinguishes the flames of self-justifying desires for the accumulation of wealth and goods masquerading as a reward for virtue.

Aquinas's conception of justice and the common good endures in Christian thinking about these matters, especially in terms of what society owes to those who are poor. In accord with Aquinas's link between individual and social good, David Hollenbach, SJ, of Georgetown University defines justice as "the minimal level of solidarity required to enable all of society's members to live with basic dignity."[25] This vision of justice demands that all members of society be able to participate in the life of society in ways that secure their human dignity. The exclusion of those who are suffering from poverty from partaking in the goods of society is a grave injustice, indeed. This marginalization is especially egregious when the overall society possesses enough resources to support all of its members but refuses to contribute what is due to other members of society, whether through payment of fair wages, provision for social welfare (such as Women, Infants, and Children, or WIC, a government program in the United States which provides food staples to supplement nutritious diets for poor women and

24. Schweiker, *Theological Ethics and Global Dynamics*, 49.

25. David Hollenbach, SJ, *The Common Good and Christian Ethics* (Cambridge, UK: Cambridge University Press, 2002), 192.

children), or charitable contributions to programs working to alleviate poverty. In accord with Aquinas, Hollenbach's definition of justice places demands on us to promote the good of others in economic, political, and social practices. Insofar as our preoccupation with accumulating our own goods obscures these demands, we sin.

Thomistic thinking about justice and the common good continues to flavor Catholic thinking about the social dimensions of virtue and vice. Weaving together the strands of his thought, Aquinas's ethics offer a multidimensional notion of justice and the common good that can navigate the tension between concerns for particular justice among individuals and general justice in society. This vision of justice and the common good will be crucial to articulating a robust rejection of the consumerist vision of the good life which often crowds out more important commitments.[26]

This analysis reveals that greed is a vice with clear personal and social implications, one which quietly infiltrates our minds and hearts, eroding our own flourishing by displacing higher goods, and disrupting the common good of the whole community through the violation of neighbors. Keeping all this in mind, we see that sins of greed are not simply a matter of personal excess. Because of this, we need to go further in naming the sins that emerge from our greed. Reasserting a critique of greed in the twenty-first century requires an examination of conscience that draws attention to greed's even wider social dimensions, especially the deleterious effects of our greed on poor people all over the world. We turn now to the way in which the social dimensions of greed become ensconced in unjust social structures that undermine the flourishing of often-invisible others in our global community.

Structures of Greed

Malls are filled with goods, but they are also filled with people. Friends converse over coffee. Shoppers fawn over expensive handbags and watches. Retail workers straighten dress displays. These people are in relationship with each other and, while it isn't always obvious, with people beyond the mall. Viewed through the lens of Catholic moral theology, the mall beckons us to ask: what is the relationship between shoppers and retail workers paid meager hourly wages? What is the relationship between luxury shoppers and poorer members of our society struggling to make ends meet? What is the relationship between coffee drinkers and those who labored to pick the coffee beans? The mall foregrounds some relationships while

26. Sandel, *What Money Can't Buy*, 9.

obscuring others. Reflecting on the relationships that remain hidden from our view can help us to recognize structures of greed that are reinforced by our actions, allowing us to name sins in which we are complicit, even though most of us would never directly commit them. These structures, fostered by our greed, reinforce the economic exploitation of the poorest and most vulnerable people in the global economy.

Social Sin and Structures of Vice

Social sin, according to Kristin E. Heyer, "encompasses the unjust structures, distorted consciousness, and collective actions and inaction that facilitates injustice and dehumanization."[27] Social sin seeps into the soil of our institutions—laws, policies, governmental and nongovernmental organizations, international decision-making bodies, etc.—perpetuating inequality and stifling meaningful participation in those institutions. And while Catholic theologians differ over the precise source and scope of social sin (i.e., social sin as an aggregate of personal sins versus social sin as consisting of nonvoluntary dimensions), there is universal concern over the power of these structures to inhibit the flourishing and violate the dignity of both the powerless and the powerful.[28]

Heyer, engaging both Catholic magisterial and liberationist pronouncements, stakes out ethical space for addressing both the personal and social dimensions of sinful structures.[29] Social sin, she argues, must account for personal human agency, calling individuals to account for discreet sinful actions that accumulate in dehumanizing systems of social sin. Thus, as we examine our consciences, we must look for personal actions and inactions that contribute to this dehumanization of others. For example, it is important for individual consumers to be aware of the effect of our personal decisions to purchase clothing from retailers who employ sweatshop labor. Upon learning that a particular retailer sells clothing made by exploited workers in sweatshops, we may decide to stop purchasing products from that store.

But personal decision making in itself does not upend historically rooted social, economic, and political structures that continue to leave their mark on human life. An adequate account of social sin must also account for

27. Kristin E. Heyer, *Kinship Across Borders: A Christian Ethic of Immigration* (Washington, DC: Georgetown University Press, 2012), 37. Heyer is a professor of theological ethics at Boston College.

28. Daniel J. Daly, "Structures of Virtue and Vice," *New Blackfriars* 92, no. 1039 (2010): 341–57. Daly's work offers a comprehensive description of the development of social sin in Catholic social thought, including developments in magisterial thinking and liberation theology.

29. Heyer, *Kinship Across Borders*, 54.

the deeply entrenched nature of unjust structures. According to theologian Karl Rahner's narration of original sin, we cannot simply purchase an item from the department store or grocery store without participating in histories of oppression. In reference to his famous "banana" example, Rahner says: "To [the banana purchaser] belongs, under certain circumstances, the pitiful lot of banana pickers, which is in turn co-determined by social injustice, exploitation, or a centuries-old commercial policy. This person himself [*sic*] now participates in this situation of guilt to his own advantage."[30] Our personal actions affect social structures, but there are also social structures beyond our immediate individual control that must be considered. In these cases, examining our consciences requires that we ask how we have failed to do what we can to address the structural problems, including moderating or changing the personal desires that really do perpetuate the oppression.

Building on conceptions of social sin in Catholic social teaching and thought, theologian Daniel J. Daly addresses the ways in which structures of virtue and vice can influence human flourishing. Social structures are potent, Daly argues, and must be interrogated for the kind of effects they have on persons and communities. He explains: "Structures have the capacity to systematically promote the human good, the common good, and human happiness, or frustrate the realization of these goods."[31] Whereas virtue can foster structures characterized by solidarity and justice, vice calcifies into unjust social structures that harm both individual good and the common good. The personal vice of greed accumulates into an entrenched structure of greed. These entrenched structures have high human costs that are often hidden from the view of everyday consumers. Yet we must trace them back to so many choices we make in pursuing the consumerist vision of the good life.

Structures of Greed and Human Trafficking

This connection, between our everyday desires and vast social structures, can be disconcerting. But we need to face these connections. Consider how human trafficking in the global economy offers an acute illustration of the ways that structures of greed undermine human flourishing, especially among the most vulnerable people of the world. Human trafficking is a form of modern-day slavery, in which victimized people are held in

---

30. Karl Rahner, *Foundations of Christian Faith*, trans. William V. Dych (New York: Crossroad, 1978), 110–11.

31. Daly, "Structures of Virtue and Vice," 353.

compelled service.[32] Those victimized by trafficking are often subject to forced labor, including in sexual, service, and agricultural economies. Trafficking is prevalent in sex work, domestic service (housekeeping, childcare), and farm work. Trafficked people are often hidden from the view of consumers, making it difficult to enforce laws outlawing forced servitude. Their labor is exploited to bring products that we love to consume, from chocolate to cheap clothes. Figures and statistics on trafficking are notoriously difficult to track, but the Polaris Project estimates that at least 20.9 million people are victimized by human trafficking today.[33]

While human trafficking elicits pity from many people, consumers generally have a shallow understanding of the relationship between personal decision making and the exploitation of others in global economic systems. As anti-trafficking activist Laura Germino explains: "American consumers don't want to have slavery woven into the fabric of their daily lives; but, unknown to most, it already is. They drink orange juice in the morning, they eat tomatoes with their burger for lunch."[34] While the role of human trafficking in commodity chains is largely unknown to consumers, this structure uses and abuses the bodies of the world's most vulnerable people, treating them as if they are disposable. Commenting on the trafficking along US-Mexico border, Nancy Pineda-Madrid points out that trafficked bodies of women, who work in the *maquiladoras* along the border, are treated as *mujeres desechables* or "disposable women" even as their labor produces products of value for the market.[35] Pineda-Madrid's description resonates with Pope Francis's critique of the "throwaway culture which affects the excluded just as it quickly reduces things to rubbish."[36]

The US bishops wrote in a letter: "We judge any economic system by what it does for and to people and by how it permits all to participate in

32. U.S. Department of State, "What Is Modern Day Slavery?" *U.S. Department of State*, accessed December 11, 2016, http://www.state.gov/j/tip/what/. The U.S. State Department offers a broad definition of trafficking: "The United States government considers trafficking in persons to include all of the criminal conduct involved in force labor and sex trafficking, essentially the conduct involved in reducing or holding someone in compelled service...individuals may be trafficking victims regardless of whether they once consented, participated in a crime as a direct result of being trafficked, were transported into the exploitative situation, or were simply born into a state of servitude."

33. "Polaris Project," *PolarisProject.org*, https://polarisproject.org/human-trafficking.

34. Quoted from interview in Kevin Bales and Ron Soodalter, *The Slave Next Door* (Berkeley, CA: University of California Press, 2009), 51.

35. Nancy Pineda-Madrid, "Sex Trafficking and Feminicide Along the Border: Re-Membering Our Daughters," in *Living With(out) Borders: Catholic Theological Ethics on the Migration of Peoples*, ed. Agnes M. Brazal and María Teresa Dávila, Catholic Theological Ethics in the World Church (Maryknoll, NY.: Orbis Books, 2016): 87.

36. Francis, Encyclical Letter *Laudato Si'* (May 24, 2015), 22.

it. The economy should serve people, not the other way around."[37] If the current consumption-driven global economy fosters trafficking and modern-day slavery, then it is necessary to interrogate this particular structure as a catalyst of dehumanization. And, as painful as this might be, we must recognize our own sins in contributing to this trafficking. Of course, it is not the case that simply wanting useful clothes or healthful OJ is greedy. But our desires for these things and so many others at the cheapest cost with little consideration of moderation (maybe tomatoes could be put on sandwiches seasonally?) is in fact what drives the way the commodities are produced. If we ourselves think that we would never treat other human beings in this way, we need to see the trafficked bodies hidden behind the shiny surfaces of consumer goods. A consumerist vision of the good life defined by inordinate desire for wealth and possessions facilitates a structure of greed characterized by disregard for the neighbor.

Reclaiming the Good Life

How ought Catholics respond to this problem? We need to cultivate both personal and social practices to dismantle structures of greed and honor the dignity of all persons. This necessitates that we supplant the consumerist vision of the good life with a Christian vision. Reclaiming this vision requires practicing a new way of seeing, looking beyond the glare of wealth, possession, comfort, and security toward a life characterized by solidarity with the most vulnerable among us. Pope Francis has defined faith as seeing with the eyes of Christ, or seeing our world as Christ sees it.[38] This way of seeing calls us toward a clear-eyed view of the way our personal decisions should be shaped by our social obligations to others.

This final section suggests practices that resist structures of greed. These practices call upon us to pay attention to the social implications of our personal economic choices. Finally, we will highlight the potential of global social movements led by everyday Catholics to resist structures of greed. These movements channel collective efforts toward generosity and solidarity toward affecting social change.

Practical Solidarity: Assessment, Confession, Transformation

The Catholic vision of the good life calls for us to resist unjust social structures through practical solidarity, or cultivation of virtuous personal and

---

37. United States Conference of Catholic Bishops, Pastoral Letter *Economic Justice for All* (November 1986), paragraph 13.

38. Francis, Encyclical Letter *Lumen Fidei* (June 29, 2013), 46.

social habits. On the personal level, practical solidarity requires taking a hard look at our daily actions, assessing them for the effect they have on the lives of others. Here are some questions you could ask yourself:

- Am I preoccupied with money and things?
- Do I lust after luxury items (expensive cars or designer clothing, for example)?
- Does my vision of a life well lived depend on whether or not I have acquired these things?
- Do I live beyond my needs (do I have much more stuff than I could ever use or really need)?

These are tough questions that can confront us with upsetting realizations about how we relate to wealth and money. Answering them honestly might reveal that our seemingly benign desire for the "finer things in life" is actually greed in disguise. These questions ask us to unmask the consumerist vision of the good life, naming our particular sins rooted in greed so that we may pursue the Christian vision.

Assessing our daily actions is but the first step in extricating ourselves from a consumerist vision of the good life. But it is also important to confess the ways in which our personal economic practices can hinder the flourishing of others in society. Returning to Karl Rahner's example of the banana, we see that our actions can have adverse effects on people whom we have never met who live in places far from our own homes. This realization beckons us to examine our consciences and to confess these harms, even if these harms are unintended and largely hidden from our daily realities. Acknowledging the ways our actions can inadvertently undermine human dignity calls us to social repentance in which we accept a new level of responsibility for the way that our actions can harm others, compelling us to pay attention to the subtle—and sometimes invisible—implications of our decisions.

This new level of awareness is key to identifying and adopting new economic habits that can help transform unjust social structures. Here are some ways in which we can begin to reclaim a truly good life that recognizes our responsibility to our neighbors near and far as commanded by Jesus Christ:

- *Get involved with your local community.* Invest time and money in local organizations that support communal thriving, i.e., local parishes, neighborhood associations, community centers, community supported agriculture, credit unions. Get to know your neighbors: those who live

next door, down the street, and in parts of town where you typically
don't go. Shop at local businesses. Getting to know your neighbors helps
you to recognize your connections to each other. Encountering your
local neighbors also helps you to conceive of the circumstances of your
global neighbors in more concrete terms.

- *Live frugally.* While often overlooked in discussions of Catholic social
  teaching, frugality is a central practice in resisting greed and promoting
  a society in which all people can survive and thrive. Frugality means
  spending less by questioning the standards for material wealth handed
  to us by our society.[39] It requires that we become less attached to material things, but also that we take a sacramental view of the world so
  we see things as part of God's creation.[40] Further, it demands that we
  think about the cost of our consumer habits on other people, especially those who are exploited in the process of production and deliv-
  ery of these goods.

- *Ask questions.* Inquire about how the products you buy were made: Who
  made this product? Where was it made? Was it produced in an envi-
  ronmentally and economically sustainable way? Was the person who
  made the product paid a just wage? Were the workers provided adequate working conditions? These questions can help us begin to notice
  the scaffolding of economic structures. Once these structures come
  into view, we can help eradicate them by imagining new ways of consuming that strive to honor basic human dignity and fundamental
  human rights.

The thought of interrogating and changing our daily practices can be
intimidating; we may wonder if such transformations are even possible.
Nevertheless, the theology of the Church realizes that living a good life
takes practice. It is not something that can be learned overnight or bought
in a store. But it can be learned by striving to live a simple lifestyle that is
mindful of how one's decisions can influence the lives of others.

Resisting Greed Together

Personal actions are crucial in resisting structures of greed, but it is
easy to feel as though one decision is but a drop in a massive ocean of
human action. Indeed, it is difficult for one person to change the world,
at least working alone. But what happens when one person committed to

---

39. See Julie Hanlon Rubio, *Hope for Common Ground: Mediating the Personal and the Political in a
Divided Church* (Washington, DC: Georgetown University Press, 2016), 133.

40. Cavanaugh, *Being Consumed*, 58.

eradicating structures of greed teams up with others who share that commitment? This is what everyday Catholics have often done by helping to forge social movements. These movements each have their own charism, a spirit that guides their action in the world and grounds them in the Word of God and the faith of the Church. But how do these movements make a difference? Kevin Ahern argues that these organizations resist "the globalization of indifference"[41] by (1) engendering a sense of social responsibility among Christians, (2) proposing social alternatives to current problems, and (3) facilitating transformative social action.[42] Working together, ordinary Catholics can promote practices and structures that eschew our society's obsession with money and wealth while offering a vision of solidarity, justice, and human relationship that resists the culture of greed.

Conclusion

"Whoever has the power to project a vision of the good life and make it prevail has the most decisive power of all." The consumerist vision of the good life has become dominant, often supplanting a Christian vision characterized by simplicity, awareness, and relationship. Greed systematically hinders human flourishing, sacrificing the good of the other for the sake of wealth and ever greater consumption. The social dimensions of greed mean that it can have nothing to do with a Christian vision of the good life that is shaped by love of God and love of neighbor, including particular obligations to vulnerable and exploited neighbors such as those victimized by human trafficking and modern-day slavery.

The consumerist vision of the good life need not be determinative. Christians can cultivate personal practices that promote structures of justice and generosity. While our personal actions often seem small and insignificant, Catholic social movements, along with all people of good will, can work together to undermine structures of sin with what Ahern calls structures of grace. It is in this social grace that there is hope for renewed social relationships in which our highest desire is for the God who calls us to share the good life with our neighbors.

41. Francis, *Laudato Si'*, 52.

42. Kevin Ahern, *Structures of Grace: Catholic Organizations Serving the Global Common Good* (Maryknoll, NY: Orbis Books, 2015), 13.

Chapter 5

Sloth

JULIE HANLON RUBIO

I HAVE A WEAK SPOT for articles about organization, efficiency, and productivity. I like New Year's resolutions, planners of all kinds, and Lenten disciplines. Self-improvement as an ongoing project is deeply appealing and laziness is fundamentally uninteresting. I am not alone. In the broader culture, sloth is understood as laziness or a failure to work hard at school or work. I call this the "hard work" understanding for thinking about sloth. The virtue of hard work is opposed to the vice of sloth and growth in virtue seems to require resolutions to be more disciplined.

While there is truth to this understanding, historically, the vice of acedia or sloth has meant something more like resistance to the spiritual work of being in relationship with God, which is remedied by surrendering one's own will, putting aside one's own plans, and allowing God to be in charge of one's life. I call this the "surrender" understanding. Study of the historical sources suggests that this more expansive understanding is the more authentically Christian account. The virtue of surrender is opposed to the vice of sloth, and growth in virtue seems to require ever-increasing sacrifice.

Yet, as a working, married mother of three, I have often wondered about the wisdom of the surrender understanding. I can remember sitting in a classroom at Back to School Night at my sons' Jesuit high school and learning that the boys regularly prayed the Prayer for Generosity ("Lord, teach me to be generous, to serve you as you deserve, to give and not to count the cost …").[1] My first (not very pious) thought was: This might be great for teen-aged boys, but I am not sure I can pray for more generosity when I'm this sleep-deprived. It turns out that some theologians worry along the same lines. Reflecting on contemporary experience, they ask if, at least for some people, doing too much for God via doing too much for other people

---

1. Jim Manney, "Teach Me to Be Generous," *Ignatian Spirituality*, February 29, 2012, http://www.ignatianspirituality.com/12297/teach-me-to-be-generous. The prayer is often attributed to St. Ignatius, but the author is unknown, and it dates from the late nineteenth century rather than the sixteenth. Yet, Ignatius "could have written it," and it remains popular in Jesuit institutions.

may be a bigger temptation. The surrender understanding may also need some expansion.

It turns out that naming sins rooted in sloth is complicated. Is there a way to recognize traditional Christian wisdom on sloth while attending to the unique experiences, contexts, and challenges that mark our times? I attempt to do so in this chapter by analyzing the "hard work" and "surrender" understandings for thinking about sloth, listening to contemporary concerns about surrender, and proposing a yet more expansive understanding based on solidarity as a contemporary virtue opposed to the vice of sloth. Yet, readers need not worry that I will offer a guilt-inducing essay designed to drive us all to despair. Philosopher Rebecca Konyndyk DeYoung writes that studying the ancient tradition of vices or sins does not have to be an exercise in negativity. Rather, the process of discovering that others throughout history have shared and named our struggles can be "not only illuminating, but also liberating"; if such recognition inspires reckoning with the human condition, it "can be a catalyst for spiritual growth," which is much better than another new to-do list.[2]

Hard Work

A recent article by a master of efficiency purported to divulge what everyone wants to know: "How do you do it all?"[3] The writer, who says he has been asked this question throughout his life, shares his secrets. Some are simple efficiency tricks: walking to work instead of exercising at the gym, taking care of email on the commuter train, mindfully employing social media, using electronic sources and planners. Others are avoiding things that typically bog people down: TV, the latest news, office politics. Some choices are more controversial: skipping most meetings and not paying close attention in those he attends, saying yes only to those things he really wants to do, only taking calls that are "pre-arranged and with people I want to talk to." By placing limits on what he will or will not respond to and limiting obligations, the writer manages to be extraordinarily productive.

The very productive among us are often lauded as virtuous while underperformers are negatively viewed, if not as vicious, at least as insufficiently virtuous. In popular accounts of the seven vices, sloth is often juxtaposed to laziness. Historically, too, sloth was often rendered as laziness, and productivity became a virtue, a recognizable part of the American middle-class

---

2. Rebecca Konyndyk DeYoung, *Glittering Vices: A New Look at the Seven Deadly Sins and Their Remedies* (Grand Rapids, MI: Brazos Press, 2009), 10.

3. Austin Frakt, "How Do You Do It All?," *The Incidental Economist*, September 23, 2014, http://theincidentaleconomist.com/wordpress/how-do-you-do-it-all/.

work ethic.[4] Sometimes, in reaction, the vice is embraced. Popular play-wright Wendy Wasserstein wrote a book on the vice of sloth in which she celebrated her own laziness.[5] A traveling art exhibit on "The Seven Deadly Sins" allows museum-goers to indulge in their favorite vice.[6] Fans of sloth are invited to sit back in recliners, view videos of the sites of other vice exhibits to which they need not travel by foot, view a refrigerator full of alcohol and soda, and read short quotes (rather than a whole chapter!) on sloth. Related events include a "Sinful Weekend" with leisure activities for the whole family.

Curators see the exhibit as avoiding a simplistic take on acedia. They provide opportunities for patrons to indulge in laziness and "busy distrac-tion," both of which have long been associated with the vice of sloth. "Sloth is not just lying around doing nothing," one of the curators said. "It's also always checking your cellphone and running from one thing to another."[7] Time spent on television, social media, shopping, reading bad fiction or lightweight news, playing cellphone games, or even engaging in mindless activities in the real world can all be manifestations of sloth. In this under-standing, those who struggle with the vice of sloth fail to work as hard or in as focused a way as they should. As the art exhibit shows, sloth can be understood to include both idleness and pointless busyness. Both qualities are associated with a failure to produce well enough to inspire people to ask about you, "How does she do it all?" Growth in virtue seems to require attempts to be more organized, disciplined, and intentional.

Contemporary fans of this understanding point back to Evagrius Pon-ticus, the Christian monk who was the first to codify the seven deadly sins in the fourth century. Evagrius worried both about the lazy monk and the distracted or hyperactive monk. Neither was living the life to which monks were called. Though they appear to be very different, both are similarly flawed. While busyness may appear virtuous, it can be "a masquerade for a kind of inattention."[8] Evagrius speaks of acedia as "the most burdensome of all the demons" and sees it as a force that makes the day appear "fifty

4. See Benjamin Franklin, "The Way to Wealth" (1758), a short essay drawing together many useful sayings from *Poor Richard's Almanac* (1732), in which Franklin juxtaposes sloth and industry (e.g., "Sloth makes all things difficult, but industry, all easy," "Never leave that till to-morrow, which you can do to-day."). Available at: Project Gutenberg, http://www.gutenberg.org/files/43855/43855-h/43855-h .htm.

5. Wendy Wasserstein, *Sloth: The Seven Deadly Sins* (New York: Oxford University Press, 2005).

6. Susan Hodara, "A Deadly Sin at the Aldrich, From the Comfort of an Armchair," *New York Times* (August 21, 2015); http://www.nytimes.com/2015/08/23/nyregion/a-deadly-sin-at-the-aldrich-from -the-comfort-of-an-armchair.html.

7. Hodara, "A Deadly Sin."

8. Hodara, "A Deadly Sin."

hours long," leads the monk to keep looking out the window to see when the sun will go down, and even "assails him with hatred of his place, his way of life and the work of his hands."[9] Alternatively, it could lead the monk to fill his day with mindless labor. Though the busy monk appears not to be slothful, for Evagrius, a restless apathy lies at the heart of sloth.[10] Lacking the conviction that life deserves serious attention can lead one to waste time looking out the window or obsessing about minor tasks.

The hard work understanding is not wrong. It is most helpful when it directs people not simply to productivity but to "mindful labor." *Apathy* lies at the core of the vice of acedia. In our current context, though laziness is one symptom of the vice, mindless busyness might be a more common manifestation. What the hard work understanding gets right is the human need for good work. Because human persons have minds and spirits as well as bodies, good work allows for all three dimensions of our selves to be fully engaged. Karl Marx famously named "alienated labor" as a key problem of modern industrial society.[11] He described a worker who "denies himself, does not feel content but unhappy, does not develop freely his physical and mental energy but mortifies his body and ruins his mind. The worker therefore only feels himself outside his work, and in his work feels outside himself."[12]

John Paul II corrects and develops this insight, saying that a person "is alienated if he refuses to transcend himself and to live the experience of self-giving and of the formation of an authentic human community oriented towards his final destiny, which is God. A society is alienated if its forms of social organization, production and consumption make it more difficult to offer this gift of self and to establish this solidarity between people."[13] Though Marx had factory workers in mind, today white-collar workers can be alienated, too. Conversely, work that connects body and soul fulfills. According to the "hard work" understanding, then, avoiding sloth requires directing one's passion and energy to *meaningful* activity. Still, as John Paul II's words suggest, the Christian tradition on acedia goes beyond alienation from work to speak of a deeper alienation that calls for a more complex response.

---

9. Evagrius Ponticus, "Praktikos," http://www.ldysinger.com/Evagrius/01_Prak/00a_start.htm.

10. Rebecca Konyndyk DeYoung, "Sloth: Some Historical Reflections on Laziness, Effort, and Resistance to the Demands of Love," in *Virtues and Their Vices*, ed. Kevin Timple and Craig A. Boyd, 177–198 (New York: Oxford University Press, 2014).

11. Karl Marx, "Estranged Labor," in *The Marx-Engels Reader*, second edition, ed. Robert C. Tucker (New York: W.W. Norton & Company, 1978).

12. Marx, "Estranged Labor," 74.

13. John Paul II, Encyclical Letter *Centesimus Annus*, (May 1, 1991), 41.

Surrender

The Christian tradition speaks about the vice of acedia not primarily under the "hard work" understanding (as simple laziness opposed to busyness) but under the "surrender" understanding, as a refusal to seek wisdom, deep sorrow, or a failure to love God and others. According to DeYoung, the problem with popular portrayals of the vices is that "sloth gets secularized and work gets spiritualized."[14] In other words, we forget the spiritual dimensions of the vice and adopt instead a near-reverence for the mere fact of virtuous productivity or hard work. However, for Christians productive work is not the answer to sloth, nor is it an end in itself. *Both* laziness and busyness are problematic, not because they lead to low productivity but because they allow us to escape from engaging with the reality and meaning of human existence. For Christians, being slothful is "going through the motions" in life without due consciousness of where we are going or what all of our activity is really for. In contrast, a virtuous person understands her ultimate end in God, consciously seeks God, and surrenders herself to God's desires for her life. Even those who affirm Christian teaching about God and human destiny may still struggle with the tendency to fall into despondency, leading us to plod through our days rather than striving to be fully human and fully alive. Beyond busyness or laziness, the Christian tradition identifies three significant kinds of resistance to living a meaningful life. Turning to these three forms of resistance helps us name sins rooted in sloth that aren't obvious if we only hold to the hard work understanding of the vice.

Refusal to Seek Wisdom

Some traditional accounts describe sloth primarily as a failure to attend to one's spiritual core by seeking true wisdom. Thomas Aquinas interprets Sirach 6:25–26 ("Put your feet into her fetters, and your neck under your yoke / Bend your shoulders and carry her and do not be irked at her bonds.") as a call to pursue wisdom and avoid being "irked" or made sorrowful by this work.[15] Thus, he says sloth, or the lack of disciplined attention to or "sorrow for" one's "spiritual good," is a sin. One does not overcome this sin simply by resistance but by perseverance, for "the more we think about

---

14. Rebecca Konyndyk DeYoung, "The Vice of Sloth," *The Other Journal,* http://theotherjournal. com/2007/11/15/the-vice-of-sloth-some-historical-reflections-on-laziness-effort-and-resistance-to -the-demands-of-love/.

15. Thomas Aquinas, *Summa Theologiae* II-II, q. 35, a. 1. In the passage from Sirach, acedia is the root of the word translated as "irked."

spiritual goods, the more pleasing they become to us, and forthwith sloth dies away."[16] For Aquinas, disciplined focus on spiritual things is virtuous while despair is morally problematic.

The wisdom of Aquinas may seem obvious, but when we look back to how it was communicated to Catholics in the nineteenth and twentieth centuries, there is a noticeable focus on rules relating to religious practices. At that time, moral theology was taught to priests using moral manuals originally designed to help priests assign penances in the confessional.[17] The primary interest of the manualists was to ascertain if a given action was permissible or sinful, and if sinful, how sinful. Most contemporary critics fault the manualists for failing to inspire spiritual growth. A more charitable reading might be that the manualists were concerned about spiritual growth but viewed their primary responsibility as steering people away from sin. Thus, they gave priests advice on how to approach common spiritual shortcomings such as the failure to go to Mass, forgetting to pray, or breaking rules about fasting during Lent. Though I do not want to go back to the deficiencies of pre-Vatican II Catholicism, I do want to bring forward the manualists' concern for ordinary Catholics who struggle to know when they are sinning. Despite their shortcomings, the manualists can help us name sins and prepare to seek forgiveness in the sacrament of Reconciliation.

If the manualists were typically too legalistic in their interpretation of sloth as a spiritual vice, Aquinas's insight about the fundamental importance of pursuing "spiritual goods" should not be dismissed too quickly. For Christians, religious commitment is not limited to fulfilling particular obligations; it includes the larger obligation of focusing energy on what is most important. What does this look like? We can think of Mary of Bethany, who sits and listens to Jesus, choosing "the better part" over distraction (Luke 10:38–42). But we can also think about the student who begins his day with centering prayer and makes a commitment to be present in his classes or the parent who prays with her child before leaving the house for work and really listens to her spouse tell about his day in the evening. Yet, acedia is more than a simple failure to direct attention to the right things. It a vice involving the heart and the will.

---

16. ST II-II, q. 35, a. 1.

17. Popular manuals included: Heribert Jone, OFM, *Moral Theology*, trans. Urban Adelman (Westminster, MD: Newman, 1945); Henry Davis, SJ, *Moral and Pastoral Theology*, vol. one, fourth rev. ed. (London: Sheed and Ward, 1945); and Thomas Slater, SJ, *A Manual of Moral Theology for English-Speaking Countries*, vol. 1, sixth rev. ed. (London: Burns, Oates, & Washbourne, 1928).

Sorrow

Aquinas claims that sloth is "an oppressive sorrow, which, to wit, so weighs upon man's mind, that he wants to do nothing." It is not simply a feeling, like sadness, but "a deliberate resistance or aversion of the will not just felt but endorsed or consented to." He also calls it "sluggishness of the mind which neglects to begin good."[18]

Consider the experience many people have of failed efforts to commit to daily prayer. I can be inspired to pray out of gratitude for the blessings of my life, out of a sense that I need to be better grounded in the source of my being, or perhaps just from reading about the prayer practices of holy people. I can know that Jesus prayed and encouraged his followers to do likewise. I can remember how daily prayer makes me feel centered in God. I can affirm in theory that making prayer a habit is necessary to enjoying its benefits. I can think, "I really want to do this." I may decide to devote a certain amount of time each day to prayer, but when the time comes, not only do I not "feel like" praying, I <u>decide</u> that I am going to check my email, straighten up my desk, or do the morning dishes instead. I may tell myself: I can pray later, but find that when end of day comes, I have failed once again to do what I say I want to do. I cannot summon the energy to direct my attention to God.

In contemporary times, some ask whether this kind of sluggishness or sadness is really a form of depression and therefore not morally blameworthy. It is important for contemporary Christians to understand clinical depression as a medical condition requiring treatment and to acknowledge that depression is not a moral failing.[19] Still, many who are not clinically depressed are still plagued by sluggishness with respect to spiritual things. For Christians, this is problematic for two reasons. First, a Christian anthropology (or understanding of the human person) claims that human beings have their purpose or end in God. We are creatures of God who are fundamentally oriented toward our Creator. Once we recognize how loved we are by God, taking "joy in God" should naturally follow. Second, Aquinas suggests that we are commanded to rest in God on the Sabbath. He thought that avoiding God could lead to hopelessness and "aversion of the mind ... from the Divine good."[20] The failure to turn our hearts and minds to the God who made us and desires to be in relation with us can be properly considered a tendency toward sinfulness.[21]

---

18. ST II-II, q. 35, a. 1.

19. See, Robert W. Daly, "Before Depression: The Medieval Vice of Acedia," *Psychiatry: Interpersonal & Biological Processes* 70, no. 1 (2007): 30–51.

20. ST II-II, q. 35, a. 3.

21. It may be possible to learn hope via connecting with the transcendent. See Warren Kinghorn, "'Hope that is Seen is No Hope at All:' Theological Constructions of Hope in Psychotherapy," *Bulletin of the Menninger Clinic* 77, no. 4 (2013): 369–94.

Sloth's Daughters

However, the vice of sloth is not only problematic on its own terms; it also has what many theologians have called "daughters" or what we might call "related effects." Aquinas draws on St. Gregory the Great's list of related effects, which includes "malice, spite, faint-heartedness, despair, sluggishness in regard to the commandments, wandering of the mind after unlawful things."[22] This list has the advantage of showing how sloth in spiritual things can lead both to acting maliciously and to *not* acting as well as to "uneasiness of mind." This can mean either that the mind wanders aimlessly or that it rushes around chasing after many things.

Of course, not everyone who neglects spiritual seeking or practice is prone to every "daughter" of sloth. However, perhaps many have had the experience of finding that a spiritual practice like praying the rosary, reading poetry, or hiking grounds them, making them less restless and less prone to mean-spiritedness. Perhaps others have seen in deeply spiritual people a generosity that allows for focused attention in work and relationships, confirming the tradition's insistence that pursuit of wisdom is both good in itself and linked to other virtues.[23] Though the particulars may vary, turning away from wisdom and giving in to sorrow can have profoundly negative effects on daily life.

A Contemporary Take on Surrender: Sloth as the Refusal to Love God and Others

Contemporary writers on sloth tend to take the traditional insight on sloth a step further—emphasizing that because the love of God and love of others are inseparable, sloth as resistance to spiritual goods has vertical and horizontal dimensions. Both lack of effort in religious practice and lack of effort in relating to other people are outward manifestations of the inner condition of avoiding rest in God. On this view, sloth is a vice "because it involves inner resistance and coldness toward one's spiritual calling or identity."[24] We resist loving God and we resist deeply loving and being deeply loved by others.

How does one "resist" loving God? According to DeYoung, this vice refers not primarily to lack of belief but rather to the tendency to resist "'participation' in God." We can go to church and intellectually affirm belief

22. ST II-II, q. 35, a. 4.

23. See M. Therese Lysaught's description of how the practice of prayer shaped Cardinal Joseph Bernardin, "Love Your Enemies: Toward a Christoform Bioethic," in *Gathered for the Journey: Moral Theology in Catholic Perspective,* ed. David Matzko McCarthy and M. Therese Lysaught, 307–28 (Grand Rapids, MI: Eerdmans, 2007).

24. DeYoung, "Vice of Sloth."

in a deity, but still refuse God's desire to make us "'like-natured' to him through the Holy Spirit's presence in us."[25] We can resist the demands of being in relationship with God, like making time for silence and spiritual reading, or letting go of anger and forgiving those who have hurt us, or being ready to abandon a job for a new calling. "Charity's joy at God's presence in us, conceived of as something good, is replaced by distaste for and aversion to it as something evil or to be avoided."[26] Professing belief does not necessarily guarantee ongoing commitment to transformation in response to and in relationship with God. This is hard work requiring vulnerability and a willingness to change.

Because we are wired for what the Christian tradition calls "sanctification," or growth in holiness, even though it can be painful, by it we are fulfilled and without it we are restless. Sloth is "resistance to the transformation that God's love works in us, and in particular the painful nature of the death of the old self—that is, our willingness to let old sinful habits and attachments die and be made new."[27] Clinging to the old self and its familiar activities and habits of mind feels more comfortable than surrendering to God. Some cling to restless activity and pretend not to think about questions of ultimate meaning. Others cannot avoid those questions but become overwhelmed and are prone to despair. Either way, avoiding God may feel comfortable in the short term but ultimately yields a restlessness that does not easily go away.

Avoiding the demanding nature of a relationship with God is intimately linked with avoiding the demands of being in relationship with other people. Just as it is easier to avoid spending time in God's presence, it is also easier to avoid having difficult conversations or spending focused time with people you love. One can stay with another person physically while refusing to grow in intimacy. Busyness offers a way out of vulnerability and a ready-made excuse for not taking the time to work through hard things. Sometimes what another person really needs from us is for us to change, but "sloth's opposition to the transforming demands of love" holds us back.[28] Theologian Richard Gaillardetz offers a contrasting vision of Christian marriage, which requires spouses to embrace the "paschal" nature of marriage by dying to their old selves and becoming the persons their spouses need.[29] Challenging the popular ideal of meeting "The One"

25. DeYoung, "Vice of Sloth."

26. DeYoung, "Vice of Sloth."

27. DeYoung, "Vice of Sloth."

28. DeYoung, "Vice of Sloth."

29. Richard Gaillardetz, *A Daring Promise: A Spirituality for Christian Marriage*, rev. ed. (Liguori, MO: Liguori Press, 2007).

who is perfect for me, Gaillardetz insists, "you always marry the wrong person" (or a person who is not a perfect fit for you), and calls for a realistic, lifelong commitment to making marriage work anyway.[30]

Overcoming sloth means refusing to take the easy way out with God and other people. Sloth is not opposed to diligence or industriousness; it is opposed to love. The problem with "comfortable indifference to duty and neglect of other human beings' needs" is not a lack of grit but "the lack of love that lies behind that laziness."[31] To overcome sloth, we have to "face up to the sources of our own resistance to the demands of our relationship to God, rather than grasping at a way out or a ready diversion any time we start to feel stretched or uncomfortable."[32] The same is true for relationships with other people. Spiritual growth seems to require overcoming "an unwillingness to surrender [oneself] to God [and others]."[33]

In sum, sloth in the Christian tradition means failing to seek wisdom, allowing sorrow to block attention to spiritual goods, and resisting the challenging demands of being in relationship with God and others. When sloth is a problem, a person lives the life of her choosing and may choose well, but she loses touch with the transcendental dimension of her personhood and thus of her true vocation. The tradition rightly names sloth a capital vice and calls believers to embrace the vulnerability of responding to what God and others ask of us.

Contemporary Questions and Challenges: Whose Experience? Which Sins?

This "surrender" understanding expands our grasp of the roots of the vice, helping us name sins far beyond simple laziness. But this understanding also raises questions in our contemporary world that call for further refinement in our naming of sins associated with sloth. For more than fifty years, Christian feminist theologians have raised significant critical questions about Christian thinking on sin, the self, and the good life. Because they have approached theology with women's suffering in mind, they have been especially concerned about the central place of sacrifice in Christian theology. Although there has been little explicit

---

30. Theologian Stanley Hauerwas has also spoken about the inevitability of marrying "the wrong person." See *U.S. Catholic* 56, no. 6 (June 1991): 6–13.

31. DeYoung, *Glittering Vices*, 81.

32. DeYoung, "Vice of Sloth."

33. DeYoung, *Glittering Vices*, 95.

feminist attention to sloth, it is important to bring feminist questions to the understandings for sloth we have considered so far. While feminist theologians pay special attention to the experiences of women, their questions uncover weaknesses in the anthropology (the overall understanding of human beings) that is often assumed in Christian discussions of virtue and vice. Hearing this critique is crucial to constructing a more balanced anthropology informed by a broader range of human experience, a more nuanced way of naming sins, and a more complex virtue ethic that can speak to all Christians.

Sin and the Self

In one of the first essays ever written by a feminist theologian, Valerie Saiving questioned the traditional Christian identification of sin with pride.[34] Saiving argued that Christians had traditionally relied on a description of human experience that was really a more typically male experience of "separateness and the anxiety occasioned by it." The Christian theological vision of "sin as self-assertion and love [as] selflessness" made sense for men.[35] But, she suggested, women are more typically schooled not in pride but in self-giving, because most grow up as daughters of caretaking mothers and become mothers who more often than not bear primary responsibility for children. Thus, women are more prone to sins of "triviality, distractibility, and diffuseness; lack of an organizing center or focus; dependence on others for one's own self-definition . . . in short, underdevelopment or negation of the self."[36] Women, according to Saiving, need to guard against excessive self-surrender that impedes true self-development. Yet the theology of sin that is meant to apply to everyone seems to encourage them to deny their aspirations while devoting themselves "wholly to the tasks of nurture, support, and service."[37] A woman who desires a separate sense of self and work of her own will, if she "believes the theologians, . . . will try to strangle those impulses in herself."[38] For as DeYoung has told us, sloth, at its root, is "an unwillingness to surrender oneself to God [and others]."[39]

---

34. Valerie Saiving. "The Human Situation: A Feminine View," *The Journal of Religion*, 40, no. 2 (1960): 100–12. See also Serene Jones, *Feminist Theory and Christian Theology: Cartographies of Grace* (Minneapolis: Fortress Press, 2000).

35. Saiving, "The Human Situation," 100.

36. Saiving, "The Human Situation," 109.

37. Saiving, "The Human Situation," 110.

38. Saiving, "The Human Situation," 110.

39. DeYoung, *Glittering Vices*, 95.

One might ask if Saiving is oversimplifying things a bit here. Does "women's experience" really differ this profoundly from "men's experience"? [40] Yet we do not have to take Saiving's claim literally to consider her challenge. *People* are different. For some (perhaps especially women and others who are less privileged), sloth may manifest as self-negation rather than self-assertion. In these cases (e.g., the man who was never encouraged to think about what he wanted to do with his life and is stuck in a dead-end job, the woman who takes care of everyone in her family but puts aside her gift for science) the remedy will not be more surrender, but more attention to the self in relation to God and others. Some of us may be slothful precisely in failing to take responsibility for our lives by attending to our own development as people of faith called into particular vocations. This does not mean that surrender will have no place in a Christian virtue ethic informed by feminist theology.[41] However, feminist theologians remind men and women that one must have a strong sense of self before one can authentically give that self away.

The Good Life

Feminist theologians also push us to ask about the nature of the good or virtuous life. Secular accounts of sloth see virtue in focused hard work, as exemplified by the efficiency expert we encountered at the beginning of this essay. For Evagrius, the monk whose days are filled with prayer and undistracted work lives a good life. For Aquinas, the person who seeks God and strives to honor duties to family and neighbors lives virtuously. For DeYoung, because love of God and love of others are inseparable, the good life involves openness to God and to the demands of others. Feminist theologians would not dispute the inclusion of focused work, spiritual seeking, and love of others in these definitions of the good life, but they also emphasize the importance of duties to others that require social action. The good life requires *both* attention to self *and* work for a better society.

Consider the problem of work. Earlier in this essay, I noted a widely shared concern about labor that is unconnected to the mind and soul or "alienation." Some of us might overcome alienation by approaching our work differently or changing jobs, but social structures may make it much

---

40. For questions like these, see Mark Douglas and Elizabeth Hinson-Hasty, "Revisiting Valerie Saiving's Challenge to Reinhold Niebuhr," *Journal of Feminist Studies in Religion* 28, no. 1 (2012): 75–114.

41. Feminist theologians do not discount the need for sacrifice for the sake of children. See Christine E. Gudorf, "Parenting, Mutual Love, and Sacrifice," in Barbara Hilkert Andolsen, Christine E. Gudorf, and Mary Pellauer, *Women's Consciousness and Women's Conscience: A Reader in Feminist Ethics* (New York: Harper and Row, 1985).

more difficult for some to find fulfilling work than others. Consequently, a desire to avoid the vice of sloth might lead me both to pursue meaningful work in my own life and to support job training programs in my community that help others prepare for fulfilling work in their lives.

In their thinking about the good life, feminist theologians recall Jesus's ministry to outcasts and sinners and ask how Christians can bring about a world where each person's capacities can be developed. This is a huge task involving both personal relationships (Who is excluded from our tables?) and structural change (What kinds of businesses receive our patronage? How are we trying to shape the institutions to which we are connected?). Living un-slothful lives requires not just a general commitment to conversion but specific attention to how personal and political choices sustain or break down structures that harm the vulnerable.

Feminist concerns about sacrifice and the good life lead many to embrace an ethic of resistance as an antidote to sloth. In the beginning of this essay, I referenced the Prayer of Generosity frequently attributed to St. Ignatius, which emphasizes giving "without counting the cost." If sloth is understood as a lack of willingness to direct attention to God and others that manifests in laziness and busyness, generosity can be seen as an appropriate response. Yet feminist theologians ask if resistance can be equally important. In a groundbreaking essay, "The Power of Anger in the Work of Love," ethicist Beverly Harrison argued that God's grace can be seen in the "power to struggle and to experience indignation."[42] She suggests that anger can be a powerful tool motivating necessary confrontation.[43] According to Harrison, faithful people are called not only to sacrifice but also "to confront, as Jesus did, that which thwarts the power of human personal and communal becoming ..."[44] Anger at injustice is connected to love (see chapter 6).

Traditional accounts of sloth rightly call us to turn with our whole hearts to God and the people around us. Feminist theologians help us remember that Jesus attended not simply to family and friends but to the poor, the sick, and the marginalized—and sometimes even expressed anger at those who ignored them. Like John Paul II, they ask Christians to see the pain caused by "social sins which cry to heaven" and commit to alleviating that pain in whatever way they can.[45] This, too, is part of what it means to live a good life.

---

42. Beverly Harrison, "The Power of Anger in the Work of Love," in *Making the Connections: Essays in Feminist Social Ethics*, ed. Carol S. Robb and Beverly Wildung Harrison (Boston: Beacon, 1986), 224.

43. Harrison, "Power of Anger," 216. For further analysis of how to distinguish the vice of anger from proper feelings of anger at injustice, see also William Mattison's chapter in this volume.

44. Harrison, "Power of Anger," 223.

45. John Paul II, Apostolic Exhortation *Ecclesia in America* (January 22, 1999), 56.

Thus, naming self-love and the sometimes-confrontational struggle for justice as essential aspects of right relationship with God and others is essential to contemporary appropriation of the vice of sloth. Because many feminists know from experience the dangers of too much sacrifice for others, they worry about uncritical demands for self-giving. In a provocative essay, ethicist Karen Lebacqz suggests that in light of the long history of male violence toward women, women must love the men in their lives as they do their enemies.[46] This means cultivating awareness of widespread problematic power dynamics within male-female relationships, avoiding the perils of offering forgiveness when men refuse to name their abuse as sinful, and being willing to leave if the situation demands it. It means changing cultures and laws that enable abuse. For some who abuse power in sexual relationships, Jason King's chapter on the dynamics of lust will help them name sin. But for others, in the face of pervasive sexual violence, we need to be very cautious about the language of surrender.

The Christian tradition rightly upholds the importance of sacrifice and notes the perils of not being willing to be stretched and changed for others. But human beings differ in their virtuous capacities and sinful proclivities, and loving distant others sometimes requires work for social change which will enable them to fully develop and utilize their capacities. With this knowledge in mind, we can better name sin and envision the good life for all Christians.

Resisting Sloth for Today's Christians: Moving toward Solidarity

We have found in the history of reflection on sloth a historical and cultural emphasis on vicious laziness and virtuous productivity along with a traditional Christian focus on the need to seek one's ultimate end in God via spiritual practices. Analyzing sloth has allowed us to see sin in our avoidance both of surrender and of transformation in relationships with God and others. I have taken note of contemporary theological concerns that surrender as a response to sloth can be overdone, because it can prevent recognition of the necessity of self-affirmation, social justice, and resistance. In this final section, I suggest that in our times, solidarity is the right virtue to juxtapose with sloth. Thus, to avoid sloth, we should embrace solidarity.

If the vice of sloth is about escaping responsibilities in relationship with God and others, solidarity is a virtue requiring commitment to God and all God's people, with a focus on the most vulnerable. Ethicist Meghan Clark

---

46. Karen Lebacqz, "Love Your Enemies: Sex, Power, and Christian Ethics," in *Feminist Theological Ethics: A Reader*, ed. Lois K. Daly (Louisville: Westminster, 1994), 244–61.

claims that in contemporary Catholic social thought, solidarity is understood not just as a description of actual human connections in a global context or "a vague feeling of compassion," but as a virtue that "involves an obligation to participate at all levels of human community."[47] The virtue is one to which all Christians are called, as it is rooted in fundamental theological claims about the social nature of the human person drawn from Genesis 1:26–27, John 17:21–22, and belief in the Trinity.[48] Through the writings of Popes John XXIII, Paul VI, John Paul II, Benedict XVI, and now Francis, the biblical foundation for solidarity has been linked to a modern tradition of human rights and to local and international development and advocacy work.[49]

What would embracing solidarity mean for the ordinary Christian seeking to be less slothful? Aquinas is not so far off: "the proper effect of charity is joy in God,"[50] and to take joy in God means thinking about who God is, spending time resting in God's presence, engaging in spiritual practices that train one to see the transcendent in the ordinary, and not failing to remember that one's ultimate end is in God. Yet love of God can never be separated from the love of other human beings. This truth is expressed in Catholic social teaching and ritualized in Catholic sacramental practice. As Catholics participate in the Eucharist each week, taking in the body of Christ "nourishes, strengthens, and orders us as we make visible his body through a praxis of solidarity, which counters the disorder of this world."[51] We practice in the liturgy by gathering together in Christ, so that we can *be* the body of Christ in the world, taking up engaged, mindful, activity in the service of solidarity. We are meant to find work that somehow connects to the Kingdom that God is slowly bringing about.[52] This work includes personal friendships and family relationships, but it does not stop there. The virtue of solidarity requires a commitment to accompany some of those who are most broken.[53]

Solidarity involves self-giving but also includes self-affirmation and development understood in relation to Christian vocation. If to be slothful

47. Meghan J. Clark, *The Vision of Catholic Social Thought: The Virtue of Solidarity and the Praxis of Human Rights* (Minneapolis: Fortress Press, 2014), 122.

48. Clark, *Vision of Catholic Social Thought*, 56–60.

49. Examples would be organizations such as Catholic Relief Services, the National Right to Life, and the Catholic Campaign for Human Development.

50. ST II-II, q. 35, a. 1.

51. M. Shawn Copeland, *Enfleshing Freedom: Body, Race, and Being* (Minneapolis: Fortress Press, 2010), 109.

52. Dean Brackley, SJ, *The Call to Discernment in Troubled Times: New Perspectives on the Transformative Wisdom of Ignatius of Loyola* (New York: Crossroad, 2004), 67–72.

53. Clark, *Vision of Catholic Social Thought*, 107–14.

is to be distracted in aimlessness or busyness, to avoid what God and others ask of us, a measure of focus and sacrifice is certainly required. We only have to look back at the history of slavery and Jim Crow to see that Christians have often been too distracted to see evil even when it was right in front of them. Theologian M. Shawn Copeland writes, "these vicious practices waged a frontal challenge to (black) bodies as mediators of divine revelation," and yet, the vast majority of white Christians remained oblivious to the self-sacrifice that was clearly their duty.[54] Still, self-actualization cannot be forgotten, as is well known by black women who remember slaves and domestic workers asked to forget themselves in service to masters and bosses and today's victims of sexual violence asked to sacrifice their own bodies for the sake of family unity or the good of an organization. It is not slothful to love one's self or to desire to live a life of one's own. In fact, doing so will often mean that more rather than less will be required of us.

Finally, the virtue of solidarity provides a remedy for sloth that is both personal and political. It calls us out of complacency; rather than endless to-do lists or self-improvement projects, we are called to a broader and deeper understanding of what it means to be a Christian in a broken world.

To be sure, solidarity *can* lead to a new version of the quest for productivity. Conscious of my connection to others and responsibility to participate in the healing of the world, I may construct endless to-do lists of service commitments, advocacy, and efforts to live more simply. However, feminist theology offers correctives to this tendency to obsessiveness in affirming the legitimacy of partial efforts in imperfect situations and the importance of self-love. I am not called to do everything but to discern in prayer what God is calling me to contribute to the project of salvation.

Solidarity asks us to focus less on productivity, efficiency, and success in order to focus more on how we can use our very particular gifts and resources to heal the world's brokenness. A college student seeking to practice this virtue might ask, "How are my studies and extracurricular activities helping me to understand and prepare to respond to the world's brokenness?" A businessperson might ask, "How might my products or services contribute to hope and healing for those who are marginalized?" A teacher or health professional might ask, "How can I direct more energy to those who lack good education or decent health care?" A parent might ask, "How can I raise my children to embrace vocations in which they are both utilizing their gifts and walking with others in need?" Citizens can ask, "How might I best use my political power to aid the most vulnerable when I vote or engage with my representatives?"

54. Copeland, *Enfleshing Freedom*, 109.

All will need to consider what sorts of things must be left behind so that energy will be available for what is most needed. One college student may give up the quest for perfect grades; another might choose to socialize less and devote more time to studying. One businessperson may decide not to measure her worth in profits; another may stop using work time to consume social media. One teacher might prioritize work with students with learning disabilities rather than the best and brightest; another may adapt his lesson plans to challenge students to think outside their own comfort zones. Parents may worry less about sports and more about service, or they may seek to learn more themselves about the faith in which they are raising their children. We can all only do so much. It is essential to name sins of sloth when they hold us back from the solidarity we seek.

When we look around at all of the broken peoples in the world, it is easy to fall into the deep sorrow of which Aquinas spoke. Yet discipleship to Christ asks us to keep striving, for "solidarity begins in an anamnesis" or a remembering of who Christ is and a willingness to see where fundamental Christian claims about God and human persons created in God's image are being attacked.[55] We can also remember that we are blessed to be part of a Body in which each plays a crucial part but no one is responsible for everything. We have the privilege of gathering each week to be formed in greater virtue together, and the ongoing opportunity to speak our sins out loud, experience reconciliation, and return once again. From this place, we can begin to love better both those to whom we are attached and those we may never know whose suffering nonetheless presses us beyond distraction or despair to action.

---

55. Copeland, *Enfleshing Freedom*, 124.

Chapter 6

Anger

WILLIAM C. MATTISON III

WHEN WE MENTION THE DEADLY sin of anger, it is easy to think of rage or wrath. As noted below, there are indeed good reasons to label the vice or sin of anger using another name such as wrath or rage. But these latter terms suggest an experience that is all-consuming, even beyond one's control. We might think of a classic story such as Homer's Illiad, where Achilles becomes enraged after he is denied of his spoils of war—in this case, a maiden—leading to his vengeful refusal to fight with his men and contributing to the havoc the Greeks suffered in the Trojan War. Or on a more domestic level we might think of the homicidal rage that is a common cause for murder among family members or acquaintances, which in this nation is the venue where most homicides occur.[1] Yet the vice of anger is far more pervasive than these extreme examples. In most cases it is less all-consuming but still corrosive of our characters and relationships. It is present in our mundane everyday activities, as when an apathetic cashier delays us while shopping or when someone cuts us off while driving. It is present at work, commonly directed toward colleagues or supervisors whom we perceive as not giving us our due. One priest told me if he had one warning to newly married couples about a vice to avoid it would not be lust or greed, but rather anger. A festering bitterness or resentment toward one's spouse can warp how we relate to one another and corrode our marriages. As suggested by these everyday contexts, the vice of anger is far more pervasive and corrosive than we might expect.

In order to understand better this ubiquitous vice, and therefore hopefully more easily avoid or quell it, this essay's first section "The Terminology of Anger" offers some clarifications of terminology to help us name this sin more accurately. Is anger an emotion, a sinful act, or both? Is it a sin, a vice,

---

1. Under 25% of homicides in the United States are committed by strangers. See U.S. Department of Justice, Office of Justice Programs, Bureau of Justice Statistics, *Homicide Trends in the United States, 1980–2008*, (November 2011): 16, http://www.bjs.gov/content/pub/pdf/htus8008.pdf, accessed July 1, 2016. Of course, not all family, friend, or acquaintance homicides are committed in a rage.

or both? And what exactly is its occasion and point? We must understand what exactly we are talking about when we address the deadly sin of anger. This exercise will lead us to two conclusions that structure the second and third sections of this chapter. Given the first section's conclusion that what specifies anger is a desire for the rectification of perceived injustice. The second section, "Rectifying Perceived Injustice" explores whether or not such a response to injustice can be virtuous for a Christian and, if so, when it becomes vicious.[2] " The third section, "Anger as an Emotion" addresses the status of anger as an emotion as well as a vice.[3] Can emotional responses properly be called virtuous or vicious, and if so, what makes them so? What does anger's status as an emotion mean for how it works, and how we can avoid its sinful and vicious expressions? Though this third section focuses on anger, many of its conclusions are applicable to other human emotions as well. Finally, the final section "Identifying Anger in Our Lives" distills the conclusions of the previous sections into practical guidance for the accurate naming and then avoidance of the sin of anger in one's life.[4]

The Terminology of Anger

In the context of a book on the seven capital sins, anger is tricky since it (unlike some of the other vices) can refer either to a sin/vice, or to a more general human experience that is *not* sinful. Let us begin with a general definition that includes all occasions of anger. ***Anger is a desire to rectify perceived injustice.*** This "rectification of injustice" has a ready name in Latin, *vindicatio*, but no suitable English translation. Candidates for such a translation would be vindication, vengeance, or revenge. Yet each of these terms suggests something inherently negative, perhaps as excessive or solely self-protective. Though *vindicatio*, the rectification of injustice, *can* be done sinfully, it need not be so. The emotion of anger is a natural human phenomenon, natural not simply in the sense of very common but natural in the sense of helping us to flourish. Like sexual desire, anger is part of how we humans are "built," and that means that there is some healthy point for our anger. To understand more about what that is, it would help to take apart the definition. Anger is: (1) a desire (2) for rectification (3) of perceived injustice. We treat these in reverse order, utilizing the thought of one of the great saint scholars in history, Thomas Aquinas, who wrote an extraordinary amount about anger.

2. Pg. 110 and following.
3. Pg. 114 and following.
4. Pg. 121 and following.

Defining Anger

Perceived injustice. The "prompt," or impetus or cause, of anger is a perceived injustice. We do not experience anger when we simply suffer. Those are occasions for sorrow or sadness or frustration. We experience anger when we suffer (however mildly or seriously) *wrongly*, when someone is perceived as culpably responsible. The term "perceived" is important, since as will be seen below, it is easy and all too common to perceive inaccurately that we are wronged. Aquinas comically notes that while we may become angry at animals or inanimate objects (imagine angrily kicking a tire that has gone flat!), these are improper occasions of anger since the animal or inanimate object did not "wrong" us even if it inconvenienced or frustrated us. We can only be angry at those with whom we are in a relationship of justice: friends, fellow citizens, parents, siblings, colleagues, superiors, even God. Justice is rendering another his or her due, and when we are angry we perceive that another has not rendered us (or someone else we care about) our due.[5] Anger thus has a particularly tight relationship to justice.

Rectification. Anger is not simply the experience of being wronged. It is more complex than that. It also entails a desire for righting that harm. It is easy to see why anger is so prone to intensity. It involves both a suffering harm and a (pleasurable) desire for that harm to be rectified. If we do not perceive any possibility of righting the harm, we do not experience anger but rather sorrow. Anger is a rising up against what thwarts us, not simply to remove the cause of harm but to restore right relations since the angry person perceives they have been harmed unjustly. As the initial injustice may be perceived rightly or wrongly, so too might the rectification sought in anger restore or actually distort right relations. We examine this more closely in a few pages,[6] but we first finish our reflection on the definition of anger by turning to desire.

Desire. Anger most properly refers to an emotion. It is not simply a cool, rational decision to rectify an injustice. We can easily imagine a judge in a courtroom meting out justice in the form of punishment without any emotional connection. It is only in an extended sense that we would describe him or her as angry, and if judging wrongly, as wrathful.[7] Unlike the judge's calm ruling, emotional responses entail bodily changes in response to the stimulus (heart racing, adrenalin flowing, and

---

5. Thomas Aquinas, *Summa Theologiae* II-II, q. 58, a. 11. Aquinas attributes this classic definition of justice "to render each one his due" to St. Ambrose.

6. "Rectifying Perceived Injustice: Is it Always Sinful and if Not, When is it Sinful?", pg. 110 and following.

7. See ST II-II, q. 158, a. 8 for the distinction between anger in this broader sense and its more proper sense.

so on), and they prompt us toward some response (rising up, fleeing, and so on). Though as seen below, our considered judgment, or reason, can be involved in such a response, emotional responses are also possible without the involvement of our distinctively human considered judgment. The fact that anger is an emotion is enormously important in determining if or how it can be expressed well in a virtuous human life, as explained further below.[8]

Anger as Sin? Vice?

Before turning to application, a few more preliminary words will help distinguish anger as an emotion, a sin, and a vice. The definition of anger presented above makes it clear that anger is, at root, an emotion. As a feature of created human nature, it can therefore be good, even though it commonly goes awry. But of course, the context of this essay on anger is a book on the seven capital sins, one of which is anger. In what sense is anger one of the capital sins? The two answers to this question correspond to the ensuing two sections.

Something is sinful when it impedes true human flourishing. Though we learn from trusted authorities (teachers, the Church, parents) what is sinful, breaking an authority's rules is not why an act is sinful. A deliberate human act is sinful because, in the words of the *Catechism*, it "wounds the nature of man and injures human solidarity." It is "an offense against reason, truth, and right conscience," and a "failure in genuine love of God and neighbor caused by a perverse attachment to certain goods."[9] Sins impede a person's individual and communal flourishing. They are truly wrong (not simply against the rules) because they reflect inaccurate assessments of what is truly good for a person, usually elevating lesser goods over more important ones. What has this to do with anger? Anger is sinful when it impedes a person's flourishing, when it reflects an inaccurate assessment of what is good for those involved.[10]

Note also above that sins are "deliberate" human acts. Some impediments to our flourishing are not rightly called sinful. Cancer, or even a common cold, are not sins even though they thwart one's flourishing. Given that anger is an emotion, can it even be called sinful? Are emotions "deliberate?" It is true that on occasion our emotions are not deliberate, something Aquinas acknowledges. However, we will see why, far more

8. The third section, "Anger as an Emotion," pg. 114 and following.

9. *Catechism of the Catholic Church*, no. 1849.

10. See the next section, "Rectifying Perceived Injustice: Is it Always Sinful and if Not, When is it Sinful?"

commonly than many people think, emotions are indeed morally praise-worthy or blameworthy. In the latter case they are "human acts" and may be sinful.[11]

What about anger as a vice? Aquinas not only says that anger can be a sin, but also cites Gregory the Great who names it one of the "capital vices" from which other vices arise.[12] What differentiates a sin from a vice? A vice is a habit, a stable disposition to act poorly with regard to a certain type of activity. So, one possesses the vice of anger when one has a stable disposition to get angry poorly, in a manner that reflects (usually prior) deliberation. Just as one can experience inaccurate anger but in a manner that is not sinful since it is not deliberate in any way, so too one can commit a sin of anger but not have the vice of anger since it is not a habit—yet! A person acquires the vice by repeated sinful acts of anger, acts that form a habit in a person inclining one to more such acts in the future. Though sins are bad, vices are even more corrosive since they are "second nature" dispositions inclining us to see with sinfully angry eyes and respond with sinfully angry hearts.

Having looked closely at what anger means, with the help of Aquinas, we can give a clear definition. In sum, anger is a desire to rectify perceived injustice. It is an emotion, but when it arises inordinately with some delib-eration, it is sinful. When through repeated sins a person develops a habit of becoming angry in a disordered way, the person is said to possess the vice of anger.

Rectifying Perceived Injustice: Is It Always Sinful and If Not, When Is It Sinful?

If anger is a desire to rectify perceived injustice, then the next logical ques-tion is, "can rectification of injustice ever be virtuous, and if so when?" As noted above, I have translated *vindicatio* by "rectification of injustice" because of the lack of negative connotations of that phrase. But common English translations of *vindicatio* such as revenge, vengeance, and vin-dication indicate how morally fraught this endeavor is. Even a thinker such as Thomas Aquinas who claims that anger can be virtuous notes the myriad ways that anger's goal—the rectification of injustice—can be wrong. Yet in doing so he delineates when it is reasonable, and to that analysis we now turn.

---

11. See the third section, "Anger as an Emotion," pg. 114 and following.
12. For anger as a sin, see ST II-II, q. 158, a. 2. For anger as a vice, see ST II-II, q. 158, a. 6.

Anger's "Object" Part One: Is There Truly Injustice?

Aquinas claims that anger can be sinful in its object or its mode. What does he mean by these two terms? In this subsection I will focus on the "object" of anger, which might be more colloquially translated as "what is anger about?" As we defined it above, anger in general is about the rectification of injustice. Anger is sinful in its object—what it's about—either when the prompt is not truly injustice, or when what is sought is not truly a rectification. That is why anger is defined here as a desire for the rectification of *perceived* injustice.[13] We turn now to the prompt of anger, and in the ensuing part to the rectification it seeks.

Justice exists when there are right relationships between people, when people are given what they are "due" by others with whom they are in a relationship with expectations of both parties. Teachers are just with their students when they carefully review the students' work and give grades that are accurate. Friends are just to each other when they honor their responsibilities and commitments to their friends. Spouses are just to each other when they speak to their spouses with respect and love. Nations are just to each other when they honor the sovereignty of other nations. An *in*justice occurs when one does *not* give another what is due based on the relationship that exists between them.

A problem comes about when we wrongly perceive we are not given our due, and this prompts anger. Given how prone we are to see things in a manner than benefits ourselves, this is all too common. A student can be angry at a grade that seems unjust. But is the grade truly unjust, or does the student think the teacher should have known what the student's work meant, or considered how well-intentioned the student was? A woman might become angry at her friend who is not able to meet as planned, or who declines to go to a concert with her. These are perceived as unjust slights. But are they? Does her friend have a compelling reason to not be able to come, or is her friend bound to accompany her to any concert *she* wishes to attend? A spouse is enraged at the dismissive and demeaning way his wife asks him to do something in the household. But is the request truly dismissive and demeaning, or is it merely perceived as such because he either regards it as inconvenient or wrongly detects a hostile tone of voice? A nation regards another nation is preparing for imminent attack. But is an attack truly imminent, or simply perceived as such due to the "threatened" nation's fear? In all these cases a person (or a people) perceives something that would indeed be a sort of injustice and legitimately

---

13. It might more exactly be defined as the desire for the *perceived* rectification of a perceived injustice.

prompt some form of anger—if perceived accurately. But if the perception of the injustice of the act is inaccurate, then any ensuing anger would be itself unjust. This is one way that anger is unreasonable in its object.

Anger's "Object" Part Two: Is There True Rectification Sought?

Another way anger is unreasonable in object is in the rectification we desire. As noted, the rectification sought in anger is wrong in object when the perceived injustice is not truly an injustice. If that is the case, no "righting" is needed and so any anger is unreasonable. Yet anger may also be unreasonable in the *vindicatio* sought in response to a genuine injustice, IF the response does not in fact rectify the injustice. Most often of course the *vindicatio* sought is excessive. How often do we exacerbate rather than rectify conflicts by an overreaction? Commonly we "punish" people excessively such that the response exceeds the initial offense, as when we verbally lash out, become vicious (even physically), or sever relations. Consider a parent becoming angry at a child who ignores a reasonable request, or who speaks rudely to the parent. This is a true "offense," and a good parent will correct it in a child. But the response should not exceed the offense. So, if the parent in turn screams angrily at the child or punishes the child severely, we have the sin of anger. In such cases, the rectification is beyond what the offense deserves, and so rather than a righting of wrong we have a new offense. The so-called *lex talonis*, "an eye for an eye," is a helpful guard against anger that is unreasonable in object, since it requires that the rectification of an injustice be properly tailored to the degree of the offense.

What makes rectification reasonable is not simply the quantitative amount of response to an injustice. It is also the point or purpose of that response. Responding to injustice is a rising up against the offender, and thus in some sense a desire for injury or harm to that person. This harm is experienced as evil to the perpetrator since it is against his will, his will being the injustice. Yet the angry person should not simply wish harm for the perpetrator; that would be hatred not anger.[14] The angry person rises up against the other in order to restore right relations. As Aquinas says, "The angry man desires the evil of another, not for its own sake but for the sake of revenge (*vindicatio*), towards which his appetite turns as to a mutable good."[15] In other words, the appropriately angry person seeks right relations, not simply harm, and any harm involved must be part of

---

14. For more on the difference between anger and hatred, see ST I-II, q. 46, a. 5 and II-II, q. 158, a. 4.

15. ST II-II, q. 158, a. 2, ad. 2. See also ST II-II, q. 158, a. 1 ad. 3: "It is unlawful to desire vengeance considered as evil to the man who is to be punished, but it is praiseworthy to desire vengeance as a corrective of vice and for the good of justice."

that restoration. This is why Aquinas insists that anger is compatible with love of the other, and with forgiveness.[16] We can—indeed we should—love those with whom we are angry and seek reconciliation. To restore right relations with someone for the good of both parties, such anger is reasonable in object since the rectification sought is a true righting. Though it may sound surprising, such anger is rightly called "virtuous."

But of course, this commonly does not occur, and the rectification sought either does not fit the offense or is not intended for the further good of reconciliation and restoration of justice. Consider again a mother who becomes angry with her child who is truly misbehaving. If, in anger, the mother responds to the misbehavior not for the good of correcting the child but to demean him or to blow off her own steam, then the anger is sinful. Or, when a man is understandably angry at his spouse for a genuine offense and responds by lashing out with behavior to "get back at her," then the "rectification" sought is not truly restoring right relations. Or, as is increasingly common today, consider occasions of "road rage." When a driver commits a genuine injustice—perhaps by cutting in line in traffic—and the wronged driver responds by flashing an obscene hand gesture or chasing down and cutting the offender off, it is difficult to see how this angry response is done to restore right relations. On the political level, consider the difference between the Black Panthers and Martin Luther King Jr. Clearly both responded to a genuine injustice, though King regarded the Black Panthers' violent response as precluding rather than enabling social reconciliation.

Virtuous anger does involve rising up against the other, and so discussion is needed as to what constitutes such response in a manner that *does* contribute to restoring right relations. For instance, what sorts of punishment of children are ultimately good for the child? How can a spouse respond to a slight in a manner that rectifies the injustice and helps restore right relations? These questions would have to be addressed on a case-by-case basis. But Aquinas's analysis equips us with the parameters of that discussion. Anger should be oriented toward the righting of injustice.

Concluding Thoughts on Anger's Object

In sum, Thomas Aquinas helps us recognize how anger may be unreasonable in its object. As he says:

> If one desire the taking of vengeance in any way whatever contrary to the order of reason, for instance if he desire *the punishment of one*

16. See ST II-II, q. 158, a. 3 ad. 3.

who has not deserved it, or *beyond his deserts,* or again contrary to the
order prescribed by law, or *not for the due end, namely the maintaining of justice and the correction of defaults,* then the desire of anger
will be sinful, and this is called sinful anger.[17]

Aquinas offers here a summary of the ways where anger goes awry. It
can be prompted without true injustice ("the punishment of one who has
not deserved it"). Or it can be prompted by true injustice but not toward
true rectification, either because the response is excessive ("beyond his
deserts") or because its goal is not the restoration of right relations ("not
for the due end, namely the maintaining of justice and the correction of
defaults"). In these cases, anger is sinful in its object because its prompt or
point is unreasonable.

The above examples are all ones of excess. In response to the question of
whether or not there is a vice opposed to virtuous anger resulting from a
lack of anger, Aquinas says, "Anger may be understood in two ways. In one
way, as a simple movement of the will, whereby one inflicts punishment,
not through passion, but in virtue of a judgment of the reason: and thus
without doubt lack of anger is a sin."[18]

Thus, a lack of anger can indeed be sinful. If one is in the presence of
true injustice and does not experience the offense with a concomitant
desire to restore right relations for the good of all involved, such a lack of
anger is a sin. Aquinas uses the term "anger" here more broadly to refer to
any movement of the will to rectify injustice. But recall from our earlier
definition that most properly, anger is a desire, what Aquinas calls a "passion." Can it be sinful not to "feel" angry, perhaps even if one responds well
to the injustice though without feeling anger? Aquinas answers that even
the lack of the emotion anger can be sinful. How he can say so is the topic
of the following section. All that has been said so far concerns seeking to
rectify injustice, regardless of whether that seeking is simply a movement
of the will (anger in its broader sense) or the emotional desire for such
rectification (anger most properly). We now turn in the following section
to matters concerning anger as an emotion, which is the root of anger and
so commonly experienced by us.

Anger as an Emotion—Can It Even Be Called Sinful or Virtuous?

It is easy to understand how a deliberate decision to correct an injustice can
be sinful (i.e., morally blameworthy) for all the reasons addressed in the

---

17. ST II-II, q. 158, a. 2, emphasis added.
18. ST II-II, q. 158, a. 8.

previous section. Yet recalling that anger is an emotion, people commonly hesitate to label an emotional response as sinful. After all, emotions are spontaneous reactions to some impetus, reactions that prompt us toward some response (to rise up, flee, seek more, and so on). They entail bodily reactions (racing heart, sweaty palms, surges of adrenaline, and so on), and perhaps most importantly, seem to arise automatically without any deliberation. How could such phenomena ever be called sinful, or on the other hand, morally praiseworthy?

Can We Be Blamed for "How We Feel?"

The mistaken idea that emotions can never be called sinful is latent in that commonly uttered expression, "That's just how I feel!" Note the assumption here is that we cannot govern or guide—let alone fully control—our emotional responses and hence they are not "moral" events. The unstated conclusion of "That's just how I feel" is "so you cannot blame me for my feelings if I do not act on them!" But since actions are assumed to be things we can govern and guide, this thinking goes, only actions are moral—not feelings. The wisdom of this approach is that it rightly recognizes we must have some ability to govern and guide our responses in order to call them sinful or praiseworthy. However, the bulk of the Western (not simply Christian) tradition has indeed affirmed that emotions can be praiseworthy or blameworthy. As Aristotle famously said, the person "who is angry at the right things and with the right people, and, further, as he ought, when he ought, and as long as he ought, is praised."[19] Note there is no mention of acting out of anger here, only being angry. In the Sermon on the Mount, Jesus mentions anger as distinguished from ensuing acts:

> You have heard that it was said to your ancestors, 'You shall not kill; and whoever kills will be liable to judgment.' But I say to you, whoever is angry with his brother will be liable to judgment, and whoever says to his brother, 'Raqa,' will be answerable to the Sanhedrin, and whoever says, 'You fool,' will be liable to fiery Gehenna (Mt 5:21–22).

Here simply becoming angry is decried, in a manner distinct from various acts that flow out of that anger. How can it be that anger itself, without any ensuing act, can be praiseworthy or blameworthy?

The claim here is that though many times emotions are not morally evaluable, they can be, and they can be not only blameworthy but also praiseworthy. If you witness someone being unjustly victimized, and you

19. Aristotle, "Nicomachean Ethics," 1125b32–33, trans. W.D. Ross, in *The Basic Works of Aristotle*, ed. Richard McKeon, 927–1112 (New York: Random House, 1941), iv.5.

feel anger at it, that anger is good! And if you experience racist emotions, it may be "just how you feel," but it is blameworthy even without ensuing action. But of course, if simply an emotion such as anger can be labelled sinful, and if emotions are not to be dismissed as always blameworthy but at times praiseworthy, then some account is needed as to how to guide or govern our emotions in a virtuous manner. In the next subsection, I will rely mainly on the work of Aquinas for an explanation of how an emotion such as anger can "participate in reason," so as to be morally evaluable.

How Can an Emotion Such as Anger "Participate in Reason?"

There are myriad ways that one can "govern" one's emotions. The most obvious way was mentioned above. If we are experiencing an unreasonable emotion, such as excessive anger, we should not act on it. This is a crucial strategy to help us avoid the development of a vicious habit, such as anger. Yet note in this case, the presence of the emotion itself is not impacted. One way we can be relieved of a vicious emotion is by removing ourselves from the presence of what is prompting it. It is good advice for us to separate ourselves from the situation making us angry. Or even more wisely, we can avoid situations where we can expect to be roused to some sinful emotion, such as anger, sexual desire, or hatred. For instance, those who struggle with lustful desires may be well served not surfing the Internet on occasions when they are alone. In these cases, the emotion may still be activated by the stimulus, but by removing oneself from the prompt or by preemptively avoiding it, one can quell or prevent a blameworthy emotional response.

Though the above strategies entail some form of guiding and governing our emotions, that influence is "from the outside," if you will. In other words, the sinful emotional response is still roused by the prompt. So if a wife is unreasonably angry with her husband, she can walk away when angry or avoid a subject that she expects will lead to her anger. Now it must be repeated that these are excellent strategies for guiding one's emotions. But assuming the anger is not reasonable (for instance, there is no real offense, or the "rectification" sought is excessive), it would be even better not to be angry even in the presence of that prompt. Is there any way to guide or govern the very arousal of our emotions, besides removing ourselves from or avoiding what prompts them?

This question is at the heart of debates in moral philosophy and theology that have raged from the classical period through the medieval period until today. Can the emotions or passions themselves be virtuous (or vicious), such that we can say "that person desires well, or angers well, or fears well?" Or are emotional responses never themselves the "seat," if you will, of virtue (or vice), such that whenever someone desires or angers or fears well, it is not the arousal of emotion that is itself virtuous, but only the decisions one makes before or after emotional responses to "rein them in" (or set them loose)? In the latter case, the emotions themselves are not virtuous, but rather our practical reasoning's decisions regarding them are to be praised or blamed. In the former case, which is the position I am endorsing here, your emotional responses themselves can be praiseworthy or blameworthy. How is this possible?

All agree that emotional responses *can* be outside the influence of our reason. The question is whether or not our emotions can at times "participate in reason" such that their very arousal is shaped or informed by our practical reasoning. All agree it is only through a connection with our reasoning that emotions themselves could be called praiseworthy or blameworthy. The question is how that happens. If it only happens through the emotions being reined in as if "from the outside" by our reasoning, then it makes sense to label a virtuous person practically wise (or prudent) rather than a good desirer, or good "angerer." But if our emotions are aroused spontaneously and automatically, on their own yet in a manner permeated by our practical reasoning, it makes sense to praise the emotional response itself, instead of simply actions ensuing from it, or actions taken to quell, avoid, or encourage it.

The key to the emotions themselves being aroused in a manner permeated by reason is the fact that they are responses to something grasped as a certain sort of prompt. When we are afraid, we grasp something as impending and causing harm. When we get angry, we grasp someone as harming us wrongly. Our senses and our instincts can enable us to grasp a prompt as something. But for humans, we also have reason. And what we know can shape how we grasp things. That is why the same event or person might prompt desire in one person but not another, or anger in one but not another. It is not just what we perceive that prompts emotions, but *how* we perceive it. This is an obvious point once we think about how we handle people experiencing emotions we find to be misperceptions of a situation. We reassure a person who is scared of getting on a plane that air travel is safe, or another anxious about speaking in public that careful preparation ensures a good presentation. We appeal to knowledge of the situation to try and influence (in this case, quell) the emotional reaction. When friends desire something we think is not good for them, we try to convince them not only not to act on their desire but hopefully to no longer desire it.

The same is true of anger, which is a desire to rectify a perceived injustice. What we spontaneously perceive as an injustice, or what we automatically desire as rectification, reflects what we think to be true about those around us, about our own importance, and about what constitutes right relations. So when we find ourselves angry at a situation at work, a colleague might try to explain how we are seeing things wrongly since the boss is just doing what is truly best for the company. Or when a child is angry at not getting something, a good parent will explain how he is really doing what is best for the child. In these cases, we assume that a better grasp of a situation will impact our emotional response. What we hold as true using our reason impacts our emotions; this fact is reflected in how we handle our own or others' emotional responses.

In these instances just mentioned, emotions "participate in reason" when they are shaped (in these cases, quelled) by knowledge we gain. So when an emotion springs up, we learn how to better perceive a situation, and the emotion subsides. Note that participation in reason can also encourage emotions. We may not have experienced anger at, say, sexual harassment because we had no sense of the harmful wrong inflicted. Yet once we hear the story of a victim and understand the injustice, we begin to feel anger.

What if we learn enough that the next time there is a similar situation, our immediate emotional response reflects the better grasp of the situation? Then the initial, spontaneous response would be said to "participate in reason." In such a case it would make sense to say that a person desires well or gets angry well. In these cases, moments of anger would be praiseworthy. And if a person became habituated as such, we'd say they have the virtue of good anger. But of course, the opposite is also true. If our moments of anger reflect poor choices and a selfish grasp of situations, then we would label moments of such anger sinful. And if a person became habituated to such moments, we'd say that individual had the vice of bad anger.

The Blessing and Curse of Emotions Such as Anger

Why is any of this debate about whether or not the emotions can be "seats" of virtue at all important? The very blessing of emotions—and this is nowhere truer than with anger—is their potential curse. That is, emotions are spontaneous responses to a perceived stimulus that prompt us to appropriate action. This quick transition from perception to action is crucial from an evolutionary perspective. When in the presence of something life-threatening, we are galvanized by our emotion of fear to flee. When we face unjustified harm, we rise up against it. More deliberate consideration of the situation followed by decision would actually endanger the person. Emotional reactions allow human persons to respond spontaneously, by serving as shortcuts "past" practical reasoning, even if they can reflect prior such reasoning.[20]

Yet emotions do not simply shortcut reasoning based on prior formation. They also impact ensuing reasoning. They "color" a situation to be seen more in line with the emotional response. So a person who is afraid is more cautious of possible threats. A person experiencing desire is more inclined to need an object or more cognizant of its attractiveness. And an angry person is more attuned to being wronged or more sensitive about being offended. The very evolutionary effectiveness of emotional responses is also why they can be so dangerous when they go wrong. For human persons, emotions not only reflect prior reasoning but skew (for good or bad) ensuing reasoning. It is easy to see how our emotions can mislead us! Nevertheless, our emotional responses can also contribute to our flourishing, even the more intense emotions like anger. Emotions grant a nimble efficiency to how we respond to our environments, enabling our snap perceptions to translate quickly into responsive action without the delay of more plodding discursive reasoning.

To understand this contribution of well-formed emotions, we should ask what we would be missing without them. Aristotle would say that when our emotions are well-formed, they provide a "pleasure and promptness" to virtuous action. The virtuous person not only does the right thing for the right reasons and in the right circumstances, but does it wholeheartedly, with pleasure and joy. This spontaneity as described above makes for effective action especially in urgent situations. But even where such urgency lacks, a person with well-formed emotions acts wholeheartedly, thus participating in the good life with one's mind and heart. As Aquinas puts it using his more technical language (where emotions = sensitive appetite):

> Just as it is better that a person should both will good and do it in his external act, so also does it belong to the perfection of moral good that a person should be moved to the good, not only in respect of his will, but also in respect of his sensitive appetite [i.e., passions]; according to Psalm 84:3, "My heart and my flesh have rejoiced in the living God."[21]

The fully virtuous life entails a person's complete participation, in action, will (intention), and emotion.

This section has required significant exploration into the hydraulics of human action and emotion. We have done this to establish that an emotion such as anger can indeed be praiseworthy or blameworthy, even in its very

20. For an accessible account from an evolutionary neuroscience perspective of the survival advantage of emotions, as well as the emotions' relationship to practical reasoning, see Antonio Damasio's *Descartes Error: Emotion, Reason, and the Human Brain* (New York: Putnam, 1994).

21. ST I-II, q. 24, a. 3. This is Psalm 84 according to present-day numbering; to Aquinas it was known as Psalm 83.

arousal regardless of any ensuing action. We have seen how an emotion can remain truly an emotion (rather than solely a deliberate judgment of reason) and arise spontaneously with all of its bodily changes, and yet be permeated by one's practical rationality. We have seen why it is necessary to attend to emotions when doing moral theology, and far more importantly, why it is crucial to attend to our emotions in our moral lives. We have even begun to see strategies for how to have our emotional responses participate in reason, strategies that will be explored further next section. To conclude here, we turn back to St. Thomas Aquinas's analysis of the ways anger can be sinful.

Anger as Sinful in "Mode"

Recall that Aquinas claims anger can be sinful in two ways. First, it can be sinful in its object, as we have already discussed. But it can also be sinful in its "mode."

> Second, the order of reason in regard to anger may be considered in relation to the mode of being angry, namely that the movement of anger should not be immoderately fierce, neither internally nor externally; and if this condition be disregarded anger will not lack sin, even though just vengeance be desired.[22]

The last phrase of this quotation is particularly noteworthy. Even if just *vindicatio* be sought (that is, there is truly an offense and proper rectification is sought and for the right reason), still anger can be sinful. How should we understand anger that is sinful in mode even as it seeks just *vindicatio*? This distinction between object and mode dominates Aquinas's ensuing analysis of anger, and we can find in that analysis other terms for anger that is sinful in mode. Aquinas describes anger's mode as its "strength and quickness,"[23] its "impetuousness,"[24] its "stubborn desire,"[25] and how it "casts the mind headlong"[26] toward things. Aquinas sees in anger an intensity that can make it sinful even when it is reasonable in its object. We commonly say of angry people that they "just won't let it go," indicating anger that is stubborn. Or we might tell someone "OK, OK, but calm down already!" when the person is justly angry but with excessive vehemence. It is admittedly difficult to distinguish "excessive rectification" from just *vindicatio* that is immoderate in mode or intensity. But once we

22. ST II-II, q. 158, a. 2.
23. ST II-II, q. 158, a. 4.
24. ST II-II, q. 158, a. 4 ad. 1.
25. ST II-II, q. 158, a. 5.
26. ST II-II, q. 158, a. 6.

are equipped with an analysis of anger as an emotion such as that offered here, it becomes clear. What Aquinas is asking for here is tuning our emotional sensitivities over time, so that even our emotional reactions to injustice is accurate in its intensity.

This intensity also helps explain why anger is a capital sin.[27] As noted earlier, what makes a sin "capital" is that it fosters other sins. One reason that anger is a capital sin (or capital vice) is the attractiveness of its object since *vindicatio* is a desirable good. But more relevant here, another reason for anger's status as a capital sin is that its "impetuosity hurls the mind headlong toward all sorts of inordinate things to be done."[28] This characteristic of anger is certainly a function of anger's status as an emotion. As seen in the next section, that status is important when trying to name the sin of anger and root it out of our lives

Identifying Anger in Our Lives

The previous sections have more precisely defined anger, examined what stimulates it and what it prompts us toward, and finally, explored how as an emotion, it both reflects and "colors" how we see things for good or bad. The analysis has at times been rather technical. The purpose of this last section is to offer more practical guidance for identifying the sin or vice of anger in our lives. It turns out that the previous two sections prepare us rather well for this task. We begin here by examining what Aquinas would call the "object" of anger, and then turn to guidance on anger that concerns its status as an emotion.

Anger is a desire for the rectification of perceived injustice. So the first place to begin is identifying those areas of our lives where we feel wronged. Whom do we feel has not given us (or others we care about) "our due"? Or, who has transgressed the parameters of right relationship with us? It is perhaps easiest to recognize anger in its more intense moments, such as the road rage case mentioned at the start of this essay. And it may also be more evident with acquaintances, say, at our workplace or in our neighborhoods, who offend or irritate us. But sinful anger commonly lurks more significantly in our relationships with those closest to us. A parent can be perceived as thwarting us. We can be wounded at a friend's perceived neglect of being there for us in the ways we hope. Especially with spouses, day-to-day relations can be fraught with perceived offenses. Even our grander hopes and dreams we might perceive as impeded by those

27. ST II-II, q. 158, a. 6. See also Thomas Aquinas, *On Evil*, trans. John Oesterle and Jean Oesterle (Notre Dame, IN: University of Notre Dame Press, 1995), XII.5.

28. ST II-II, q. 158, a. 6, translation mine.

with whom we share our whole lives. Anger is at least as commonly found at home as it is toward the outsider. Indeed, when Jesus instructs us to "love your enemy," this includes not only the outsider, but also the loved one who is perceived as acting like an enemy to us in some facet of life.

Seeking out such perceived injustices is a first and crucial step in tending to anger in our lives. Sometimes simply the honest recognition of what offends us, when articulated even inwardly to ourselves, evaporates anger once we see how petty or unreasonable our perception of slight is. Or we realize that despite the existence of real pain, our attribution of that pain to the fault of another is not reasonable. But of course, sometimes offenses are real, in which case we need to examine that other facet of the "object" of anger, rectification. Do we really seek the restoration of right relationship, or is our anger more an occasion to vindicate ourselves? In anger we may lash out and try to "get back" at the one who harms us. But that should not be an end in itself. The proper goal of anger is reconciliation, and any rising up or resistance to the offender should be tailored toward that goal. One way to help determine our true goal is to ask if we truly hope that right relations are restored, or whether we simply hope for harm to befall the other. Even further, would we be able to let go of that resistance if true reconciliation could be achieved without it? It is worth pausing here to look at Jesus's words on precisely this topic.

In the Sermon on the Mount, Jesus says "You have heard it was said 'an eye for an eye and a tooth for a tooth.' But I say to you offer no resistance to one who is evil. When someone strikes you on [your] right cheek, turn the other one to him as well" (Mt 5:38–39). Jesus here refocuses us during occasions of injustice on the goal of reconciliation. The often-misunderstood Old Testament law "an eye for an eye" (Ex 21:24) is a way to limit response to injustice rather than escalate it. Though the goal of the law is clearly restoration of right relationship, it is easy to see how "an eye for an eye" can lead to a simple "tit for tat" response to injustice without a further eye toward reconciliation. Jesus' injunctions to "offer no resistance" and "turn the other cheek" are not an abdication of the pursuit of justice, something that does not at all fit with the rest of his ministry. They are rather a radical relativization of punishment or resistance in relation to its proper further goal of reconciliation. Good resistance or punishment has as its point the cessation of the will and unjust activity of an offender. The rectification of injustice requires such a change, but if this can be achieved without punishment, then all the better. Indeed, as figures such as Martin Luther King Jr. have witnessed and any parent of young children knows, at times the relinquishment of punishment may be most effective toward the end. So while in anger even against a true injustice, we must ask ourselves what exactly we seek in our anger. And if restoration of right relations requires a rising up and resisting, then we must ensure that resistance is truly oriented toward and governed by the goal of reconciliation rather than an added impediment toward it.

Awareness of the "object" of anger enables us to reflect on whether or not there is true offense and if so, whether or not our response is truly oriented toward the restoration of right relations. A rising up in anger can indeed be so oriented, which is why the Christian tradition has by and large affirmed its compatibility with love and forgiveness. But so often it is borne out of self-pity or pride, and oriented not toward forgiveness but rather self-vindication or bitter harm of the other. In these cases, anger is sinful and must be surrendered. Since this is easier said than done, I offer two pieces of practical advice here.

First, for reasons even more evident below, honest recognition of whether or not there is true offense, or whether or not we truly seek reconciliation, can be very difficult. There may be no better aid to this than friendship. When we can discuss such occasions with a friend who cares for us enough that they will also tell us when we are misguided, we are more likely to see these occasions correctly. Conversations with friends provide occasions for us to narrate aloud what occurred, to specify and clarify often inchoate emotional responses. Such an "airing" of the story can lead to an honest recognition that our anger is unreasonable, a recognition less possible when anger is left to fester interiorly and unscrutinized. It can also provide occasion for our friend to help us see more clearly that our version of the story is skewed.

Second, anger is inextricably bound to justice and relationships of desert. Though part of justice is discerning what we are "owed," at least as important a part is gratitude for what we have been given. Gratitude helps keep "what we are due" in proper context of what we have been given. The positive effects of gratitude are increasingly recognized in popular literature.[29] Being grateful does not mean that we never suffer injustice or cannot experience virtuous anger. But it does contextualize our standards of justice, which are so easily warped in a manner that overestimates what we are due.

The above reflections correspond with the "object" of anger. The status of anger as an emotion also offers blessings and challenges. Anger is a very embodied response to perceived injustice and desire for *vindicatio*. Yet the arousal of this emotion further galvanizes our perception of injustice

---

29. See Robert Emmons, *Thanks!: How Practicing Gratitude Can Make You Happier* (Boston: Houghton Mifflin Co., 2007; repr. New York: Mariner Book, 2008).

and desire for *vindicatio*. This dynamic may be effective from an individual survival standpoint. It also works well socially on occasions of true injustice, as when famous prophetic figures seem to recognize better than others the presence of injustice as well as what needs to change to redress the situation. We might think here of Rosa Parks or Martin Luther King Jr. But due to our broken human condition, so often this response is vitiated by self-serving perception and redress that is mere self-vindication. Worse yet, our emotion of anger is so effective in attuning us to rectification of perceived injustice that it is difficult to get out of its cycle and begin to see things rightly and respond accordingly. How can we break this vicious cycle?

The earlier examination of the ways anger can participate in reason is a great place to start. First, when we find ourselves angry it is nearly always good advice to not act immediately. Do not fire off that email to a colleague, scream at a misbehaving child, or lash back at a spouse. Though this does not quell your anger, nor does it foment it further. Second, it is almost always good advice to quell one's anger by removing oneself from or avoiding occasions of anger. Separate oneself from the situation in order to think about the situation more calmly, not "colored" by anger given how effective it is in attuning us to harm suffered and the goodness of *vindicatio*. Sometimes such separation is not possible, and immediate reaction is necessary. But if it is, it is almost always wise. Think of the difference between an angry mob looting in response to racial injustice versus the more thought-out protests, marches, and boycotts of Martin Luther King Jr.

These two pieces of advice do not necessarily mean that an action out of anger, or the arousal of one's anger, is always a sin. They simply acknowledge the power of anger's impact on our evaluation of a situation. We say that those in love see the beloved through "rose-colored glasses," accentuating the positive qualities and neglecting the negatives. But those in the heat of anger are said to "see red." When angry, we renarrate our relationships accentuating other times we perceive we were wronged. We dwell on, even fantasize, ways we will "rectify injustice," even though too often these are ways of lashing back rather than true rectification. Calmer moments are needed to assess the situation without the "tint" of anger so as to ensure that anger is not distorting that assessment.

These two strategies are really ways of having the emotion of anger cease to distort the sort of analysis of the object of anger outlined in the above. As noted, such analysis is difficult even in calmer moments given how prone we are to evaluate situations in ways that favor ourselves. Self-deception is a formidable enemy to the virtuous life. This is why the sacraments and prayer are so important. The sacraments enable us to narrate our lives properly within the broader story of God's salvation. They enable us to see the extraordinary goodness and giftedness of creation. They remind us of our persistent sinfulness in turning away from God and living our stories with ourselves as the center of attention. And they remind us of God's never-ending love, mercy, and forgiveness, as well as offer of the grace needed to live most fully, in the true story with God at the center.

Prayer is also crucial. I mentioned how important friends are for the virtuous life. Our truest, wisest friend is Jesus, who calls us not servants but friends (John 15:15). Prayer is another venue where we encounter Christ our Friend who helps us see and live truthfully. And of course, Christ is present in His Body, the Church, that community of people living lives narrated primarily by God's story. When our friends help us in occasions of anger, they are the hands and feet of Christ our Friend.

All of this guidance helps us more accurately reflect on possible sins in relation to anger. Many times we realize that there is no real slight present. Or we realize that there was, but we are not honestly seeking true reconciliation. Yet at times our reflection reveals that our anger is good in its object. At this point it helps further to recall Aquinas's words on the other way that anger may be sinful, namely, in mode. Even if I seek true rectification of genuine injustice, is my anger immoderately intense? For instance, is it excessively fierce in intensity? Is it consuming my energy? Is it stubborn in its duration? When anger is immoderate in mode, even if reasonable in object, it can itself become an impediment to right relationships.

This reflection on our anger is all oriented toward a more accurate grasp of occasions of possible injustice. It helps build a habit of not "flying off the handle," of seeing relationships of justice in gratitude—not self-centeredness—and of seeking true reconciliation in situations of offense. Making these practices part of our lives engenders a good habit. One "angers well." Most often this will result in a virtue one might call calmness. With such a virtue, even when anger does arise it will participate in reason in the fullest sense, where the very arousal of the emotion is "shot through" with good practical reasoning, such that the person is "angry at the right things and with the right people, and, further, as he ought, when he ought, and as long as he ought."

Chapter 7

Envy

DANA L. DILLON

WHEN I WAS A CHILD, my parents would pile the whole family into the station wagon the first Saturday of every month and drive us to confession at our parish, Our Lady of Perpetual Help. As we grew up, we did this a bit less, but I made a lot of confessions as a child and teenager. Most of my early examinations of conscience used the Ten Commandments as a guide. I recall no worshipping of false gods (1), but I definitely had occasion to confess swearing (2), some resentment of going to Mass (though we always had to go in my household) (3), some failures to honor my parents (4), lots of fighting with my brothers and occasionally wanting to kill them (5), an array of sins around sex and lust (6), a few petty thefts (7), and quite a few lies (8). Yet I don't ever remember confessing anything related to the ninth or tenth commandments. I don't even remember seriously considering whether I had coveted anyone or anything that was my neighbor's.

In hindsight, however, envy was probably the defining sin of my childhood. As the sibling of a brother fifteen months my elder, I wanted everything he had, I wanted to do everything that he did, and I certainly wanted my fair share of any privilege my parents bestowed upon him. I would not have called it envy at the time; I know I didn't confess it at all—neither as envy nor as covetousness. Yet I can remember resenting that my brother got to go to school before I did, rode a bike first, was stronger and faster, had more interesting toys, got more of our father's attention, and on, and on; the list was nearly endless. As we got older, the items on the list changed to cars and curfews, college admissions and job offers, but there was still a list. As I grew up, I learned to see my brother not simply as a brother, but also as a measuring stick for the things I should have, the things I should be able to do, the things I should value. In short, I came to see him as the model and measure of the person I should be. In some ways, this was a good thing as it spurred me to successes I might not have found on my own. But it also nurtured some unhealthy and unnecessary resentments of my brother, in addition to skewing my vision of myself and who I was called to be. What is worse, it created certain habits of mind where I learned to reflect upon myself, my accomplishments, my desires, and even my worth by using others as measure. In fact, I came to see this as normal and natural, to want to be the best, smartest, the favorite as compared to others, rather than wanting simply to develop my own gifts, my own relationships, my own virtue simply to become the fullness of the person I am called to be. My three brothers, whom I might have seen as cooperative partners in learning to be people of love and charity, were often instead my competitors for my parents' affection and approval. This envious way of seeing and engaging one another would haunt us into our early adulthood, making it harder than it should have been for us to offer one another help when it was truly needed. Envy springs from and reinforces this distorted vision, where we see ourselves and others as fundamentally in competition with one another, rather than seeing ourselves in a community of love, where we are all committed to one another's good.

The *Catechism of the Catholic Church* is not as helpful as it might be in directing the faithful to see the pervasive power of envy in our lives. It treats envy within its attention to the tenth commandment ("you shall not covet your neighbor's goods"). After attending to the commandment as primarily about a covetousness that connects more directly to greed and the desire to accumulate wealth and power even at the expense of justice and reason,[1] it turns to envy, which it defines as "sadness at the sight of another's goods and the immoderate desire to acquire them for oneself."[2] The context of the commandment makes it understandable that the focus is on the neighbor's goods (that is, her stuff) rather than on the neighbor's good (all the things she has and is and that happen to her that lead to her flourishing), but this is a narrowing of what envy has typically meant. As Rebecca Konyndyk DeYoung points out,

> Covetousness, like greed, tends to be more focused on possessions— things we *have* or own—than envy does.... Envy, on the other hand, is typically more concerned with who we *are*. Envy targets the internal qualities of another person, qualities that give a person worth, honor, standing, or status. If the envious do desire an external thing, it is because that object symbolizes or signifies its owner's high position or greatness.[3]

As we shall see below, DeYoung's broader and less material focus is more in keeping with the way that envy was treated in the Christian tradition, particularly as expressed by the theology of St. Thomas Aquinas and the poetry of Dante Alighieri.

1. *Catechism of the Catholic Church,* no. 2535–36.

2. *CCC,* no. 2538.

3. Rebecca Konyndyk DeYoung, *Glittering Vices: A New Look at the Seven Deadly Sins and Their Remedies* (Grand Rapids, MI: Brazos Press, 2009), 43. Emphasis in original.

For those who would live a life rooted in Christ and directed toward union with him, it is crucial to live a life ordered to love and truth. Love and truth are more than important values or principles for Christians; they are claims about who God is. Jesus claimed to be "the way and the truth and the life" (John 14:6) and St. John the Evangelist proclaimed that "God is love" in the context of exhorting his fellow Christians to love one another because love of one another is deeply connected both to love of God and knowledge of God (1 Jn 4:7–8). The *Catechism of the Catholic Church* defines charity as "the theological virtue by which we love God above all things for his own sake, and our neighbor as ourselves for the love of God."[4] Envy is so deadly a sin because it stands in direct opposition to the virtue of charity and to a truthful vision of ourselves, our neighbors, and our interconnectedness. The love and charity we owe to our neighbors means that we should rejoice in their good, but the mark of envy is sorrow at our neighbor's good. Envy reverses the charitable response. Perhaps even more dangerously, envy has a way of corrupting our vision, so that we see our neighbors, siblings, colleagues, and even spouses not as persons in whose good we both share and rejoice, but merely as measuring sticks for our own successes or failures, our own acquisitiveness, even our own identities. Joseph Epstein points out that "entire bodies of theory exist founded on envy as normal human conduct."[5] After pointing out Freud's normalization of such concepts as the Oedipal complex, penis envy, sibling rivalry, and sublimation, he observes that "In the Freudian cosmos, envy, it could be said, makes the world go round."[6] In *Sinning Like a Christian: A New Look at the Seven Deadly Sins,* Will Willimon points out that, because of these and other normalizations of envy, it has come to be seen as "a perfectly natural, utterly pervasive human tendency, not a sin."[7] He goes on to point out that, although envy may be the most pervasive of the seven deadly sins, affecting us all in subtle and destructive ways, "it represents us at our most vile, not at our most 'natural.'"[8] We must remember that, as Christians, we believe in a God who is love, who made us in God's own image and made us for union both with God and with one another. That is our true nature; that is our true calling, and Christ himself has shown us the way to live up to that calling. If we want to live holy lives worthy of Christ, it is imperative that we name envy as the distorting sin it is, that we

---

4. *CCC,* no. 1822.

5. Joseph Epstein, *Envy* (New York: Oxford University Press, 2003), 12.

6. Epstein, *Envy,* 12.

7. William H. Willimon, *Sinning Like a Christian: A New Look at the Seven Deadly Sins* (Nashville: Abingdon Press, 2005), 61.

8. Willimon, *Sinning Like a Christian,* 61.

learn to see its subtle but pervasive effects on our moral lives and especially on our vision of ourselves and others, and that we commit ourselves to an alternative vision more deeply grounded in truth and charity.

The chapter that follows seeks to do exactly this. Drawing primarily from the analysis of St. Thomas Aquinas, we will explore envy both as a willed sin and a passion that works on us in ways that are subtler but also potentially more morally debilitating. Then we will turn to Dante's *Purgatorio* to discover envy as a distracted and distorted vision in need of being tamed through vulnerability and community. The final part will draw from these as well as more contemporary resources to point to some practical tools to aid us both to see and to name better the role of envy in our moral lives and turn toward a life more deeply grounded in truth and love.

Aquinas on Envy

Careful analysis of Aquinas's treatment of envy will be instructive in displaying the deeply damaging nature of this vice as well as its subtlety. For Aquinas, envy stands directly opposed to charity, which is the greatest of the theological virtues. Charity is the virtue by which we love God above all else and love others as we love ourselves. Aquinas also calls charity the "form of the virtues," because in a soul truly infused with charity, it orders every act and every virtue of the soul toward union with God. Though often reduced to small philanthropic gifts in modern English, charity actually names the virtue that disposes us to love of God and love of neighbor, as well as the love that animates those acts. For Aquinas, envy is a capital vice directly opposed to the theological virtue of charity. What makes a vice a capital vice (that is, a deadly sin) is both its deadly nature (as in, deserving of capital punishment) and that it takes root in a person and gives rise to other vices and sins.[9] Aquinas defines envy as "sadness about another's good as being a hindrance to one's own excellence".[10] This means that envy is a disordered form of sorrow, which we will discuss more below. For now, suffice it to say that, when sorrow is well-ordered, it is drawn from us by things that are actually bad for us and for those we care about.[11] However, when we are envious, we sorrow in our neighbor's good and since "charity rejoices in our neighbor's good",[12] this vice of envy and this virtue of charity share an object, the neighbor's good, responding to it

9. Thomas Aquinas, *Summa Theologiae* I-II, q. 84, a. 3.
10. ST I-II, q. 84, a. 4.
11. ST II-II, q. 36, a. 1.
12. ST II-II, q. 36, a. 3.

in precisely opposite ways. As such, envy is a sign of a deeply disordered soul. It stands directly opposed to charity, the greatest of the virtues. This is why Aquinas classifies it as a mortal sin according to its genus. Although further analysis of any particular act is needed to call it mortal sin, any act that has envy at its root is fundamentally opposed to charity and therefore is morally very serious. Whether a particular act is a mortal sin depends also on how deeply engaged the person's will and intellect were in the act. Aquinas makes clear that one can be moved in small ways toward envy that are merely venial sin, because the agent has not fully or directly acted upon them.[13] In other words, although the sin of envy is always serious, small movements of envy, though still sinful, are not mortally sinful. But for those who seek a life of virtue and holiness, it is crucial to root out even these venial sins. Because of the primacy of charity in the virtuous Christian life, avoiding every kind of envy is essential.

Recall that Aquinas defines envy as a disordered form of sorrow; it will be helpful to look at what he means by sorrow. He treats sorrow and pain together in a question among several others on the concupiscent passions.[14] The crucial thing to understand about passions in general is that they are, at their most basic level, the unreflective, natural responses to certain things. We see something good and worthy, and we respond with love; we see something evil, and we respond with hatred. Something good happens for ourselves or those we care for, and we respond with joy. Although we can reflect and turn these passions to more intentional actions, they are our unreflective responses. So, when Aquinas says that the proper object of sorrow is one's own evil,[15] what he is saying is that sorrow is what is drawn from persons who apprehend their own evil (such as a loss experienced or a sin committed). The knowledge of the evil or loss draws sorrow from the one who apprehends it, without the person consciously willing or choosing that response. Passion in this sense shares the root of the English word "passive," because the person here is (at least initially) not active but passive. Consider sorrow in relation to its proper object, one's own harm. When we realize that a loved one has died or that something we did has hurt someone we care about, we feel sorrow without any form of conscious choice entering in. The knowledge of the loss experienced or harm done evokes the feeling of sorrow from us without an act of the will. We may choose to express the sorrow or not, or to act on it in a variety of ways, and the will becomes involved in those choices, but at a basic level, a passion

13. ST II-II, q. 36, a. 3.

14. ST I-II, q. 35. The "concupiscent" passions are the ones related to our desire to seek good and avoid evil.

15. ST II-II, q. 36, a.1.

like sorrow is drawn from us by its object rather than being a response that we choose. (Of course, as noted in William Mattison's earlier chapter on anger, these responses are susceptible to formation or a lack thereof. We know, for example, that one who has become "hardened" may come to lack the feeling of sorrow, even at one's own loss.)

Let us note here a more general point about how the passions fit into the life of virtue as Aquinas understands it. Each passion is a disposition of the soul toward certain things. The concupiscible passions (such as joy, sorrow, love, hatred) are disposed toward good and evil themselves; the irascible passions (such as daring, fear, hope) are disposed toward the effort required for achieving a good or overcoming an evil.[16] These passions are evoked in various ways, but once a disposition becomes stable, it is a habit. Good habits are virtues, and bad habits are vices. For Aquinas, "like acts dispose like habits." The more you are drawn to a certain direction, the more stable your disposition will become. So, if I very occasionally find myself drawn to sorrow when I see that something good has happened in my neighbor's life, and I quickly chastise myself for that feeling and repent of it, I have hardly sinned at all. But if I fail to notice this disposition to sorrow at my neighbor's good, it becomes habitual and vicious, even if it seems to be unconscious or unchosen. For Aquinas, the path toward virtue involves ordering one's passions and acts according to reason and to charity, so the failure to rein in my envious disposition is itself a serious sin of omission.

In this context, it becomes clear what Aquinas means when he talks about envy as always being a mortal sin according to the genus even though there are "certain imperfect movements" of envy which are venial but are still sinful.[17] Certainly our modern instinct is not to hold someone accountable for things that they do not particularly intend to do. However, consider what it means to say that a person might see a neighbor's good and be drawn to sorrow as the seemingly natural response. Remember that one's own evil is the proper object of sorrow. So this person is drawn as instinctively toward sorrow by the good of another as by his own evil. It is evident that such a person is not ordered toward charity, the source and summit of the Christian life and the form of all the virtues. Being the form of the other virtues, charity should help direct every virtue toward the love of God, or toward love of neighbor for God's sake.[18] Since charity is "the effective willing of the good of another," envy stands in direct opposition to it. For Aquinas, charity should order every aspect of our lives

16. ST I-II, q. 23, a.1.
17. ST II-II, q. 36, a. 3.
18. ST II-II, q. 23, a. 8.

toward love of God and neighbor. Yet envy means that the other's good is perceived and responded to as a harm to the self. This results from a fundamental failure either to comprehend or to embrace the intrinsic connection between one's own good and the good of another. This failure can even be seen in larger social and economic relationships, as Nichole Flores's chapter on greed has explained.

The deep moral danger of the passive, subtle form of envy becomes apparent when Aquinas explains the ways that the sensitive appetite causes sin. Envy, as a disordered form of sorrow, is a passion that cannot move a person's will directly, but it can impede our attention to the good through simple distraction, or, more importantly, by driving "the apprehension of the imagination and the judgment of the estimative power".[19] This means that envy not only impacts the way that we understand and imagine the world, including our understanding of ourselves and our relationships, but it can also drive the judgment of the reason which in turn drives the will.

> Now when anyone proceeds from passion to a sinful act, or to a deliberate consent, this does not happen suddenly: and so the deliberating reason can come to the rescue here, since it can drive the passion away, or at least prevent it from having its effect, as stated above: wherefore if it does not come to the rescue, there is a mortal sin; and it is thus, as we see, that many murders and adulteries are committed through passion.[20]

The point of this should be somewhat terrifying. If envious responses are being drawn from us in response to the good of our neighbor, our ability to reason is what can rescue us from falling prey to that passion and being led by it into mortal sin. Sadly, however, if we do not use reason to rescue ourselves early enough, the passion itself has the power to compromise our reason. It is often much easier to see this in others than in ourselves.

Consider William Shakespeare's *Othello*, which tells a tragic story of envy run amuck. Seeing Othello promoted and well married, his standard bearer Iago decides to take advantage of Othello's "free and open nature / That thinks men honest that but seem to be so"[21] in order to take his own jealousy-inspired vengeance upon Othello. The audience knows from Iago's early speeches that his loyalty is false and that he is manipulating Othello, but Othello cannot see it. Iago proceeds to manipulate his fellow soldier Roderigo to fight with Michael Cassio, causing Othello to punish him with

---

19. ST I-II, q. 77, a. 1.

20. ST I-II, q. 77, a. 8.

21. Barbara Mowat, Paul Werstine, Michael Poston, Rebecca Niles, eds., *The Tragedy of Othello, the Moor of Venice* (Washington, DC: Folger Shakespeare Library, n.d.), accessed May 24, 2017. www.folgerdigitaltexts.org, Act I, Scene 3, lines 443–44.

loss of rank. This positions Iago to begin manipulating Othello directly. Even while Iago suggests to Cassio that the soldier should ask Desdemona to plead for him to be restored to his rank, the crafty standard bearer also begins to speculate that Desdemona may be having an affair with Cassio. By asking simple questions, Iago gets Othello not only to beg him for his speculations, but to ask him directly for his worst thoughts. Though Iago truthfully dismisses his worst thoughts as "vile and false," he nonetheless suggests not only the affair, but that Desdemona's success in deceiving her father in order to be with Othello indicates a giftedness in deception that is likely now directed at deceiving Othello.[22] Once these seeds are planted, Othello reads every kind word Desdemona says about Cassio as proof of her infidelity. This is precisely what Aquinas means when he explains how envy affects the abilities of reason by distorting its imaginative powers. For example, the handkerchief that was an early token of love from Othello to Desdemona is stolen and carefully placed in Cassio's quarters by Iago, which Othello takes as conclusive proof of their affair. Part of what makes the play such an effective tragedy is that the audience can see at once both the truth of Desdemona's love and faithfulness to Othello and the fact that it has become impossible for Othello to see this. Once the passion of envy has been stirred up in him, he cannot see the facts in any other light. The audience sees the plain facts and how Iago has manipulated them, as well as how deeply Othello's jealousy has compromised his ability to think clearly and to examine the facts.

Envy works in very much the same way in our lives. Once we are consumed by it, it is often very difficult to see its impact on our thinking. We believe that we are calmly, rationally coming to judgments about the other person. Since it is easier to notice this in others than in ourselves, we might notice envy at work in a friend who complains about a coworker or a sibling. We can see that they are jumping to conclusions that are not justified by the facts, and we can see that their passions are leading their judgment, but it is often difficult to get them to see this. And of course, the same is likely to be true of us sometimes. Remember, too, that the occasional disposition to envy is one thing, but if we allow it to become a more stable disposition such that it becomes a constant, vicious habit, we risk compromising our ability even to see how deeply it impacts our reasoning about ourselves, our neighbors, and our relationships with them.

In his *Summa Theologiae*, Aquinas treats four causes of envy and how they fit into this description of sorrow at another's good.[23] These also pro-

---

22. *Othello*, Act 3, Scene 3.

23. ST II-II, q. 36, a. 2.

vide interesting illuminations of the way that the stable disposition to envy might dovetail with other passions, disguise itself, and impact our reasoning. Aquinas first considers the case where the sorrowful response that is envy comes from fear that the other's good will lead to our own harm, as in the case where an enemy's (or a rival's) achievement of power or wealth is something that we fear he may use to harm us or others who might suffer unjustly. For Aquinas, this is not truly envy, and can even be without sin, insofar as it denotes a proper concern for justice and is related to one's natural inclination to self-preservation.[24] But given the impact of the passions on reason that we discussed above, it is essential to examine our consciences very carefully in moments such as these. Aquinas suggests (rightly, of course) that if the fear of harm is legitimate and reasonable, then this is not truly envy. On the other hand, if we have long failed to examine our envy and the ways that it has led to a destructive relationship with a coworker, for example, we might be convinced that the promotion of that coworker will be to our harm and perhaps even to the harm of the company and everyone connected to it. We might be convinced that this is a legitimate concern about the injustice of the promotion. It is crucial, however, to consider the possibility that it is envy, rather than reason, that is leading our assessment. Because charity is the chief virtue of the Christian life, it is crucial that we try to see things in the most charitable light.

Aquinas's second cause of envy is where one's sorrow comes from a neighbor's having a good that one wants. But Aquinas insists that if the good is a virtuous good, this is not proper envy but zeal, particularly if it spurs one to develop the virtue or pursue the particular good oneself. This sort of envy is not proper envy. Although it can be sinful if it leads one to seek sinful or disordered things, it is not sinful in itself. When I sorrow that my neighbor has a good that I do not have, if I am willing to work to develop that good, my sorrow turns into a passion to develop my own good gifts, my own virtues, or to seek legitimate temporal goods. The key questions to ask when experiencing this cause of envy is whether the good is a legitimate good to pursue, whether we are pursuing it justly and well, and whether there is any failing in charity in our attitude toward the neighbor who possesses it. I think back to my envy of my brother. I envied him for his success in school and our parents' affirmation of it; insofar as this inspired me to work harder in school and to do so legitimately, it was more zeal than envy. If, instead, it had inspired me to cheat, or perhaps feed my brother's homework to the family dog, it would be envy. The harder measure may be the last one. I think that, even though our rivalry in academic

---

24. ST I-II, q. 94, a. 2.

achievement led us both to be quite successful in school and beyond, there was a real failure in charity in my attitude toward my brother. Although I never would have given the dog his homework, I probably would have rejoiced a little if that happened. I think this was *a failure to understand that his good and my good were not fundamentally opposed to one another, but in fact were (and are) ordered toward one another as part of the common good.* We will return to this theme below.

The third cause of envy that Aquinas considers is the sorrow that comes when we see that the person who has a particular good is not worthy of it. As with the fear of harm to ourselves considered above, this may seem to us like a reasonable judgment to make. In fact, it is much like what we might call righteous indignation, when we have a sense that our sorrow (or anger) is not out of envy but out of a legitimate sense that the good the person has received is not deserved. Interestingly, Aquinas leaves little room for such a sense of righteousness here. He points out that such a judgment (that the other is not worthy) can only apply to temporal goods, which are "disposed according to God's just ordinance, either for the correction of those men, or for their condemnation, and such goods are as nothing in comparison with the goods to come."[25] In other words, we should not really expect that worldly goods are handed out to those who deserve them, so we should trust that God has reasons for distributing them as they have been distributed, even if we fail to see or understand those reasons.[26] It is important to note, however, that Aquinas seems to consider malicious use of power under the first cause of envy; this seems to be the place where he might have considered those who rise to power but, for reasons other than malice, are unworthy of it. Some might simply not have the competence; others may lack a moral compass; still others may be distracted from their role and responsibilities. It seems possible that one might judge someone elected to office or promoted to a leadership role of some kind to be unworthy of the privilege (the good) that she or he has been given. It seems that, much like in the first case above, there is room either for this to be a legitimate, well-reasoned judgment or one in which reason has been distorted by envy. Again, it is crucial for us to consider deeply the possibility that our

---

25. ST II-II, q. 36, a. 2.

26. Aquinas has a sense of both the common good and justice that make leaders responsibility for distribution of common goods with genuine fairness, though his sense of distributive justice is deeply hierarchical (see ST II-II, q. 61, a. 2). However, he also holds the right to private property as conditional to the common good, such that a holder of a good should be willing to give it to the use of another (see ST II-II, q. 66, a. 2). Modern Catholic social thought has made these ideas more explicit by putting the concepts of the universal destination of goods and the preferential option for the poor at the service of the common good (See chapter 4 of the *Compendium of the Social Doctrine of the Church*, especially no. 171–84).

judgment is unbalanced by our passions and vices. To be thorough in our self-examination, we need to seek to see and assess things with charity and to seek the help of people who do not share our biases.

The fourth sort of envy is envy proper, as Aquinas understands it, and entails grief over our neighbor's good, simply because it surpasses our own. The deep failure, as noted above, is to respond with sorrow to that which should cause us to rejoice, if we were properly disposed to our neighbor's good in charity. When one sorrows at a neighbor's good, it is a sign of multiple forms of disordering. First, of course, is the failure to truly love one's neighbor. Since love is the effective willing of the good of the neighbor, to fail to rejoice in that good when it is realized constitutes a failure to love one's neighbor. But the Catholic concept of the human person holds that, because human beings are created in the image and likeness of a Trinitarian God, we are made in union with one another, intrinsically connected to one another so deeply that our good is a common good. In fact, the *Compendium of the Social Doctrine of the Church* makes it clear that the common good is rooted in "the dignity, unity and equality of all people,"[27] and to aim at the common good is to aim at "the good of all people and of the whole person."[28] In other words, the good of all people and the good of the whole person are two mutually reinforcing aspects of the single, unified concept of the common good. Despite our tendency to think of life as a competition for goods, where the good of one person is balanced against the good of another person or group of persons, where any gain for one is a loss for another, this is not the way the Catholic tradition sees it. The common good is more like the shared good of teammates than of opponents. Improved performance in any one team member is more likely to improve the teammates' play than to harm it, and certainly this improvement will be to the good of the team as a whole. So too, the Catholic concept of the common good sees the good of all and the good of each person as each contributing to the other, not goods in competition with one another in a zero-sum game. In light of this, my neighbor's realization of his own good is a part of our realization together of our common good, so the good my neighbor has attained is in the service of my own good. To sorrow in my neighbor's good is to fail to see the depth of our connectedness. It is to fail to live the vision of our shared life in God that we are invited to. To display envy's damaging role to that vision, as well as some of the means to remedy it more fully, we now turn to Dante Alighieri's *Divine Comedy*.

27. *Compendium of the Social Doctrine of the Church*, no. 164.
28. *Compendium of the Social Doctrine of the Church*, no. 165.

Dante and Vision

For Dante, as for Aquinas, envy is the vice most directly opposed to charity. Charity, of course, is the animating principle of all virtue, and the goal of Christian life. At the very end of his *Divine Comedy*, Dante has a vision of all the blessed drawn together, their will and desire moving together with "the Love that moves the sun and all the other stars."[29] But before he gets there, he must pass through hell and purgatory, as well as the lower levels of paradise. As he makes his winding way up Mount Purgatory with Virgil as his guide, he notes very early in the canto that he can hear but not see spirits "sounding courteous invitation / to the table readied for the feast of love."[30] He notes three specific voices: one that says, "they have no wine";[31] one that says, "I am Orestes";[32] and one that says, "Love him who has done you wrong."[33] According to Anthony Esolen, it is no accident that Dante moves here so quickly from the "feast of love" to the line "they have no wine," drawn as it is from Mary's comment to Jesus at the wedding feast at Cana (John 2:1–12). Esolen poignantly connects Mary's ability to see the lack of wine as everyone's problem, including her own, to the way each sinner's need for forgiveness, grace, and mercy is embedded in a web of relationships:

> Mary feels the loss as if it were her own, because in fact it is her own, and everyone else's too: no wine, no feast, no community.... They have no wine, she says, and before Jesus passed the cup of his blood round to his disciples at that first Eucharist, we, his enemies, his scattered sheep, each going our own separate way to destruction, had no wine either.[34]

For Esolen, the feast that we are invited to, both in the Eucharist and at the end of the *Paradiso*, is the communion that likewise should be the model for our relationships with others. There is much debate about whether the voice that says "I am Orestes" in line 33 is that of Orestes himself or of his friend Pylades. Pylades had claimed that he was Orestes to save his friend from a death sentence. Orestes likewise claimed his true identity to save Pylades's life. By using this simple line even without clarifying the identity of the speaker, Dante points to a relationship in which,

---

29. Dante Alighieri, *Paradiso*, trans. Jean Hollander and Robert Hollander (New York: Anchor Books, 2007), XXXIII.142–45.

30. Dante Alighieri, *Purgatorio*, XIII.26–27.

31. Dante, *Purgatorio*, XIII.29.

32. Dante, *Purgatorio*, XIII.33.

33. Dante, *Purgatorio*, XIII.36.

34. Anthony Esolen, "What Dante Can Teach Us about Envy," *Catholic Answers Magazine* 20, no. 8 (September 1, 2011). Accessed online at https://www.catholic.com/magazine/print-edition/what-dante -can-teach-us-about-envy May 21, 2017.

in Esolen's words, "the friendship itself, the greater good of communion, prompts each young man to desire the good of the other as if it were his own. Again we are presented with an order, a communion, that embraces the good of the individuals and transcends it."[35] The third voice is that of Jesus, drawn from Matthew 5:44 and the larger context of the Sermon on the Mount. His words, of course, are both a command to love and a summons away from envy. If we must love those who have done us harm, how much more are we called to love those whose good is connected to ours, whether they have harmed us or not.

Before the reader learns (if we don't recognize) anything about these speakers or their significance, Dante has asked, and Virgil has responded:

> This circle
> scourges the sin of envy, and thus
> The cords of the scourge are drawn from love.
>
> To rein in envy requires opposing notes.
> Such other voices you will hear, I think,
> Before you reach the pass of pardon.[36]

According to Robert Hollander, Virgil's words here represent the first verbal instance of what will be "the mode of purgatorial instruction by examples: first one is spurred to imitate the good, then dissuaded from following the bad."[37] So, in this circle where the envious are scourged of that sin, Dante will be exposed both to the exemplars of love and to those of envy. He will encounter models both of what to do and what not to do. The three voices that he has already heard represent models of and exhortations to a charity rooted in communion, in genuine connection to those whose good is tied to our own. And for the reader who ascends with Dante, the exhortation is the same: come to see yourself as rooted in a community of love, where your good and your joy are tied to that of those around you; rein in the envy that stands in the way of love.

As Virgil finishes this speech on the circle of envy, he directs Dante's attention to a group of figures ahead. Dante is moved immediately to compassion, seeing a group of people "covered with coarse haircloth"[38] and

---

35. Esolen, "What Dante Can Teach Us about Envy."

36. Dante, *Purgatorio*, XIII.37–42.

37. Robert Hollander, "Notes to *Purgatorio* XIII," in Dante Alighieri, *Purgatorio*, trans. Jean Hollander and Hollander, 286.

38. Dante, *Purgatorio*, XII.58.

propped up against one another.[39] As he gets closer, he realizes that they are not simply hunched together resembling blind beggars, but have actually been blinded, and quite unnaturally:

> for iron wire pierces all their eyelids,
> stitching them together, as is done
> to the untrained falcon because it won't be calmed[40]

This image evokes how powerfully envy leads vision astray. The well-trained falcon has learned what it should be focused on and what things it must not be distracted by, but until it reaches that stage, its eyelids are wired together so that it learns to pay attention to the signals of its trainer. So too a well-ordered soul is drawn to the good and the true. A virtuous woman, for instance, sorrows in harm to her neighbor and rejoices in her neighbor's good as she would in her own. Because, like Mary at Cana, she knows that she and her neighbor share a common life and a common good. A vicious woman with a soul distorted by envy would fail to see the deep interconnection between the neighbor's good and her own. She is more likely to be distracted—or worse, distressed—by the goods of her neighbor than to rejoice in them. She is too focused on her own pleasures and desires to seek her true good and to see its deep connection to the good of those with whom she is (or ought to be) in communion.

As Dante talks with these souls, he sees that their blindness works in multiple ways to correct their sin of envy. First, the closing of their eyes takes away their vision of others that had so distracted them with comparisons during their earthly years. Second, it puts them in a position of vulnerability and dependence that remakes their relationship with the community. They are put in a position where it is much more essential to ask, "how can we work through this together and help one another?" than to make petty comparisons or jostle for position and privilege. Just as the falconer seals the eyes of the falcon while it is trained in what it must focus upon, the limitation on the vision of the envious offers them a new way of seeing what is truly important. It places them in a community of interdependence, where each of them only flourishes when all are cared for. In their blindness and vulnerability, they are made into a community that helps them learn the importance of charity and solidarity and live in new ways of seeing and acting.

---

39. Dante, *Purgatorio*, XIII.59.
40. Dante, *Purgatorio*, XIII.70–72.

Cultivating A Vision of Solidarity

If we are to resist the forces in the world that push us to see competition as the normal relationship among us, and rivalry and envy as the normal way of things, we need to immerse ourselves in the stories and vision of the deep communion among all people, and particularly the communion that we share with our fellow members of the Body of Christ. In addition, it is crucial for us to cultivate the habit of careful attention to how we see both others and ourselves. Finally, we need to turn to Christ and to scripture for some help in letting go of envy's hold upon us and seeing through eyes of mercy and charity.

In his 1987 encyclical *Sollicitudo Rei Socialis*, St. John Paul II elevated the concept of solidarity to a moral virtue, insisting that the solidarity that Christians are called to is "not a feeling of vague compassion or shallow distress at the misfortunes of so many people, both near and far. On the contrary, it is a firm and persevering determination to commit oneself to the common good; that is to say to the good of all and of each individual, because we are all really responsible for all."[41] This is a rich statement, and one piece of it not to be missed is that his vision of the common good is "the good of all and of each." These are not in competition with one another but are mutually constitutive of one another. This is part and parcel of a vision where we are made intrinsically social, with interconnected goods, so that we all flourish best when we each flourish. As he continued describing the solidarity he was calling for, he described a way of seeing one another:

> Solidarity helps us to see the "other"—whether a person, people or nation—not just as some kind of instrument, with a work capacity and physical strength to be exploited at low cost and then discarded when no longer useful, but as our "neighbor," a "helper" (cf. Gen 2:18–20), to be made a sharer, on a par with ourselves, in the banquet of life to which all are equally invited by God. Hence the importance of reawakening the religious awareness of individuals and peoples. Thus the exploitation, oppression and annihilation of others are excluded.[42]

If I am seeing my neighbor through the eyes of solidarity, I see someone called by God to share in the banquet of life with me. I cannot see my neighbor this way and sorrow at his good. And yet, St. John Paul goes even further, calling Christians to a level of solidarity worthy of Christ's own Paschal sacrifice:

> In the light of faith, solidarity seeks to go beyond itself, to take on the specifically Christian dimension of total gratuity, forgiveness and

---

41. John Paul II, Encyclical Letter *Sollicitudo Rei Sociallis*, (December 30, 1987), 38.
42. John Paul II, *Sollicitudo Rei Sociallis*, 39.

reconciliation. One's neighbor is then not only a human being with his or her own rights and a fundamental equality with everyone else, but becomes the living image of God the Father, redeemed by the blood of Jesus Christ and placed under the permanent action of the Holy Spirit. One's neighbor must therefore be loved, even if an enemy, with the same love with which the Lord loves him or her; and for that person's sake one must be ready for sacrifice, even the ultimate one: to lay down one's life for the brethren (cf. 1 Jn 3:16).[43]

This is St. John Paul's call to love our neighbors, even our enemies, with the kind of love that would be willing to lay down our lives for them. This is his vision of how deeply connected we are, of how totally we are called to live for Christ and for one another. This is the kind of love and the kind of vision that can drive out our envy. We should cultivate that love and the vision both of ourselves and of our neighbors that it offers us.

We also need to recall the basic principle that how we see the world is not simply a given. As the philosopher Iris Murdoch points out, "It is a *task* to come to see the world as it is." She goes on to say that any approach to the moral life that "ignores this task ... obscures the relation between virtue and reality."[44] Murdoch claims that "the characteristic and proper mark of the active moral agent" is "[directing] a just and loving gaze ... upon an individual reality."[45] It is essential, if we are to be virtuous at all, and particularly in a Christian context, that we strive to see the world and the people in it both as truthfully and as charitably as possible. This takes work, commitment, and discipline. Because of the dangers of envy and its tendency to disguise itself and distort our reason, it is crucial that we practice Murdoch's attentive, loving gaze on those we find it difficult to love. We need to get to the heart of our obstacles to charity and try to root them out. Community can also help immensely, though it can hinder it as well. If I am struggling to see the good in a certain coworker, whether from a reasoned judgment or out of envy, I know exactly to whom I can go who is even more negative than I am, who will affirm my every complaint and add fuel to the fire. But I often know someone who values that person and could help me see them in a better light. Immersed in negative feelings, it is so easy, affirming, and comfortable to vent with someone who shares our perspective. But if we are committed to developing the truthful, loving gaze that Murdoch commends, we need to seek out the conversation partner who will help draw us to a more charitable view and avoid or shut

43. John Paul II, *Sollicitudo Rei Sociallis*, 40.

44. Iris Murdoch, *The Sovereignty of Good* (New York: Routledge Classics, 1971), 89.

45. Murdoch, *The Sovereignty*, 33.

down the conversations that fuel negativity. We need to seek out conversation partners who can help us see their positive qualities, and nurture us in seeing them charitably, or who at the very least will remind us that they are God's beloved children as well. We also need to seek to become such conversation partners for others.

Perhaps one of the best ways to develop this loving, attentive gaze is to try to see the person not through our own envious eyes but through the eyes of Christ. Pope Francis has spoken much of his episcopal motto, *miserando atque eligendo*, drawn from St. Bede's account of the call of St. Matthew. Pope Francis says, "I like to translate *miserando* with a gerund that doesn't exist: *mercifying*. So, 'mercifying and choosing' describes the vision of Jesus, who gives the gift of mercy and chooses, and takes unto himself."[46] That gaze of Jesus, who looks upon the tax collector Matthew and sees a disciple, an apostle, and an evangelist looks upon each one of us as well and sees the person who, with his mercy and grace, we can become. What a prayerful exercise to consider the one we look at with envious eyes and contemplate what Jesus might see through his gaze of mercy. We might also reflect upon what Jesus sees when he looks at us with his mercifying gaze. That gaze has the power to turn our envy into mercified charity.

My own relationship with my brothers changed definitively over the course of a few brief years. We lost our mother and then our father over the course of about three-and-a-half years. Wounded by these losses, to some extent I clung to my brothers, like the envious souls clung to one another along the slopes of Mount Purgatory. In the midst of this, however, it became clear that Paul, the middle brother who lives with schizoaffective disorder, would need some significant support from one of his siblings in order to avoid becoming lost in the woefully inadequate mental health system. There were good reasons why one of our other brothers should have done this; one was in the same city as Paul, the other in the same state, and I was in neither; I was in graduate school and likely to move again in less than two years. In the midst of many phone calls trying to figure out something, one brother put it very plainly: "I'm not my brother's keeper, and I'm not going to give up my life to become his social worker." I realized that we were in a conversation of measurement and scorekeeping; whose turn was it to deal with this? Whose life, and work, and other responsibilities were the most important? This was the kind of tallying that came from the gaze of envy, not the mercifying

---

46. Pope Francis, *The Name of God is Mercy: A Conversation with Andrea Tornielli*, trans. Oonagh Stransky (New York: Random House, 2016), 11–12.

gaze of charity. It was at that moment that I knew that I could not argue about it; I had to simply say yes. I could not be the kind of person I want to be—the kind of Christian I want to be—and continue to argue about it. I had to respond to this brother in need with love, and to these other brothers who felt that they had too much going on to care for their brother with love. I immediately began making plans to bring my brother Paul to me. When I wired money to a social worker to have him put on a bus from Texas to North Carolina, I had no idea what it would mean for me. I thought it might derail my graduate studies (my degree only took a little longer than I had planned) or my job prospects (I accepted a great tenure-track job offer before I finished my dissertation) or complicate my life in other ways. Before my brother set foot in North Carolina, I discovered that I could rely on friends in ways I hadn't imagined. One drove from Birmingham to Montgomery to find my brother at a truck stop where the voices had urged him off the bus and drove him to my house in North Carolina. Another connected me to NAMI (the National Alliance on Mental Illness) in Durham, and they directed me to resources for crisis housing and mental health care. I found community support and resources (both internal and external) that I did not know I had.

That moment was transformative for me. It felt like in choosing the loving response, I was given what I needed to offer the loving response, and I became a more charitable person in the process. It is strange. Envy of my elder brother was such a defining sin of my childhood and young adulthood. And the old habits of the soul are hard to shake off. I have moments where, distracted by my brother Paul's needs in the midst of my other commitments and responsibilities, I am tempted to envy our other brothers' ability to focus on other things and forget about Paul. But I tend not to want to be like my elder brother anymore, nor to engage in a calculus of who is better or whose responsibility something is. I am more likely to aim to be like Paul, or like those who became a loving community to support both him and me. Sharing life with Paul, I realize it is quite ordinary for him to rejoin me in a restaurant after a smoke break and ask me to order something for someone who is hungry waiting just outside. Sometimes I will come out of the grocery store and Paul will introduce me by name to a woman who just needs a couple bucks of bus money to get home with groceries for her kids. My brother, who lives so much of his own life on the margins, helps me see and give to those on the margins, and to do so with a dignity and humanity that would probably not be possible for me without him in my life.

For most of my life, as I have gone to confession, I have focused on concrete sins that I had committed. Because of its subtle and pervasive nature, envy was likely at the root of many of my other sins, but I failed to examine deeply under the surface to recognize and name the ways that envy formed me, my actions, and my ways of seeing the world. More careful attention to the ways envy formed my vision of myself and others might have helped me move beyond the petty comparisons that dominated so much of my early life. The pervasive sense of envy and rivalry as normal and natural hid from me for far too long the much different vision of relationship that Christianity calls us to: that deep, constant solidarity embodied consistently in acts of love and mercy. Perhaps if I had been able to name envy in my life more clearly and more thoroughly, I would have been able to see and enact the depth of the love to which Christians are called.

The overwhelming vision of the shared Christian life, whether from scripture, Aquinas, Dante, or others in the tradition is of a banquet to which all are invited. The Eucharist we share in weekly (at least) is a foretaste of the heavenly banquet we will share. Since envy sorrows at the neighbor's good, it sorrows at the neighbor's presence at that banquet. Or, perhaps, it is the disposition of the soul that would draw us to ask "who deserves to be here less than me?" Yet this envious question stands in opposition to the charity to which Christians are called, and to the love the feast enacts. In this way, the envious person risks excluding herself from the feast. The older brother in the parable of the prodigal son is therefore an interesting figure for us to consider when we are consumed with envy. He is out working in his father's fields when his brother returns home from his time of dissolute living. The older brother comes home from the fields, hears the sounds of the feast, asks a servant what is happening, and gets really angry. When his father comes out to plead with him, he says, "Look, all these years I served you and not once did I disobey your orders; yet you never gave me even a young goat to feast on with my friends. But when your son returns who swallowed up your property with prostitutes, for him you slaughter the fattened calf" (Luke 15:29–30). This, plain and simple, is envy. His brother is home, safe, and forgiven. All of this is good. And yet he sorrows at that good. His father reassures him of his love and his property ("all that I have is yours"), and calls him very specifically to rejoice rather than to sorrow at his brother's return. God our Father, like the father in this story, is generous to a fault and will never tire of forgiving the sinner who seeks his mercy. As we approach the sacrament of reconciliation, perhaps we can ask ourselves what are the ways that we, like that elder brother, have failed to see with the loving and mercifying gaze of the Father. What are the ways we have seen ourselves as competitors and measuring sticks for one another's worthiness for a job or promotion, or even a place at the Eucharistic feast? Like the prodigal's father, God comes to us and pleads with us to let go of our envy and resentment of our brothers, our sisters, our neighbors and come into the feast. May we have the strength to name our envy, confess the ways it divides us from one another, and choose the path of charity instead, that we may say yes to the feast and the communion it embodies.

Chapter 8

Pride

CHARLES C. CAMOSY

Is Pride Even a Vice?

O NE USUAL ADVANTAGE OF writing about the vices is that almost everyone—even people with very different theological and political commitments—can agree they are morally bad. Fictional characters like Gordon Gecko notwithstanding, people do not think that greed is good. There is no "pro-gluttony" advocacy group. Sexual desire is a positive thing, but the point of naming a particular desire as "lust" is to highlight that something is morally out of place.

But when speaking about the topic of this chapter, pride, things gets more complicated. Far from a calling it a vice, we in the developed West (and especially the United States) tend to think of pride as a virtue—perhaps one of the most important virtues. Taking pride in ourselves and in the people, places, and institutions with which we are connected is, without much thought, understood to be a good thing. Taking pride in one's country, one's favorite sport or team, one's school, one's family, and *especially* one's self is simply the way most of us live. Indeed, there is thought to be something wrong with you if you don't take pride in these things.

The concept also has an almost uniformly positive place in popular culture. The Pride movement is perhaps the most important (and definitely the most public) association of gays and lesbians, and the title of the movement is meant to underscore the positive nature of same-sex sexual orientation. As another example, I grew up a huge fan of Larry Bird, Robert Parish, Kevin McHale and Boston Celtics NBA basketball back in the 1980s, and the phrase most associated with the love their fans had for those teams (a phrase that would eventually become the title of a movie) was "Celtic Pride." Still to this day, some of the most important moments of my life have been when a teacher, friend, or family member I deeply care about and respect makes it clear that they are proud of me. Sure, many of us still have a general sense that someone can be *too* proud, but pride itself seems nevertheless very clearly a good thing—perhaps even an essential thing, especially for our flourishing as individuals and communities.

Speaking of pride as a vice, then, is quite a counter-cultural challenge. In this chapter, I hope to do so by building on the views of giants in the tradition like Augustine, Thomas Aquinas, and C.S. Lewis on the vice of pride. What they mean by pride is significantly different from what is meant in the modern secular West. While these thinkers acknowledge that healthy, rightly-ordered pride is important (Aquinas even warns of the sinfulness present in a false humility), they are far more skeptical of the good present in human nature—and especially of *our ability to discern* what the good is. We are flawed, finite creatures—prone to making errors and mistakes—who are especially good at deceiving ourselves. Human persons see what they expect to see, and this often blinds us to reality—especially to reality with which we find it difficult to come to terms. Because of our self-deception, without help—and especially the kind of help which comes from genuinely diverse communities—we may not have the kind of perspective necessary to properly name the things in which we should take pride and distinguish them from the things in which we should not take pride. And, relatedly, we may not have the strength to confront those latter realities—again, especially when they are so difficult for us to come to terms with on our own. These blindnesses make it difficult for us to name some of our own sins.

After articulating the traditional view of pride as a vice, the chapter will turn to some practices of resistance to the vice of pride. The corresponding virtue, or good habit, is humility, and we will explore what that might look like—in a very general way—in today's culture. This includes listening first, reserving the right to change one's mind, keeping in close contact with people who think differently and have permission to challenge one's assumptions, and seeing disagreements and conflict as something other than "us vs. them" opposition. The chapter will then conclude by naming some contemporary sins where the vice of pride plays a significant role: everything from our uncritical nationalism, to how we use social media, to our general allergy to exceptionless moral rules.

Some Alternative Ways of Thinking about Pride

In *Mere Christianity* the great C.S. Lewis has an entire chapter on pride, and titled it "The Great Sin."[1] He argues that it is the sin which most of us fail to see in ourselves—and yet, paradoxically, the more we suffer from it ourselves the more we are annoyed by pride in others. For Lewis, this is

---

1. Material on Lewis cited from C.S. Lewis, "The Great Sin," in *Mere Christianity* (New York: Harper-Collins, 2001), 121–22.

the essential vice and the height of evil. Pride, the vice which felled Lucifer himself when he decided to put his own judgment in the place of God's, is the source of all other vices.

St. Augustine also had a particular focus on pride, noting it as the source of Adam and Eve's rebellion against God. Pride, the primordial sin, is deep within the fallen nature of every human being. Augustine asks us to see the places where we sometimes explicitly, and often due to self-deception, pridefully replace God's values and power with our own. In his *Confessions*, Augustine takes himself to task for the sin of pride. It was behind every one of his failings. Only in a genuine, soul-emptying relationship with the humility of Jesus, Augustine said, was he able to understand what "[Jesus'] weakness was meant to teach."[2]

St. Thomas Aquinas insists that pride, insofar as it is a choice to turn away from God and replace God's will for us with what we deem appropriate, is by definition a mortal sin. That is, it is a sin which risks radically severing our relationship with God.[3] Pride, for Aquinas, comes when we think of ourselves and our capacities as "above" where we and they actually are. (The mortal sin comes when, again, we crowd out God with our own judgment.) Contrast this with, say, our usual use of pride in terms of taking pleasure in justified praise from others and for feeling good about our genuine accomplishments. Indeed, Aquinas insists that taking credit where credit is due is a matter of justice, and a kind of "false humility" is actually yet another example of pride.

Pride, then, is *inordinate and unjustified* belief in yourself. It is essential to have good self-esteem, but this view of pride also invites us to critical-self-awareness of our limitations. We are finite, sinful, often self-deceived beings—beings who have the primordial temptation to put our own self-interested reasoning ahead of God's. Far too often, we simply assume that what we experience—or, perhaps more precisely, what we conclude must be true on the basis of our experience—must be correct. And here is a critical point: what we experience is often tainted by sin. That means that even our own perceptions of ourselves and what might be prideful or not, can be muddied by pride! Pride is therefore a difficult sin to discuss and name.

We will discuss specific examples of the difficulty of naming the sin of pride in some detail in the final section of the chapter, but let's pause for just a moment here and initially name some instances. Consider someone who says, "I experience my wealth as a sign of God's gifts and favor" or "I

---

2. Augustine, *Confessions*, trans. Henry Chadwick (New York: Oxford University Press, 2008), 128.

3. Thomas Aquinas, *Summa Theologiae*, q. 161, a.1 ad 2, and II-II, q. 162.

experience sexual attraction for person X as romantic love." To conclude that one's experiences must be indicative of something good to be pursued, without even pausing to consider that they might instead be the result of our fallen, sinful natures, comes from pride. The writings and advice of holy women and men of God, along with the witness of Scripture, might offer wisdom that would call such conclusions about these experiences into question, but pride often hinders our ability to be genuinely challenged in this way.

Also consider that (even after careful reflection and prayer), though we may rightfully decide that a goal is worth pursuing, pride can also cloud how we think about the morality of *the means* by which we accomplish that goal. For instance, the developed world has experienced startling advances in technology and science over the past several decades, and our appreciation of those achievements may lead us to the questionable conclusion that we may pursue our goals with whatever means that we have available to us. Consider the good of having a healthy child. May this good be achieved by any means necessary? We now have the technology to create embryos in a laboratory, determine which ones are likely to be sick or disabled and which ones are healthy, and throw away those who we think are sick or disabled. In a culture that is dominated by a prideful belief in what is sometimes called the "technological imperative" or "scientism,"[4] we are told that simply because we *can* do something means that we *should*. Those who have cautions or objections are often rebuked as "anti-science" or somehow against progress. But, again, this kind of uncritical confidence in ourselves refuses to consider the fact that we might be blinded by our technological and scientific success—thus failing to see those who are (or may be) hurt in the process.

Pride can also come from inordinate and unjustified belief in one's associations, including national, religious, and political. Good feelings about one's country can be justifiable, of course, but uncritical attachment risks those feelings becoming prideful. For instance, the belief many Americans have that we live in "the greatest country on earth" often comes from a prideful point of view—a view which misses the fact that GDP, the strength of one's military, and influence over the world's popular culture are questionable measures of greatness, especially in light of the Gospel. It may also lead to an undue confidence when it comes to exporting our values and practices around the world—especially when such export is done with the use of violence.

---

4. This is nicely articulated by Pope Francis in Chapter Three of his encyclical letter *Laudato Si'* (May 24, 2015), 101, when he speaks of "technocratic paradigm."

Something similar is often true of our religious associations as well. We can become so attached to a particular church—or even a particular group within a particular church—that we lose our critical lens. I know fellow Catholics, for instance, who seem literally unable to accept the horrific reality of the widespread sex-abuse crisis because it conflicts with the pride they have in the Church. Furthermore, not a few progressive Catholics are unable to see the sex-abuse crisis as anything other than a failure of the Church's outdated and hierarchical social structures, while some traditional Catholics are unable to see it as anything other than the result of poor formation of priests and relaxed attitudes toward gay sex. It is not wrong to have good feelings about one's religion—and even about the subgroups of one's religion—but when those feelings turn into the kind of attachment which keeps us from responding to the reality of injustice, as God insists we do, then these good feelings have become prideful.

Our political affiliations are chock-full of pride. And at least in the United States, they are prideful in a very particular way. Though the reality of what people actually believe is much more complex (especially among younger people), our political imagination conjures up a binary "us vs. them" struggle or war. "Our side" is, by its very nature, set up against "the other side." So we may not only struggle with inordinate and unjustified belief in "our side" (in the same way we might with our country or our religion), but we struggle with an inordinate and unjustified opposition to "the other side." Indeed, if we are conservatives, much of our identity comes from being directly and strictly opposed to liberals. If we are liberals, much of our identity comes from being directly and strictly opposed to conservatives. In such cases, the pride we have for our political associations leads us to imagine—again, without self-aware critical analysis—that "the other side" must be obviously wrong and even evil. In this context, pride shifts justified love of one's political associations into contempt for a group of fellow citizens—and this contempt becomes essential to our personal identity. In the context of the 2016 presidential election, for instance, this mindset led millions of people to support a candidate—in either major party—they thought would actually be bad for the country (both Donald Trump and Hillary Clinton had record-high unfavorability ratings) simply because their identity was more strongly connected to hatred for the other candidate!

Practices of Resistance

So how do we resist the vice of pride? Given what has just been laid out, it seems like a pretty tall order. It is especially important to be mindful of the point I raised at the beginning of this essay: we are very good at deceiving ourselves, and it can be difficult to determine whether even our "resistances" might be instances of pride!

That said, the first and foundational practice of resistance has been exemplified by Pope Francis. Not long after he became pope, Francis was asked about who he was, and his answer could not have been more clear: "I am a sinner."[5] This basic acknowledgment is the starting point for living a humble life that is capable of resisting our prideful natures. The Pope compared himself to St. Matthew, a tax collector who—empowered by Jesus' gaze and call—was not only convicted of his own sin, but resolved to follow a radically different path from the one he had chosen for himself. The pope's frank admission of identity challenges us to consider all the ways we are tempted to aggrandize ourselves. The essential foundation of resistance to pride is a humble acknowledgement that we are finite, flawed, sinful people.

Many important things follow from this starting point.[6] It is important, therefore, to have conversation partners and friends who display other points of view, and who have very different perceptions of who we are. When we engage in political and theological reflection and discourse, we will not only become more comfortable with someone challenging our point of view, but—knowing there is a significant probability that we are wrong—we will reserve the right to change our mind. Instead of an "us vs. them" binary where we set ourselves up against those with whom we think we disagree, we will be guided by the humble, Christ-like love which insists on solidarity with our perceived enemies. This involves active listening and—again, given our fallen, sinful natures—presuming that one has something to learn. It will mean never reducing others' ideas to their gender, race, level of privilege, sexual orientation, or social location. Similarly, it will mean never casually dismissing them on the basis of what you suspect are their "secret personal motivations." To resist the vice of pride, we must allow ourselves to be challenged by the actual idea or argument being offered for our consideration—and, again, being open to changing our mind as a result.

Recognizing our sinfulness and finitude also means making a conscious effect to live within politically and theologically diverse communities—and with people who feel comfortable calling out our blind spots and biases.

5. Antonio Spadaro, SJ, "A Big Heart Open to God: An Interview with Pope Francis," *America: The Jesuit Review*, September 30, 2015, http://americamagazine.org/pope-interview (accessed November 30, 2016).

6. Much of what follows in Charles C. Camosy, "5 Tips for Creating Civil Discourse in an Era of Polarization," *Seattle Times*, July 10, 2012, http://www.seattletimes.com/opinion/5-tips-for-creating-civil-discourse-in-an-era-of-polarization/ (accessed November 30, 2016).

The unity of our communities, especially if they are Christian, should not prioritize uniformity over diversity. A conscious effort to live with genuine political and theological diversity cultivates our humility—not only in seeking out positions and approaches different from our own, but also in living in close proximity to people who may, frankly, be quite annoying. Theologian Julia Brumbaugh, in an interview at a conference dedicated to working on polarized disagreement within the Catholic Church, said she wants to attend Mass "with people who make my blood boil."[7] If our quest for genuine humility is a serious one, we must work on being in the presence of people who challenge us—even on matters we hold dear.

As we saw above, operating with awareness of our finitude and sin will also means paying close attention to *the means* by which we accomplish our goals. Far too often we can become so blinded by the genuine goodness of our goals that we uncritically assume the means by which we pursue them must also be good. Helping infertile couples have children is an overwhelmingly positive good, for instance, but far too often the practices we use to achieve this goal involve deep injustice for the most vulnerable. From the embryos who are thrown away after *in vitro* fertilization, to the impoverished women who are often used simply as incubators, there are many populations who get overlooked in our prideful attempts to pursue this good goal. Or consider the good goal of lowering the prices of goods so that those without substantial resources can have access to them. Far too often, attempts to achieve this goal overlook the worker who is not paid a living wage or the long-term ecological impact of the way the goods are produced. Resisting pride in these contexts means taking a hard look around for those whose voices and interests are absent from consideration giving them their full due and weight. It also means acknowledging the difficulty of anticipating the medium- and long-term results of our actions. What may seem to be harmless practice to us may, in fact, turn out in the long run to be quite harmful.

But, again, this seems like a tall order, especially in terms of naming specific actions as sins. Can we really take into consideration the results of our actions that are so difficult to anticipate? Here, I think, is where the virtue of faith looms large. Without checking our consciences at the door, we should lean on the Wisdom of God and God's Church. We should listen to God during time spent in quiet prayer and discernment. We should listen and wrestle with God's Holy Spirit working through Scripture and the teachings of the Church Christ gave us, perhaps especially when these

---

7. Una Ecclesia, "Una Ecclesia," from the Polarization in the U.S. Catholic Church: Naming the Wounds, Beginning to Heal Conference, filmed September 2015, YouTube video, 12:07, posted September 15, 2015, https://www.youtube.com/watch?v=yDmpWp_X7o0.

teachings seem deeply "inconvenient" in our lives. We should learn and wrestle with the tradition of the holy and learned women and men of God. There may be rare circumstances in which our well-formed, humble conscience calls us to something at odds with these sources, but if we are truly resisting the vice of pride with the virtue of faith, we will give them every benefit of the doubt we possibly can.

How might this play out in the real world? Discussion of "our sinfulness" and "self-deception" and "undue" pride are necessary starting points for this discussion, but now let's explore how this plays out in practical situations, so that we are better able to name precisely the sins we commit rooted in pride.

Exceptionless Moral Rules

Our pride may affect how we think about and reflect on moral rules. Moral rules aren't exactly popular in the culture of the contemporary West. This is especially true when such rules don't allow for exceptions. For many people, accepting a rule without an exception signals a kind of unthinking, simplistic reliance on institutional authority. And those who advocate for such rules are often looked at with suspicion. Why do they want to control people's lives? Why don't they respect the autonomy and freedom of the individual to make her own decisions? And why do these rules always seem to have something to do with sex or other "conservative" obsessions?

But given the chance to reflect more deeply, many of these same people end up agreeing that we need exceptionless moral rules. For instance, most are rightly horrified when thinking about exceptions to the rule against torture, killing the innocent, or having sex with someone without their consent. Some goods are just so important, and some evils just so terrible, that we need exceptionless rules in order to uphold the values and resist the evils in every circumstance.

Catholic moral theology insists on a host of rules which uphold these values and resist these evils. And it turns out the rules are neither politically "conservative" nor obsessed with sex. Here are a few examples:

- It is always wrong to kill the innocent.
- Sex must always be open to procreation.
- It is always wrong to torture someone.
- War must always be defensive.
- Rape is always wrong.
- Racism is always wrong.
- Slavery is always wrong.

- Sex is only morally acceptable with one's (sole) spouse.
- Lending of money at interest which exploits the borrower is always wrong.

Many readers will find rules here that they like *and* don't like. Their objection is not to *the very idea* of exceptionless moral rules, but rather to the supposed exceptionless nature of moral rules *they believe* should have exceptions. Perhaps a banker should be able to lend money however the market demands, and if the borrower makes a poor decision that isn't the banker's problem. Perhaps assisted suicide, though it kills an innocent person, is sometimes necessary to avoid suffering. And, for the love of all things holy, perhaps the Catholic Church—and its celibate leadership—ought to stay out of people's bedrooms and let them make their own sexual choices.

These objections lift up our individual powers of conscience and reason over the Church's exceptionless moral rules. But if one doesn't first wrestle with the wisdom of the Church and the holy women and men of God throughout the ages, then our prideful nature risks deceiving us as to what is actually going on when we appeal to conscience for exceptions to these rules. Are we really doing the right thing or merely acting out of self-interest? Are we making a genuine effort to look around for the vulnerable and voiceless populations who may be hurt and giving adequate weight to their interests? Have we sufficiently thought about the long-term consequences of our actions? Far too often the answers to these questions is no. Self-interested and short-sighted reasoning—as noted above, driven by the blindness induced by pride—turns out to actually be running the show.

Resistance or disagreement on these issues may not involve the sin of pride. It may be a genuine wrestling in conscience with difficult questions. Yet because of our own tendency to deceive ourselves, it is important to allow the tradition to make us uncomfortable on these points. Thus, to examine ourselves for the sin of pride, we need to pay close attention to the arguments the tradition presents in defense of these norms. Let's take a closer look at a few.

Usury

Though moral theologians disagree about the precise definition of usury, in general it refers to the lending at money in ways which exploit the person who is borrowing money. The *Compendium of the Social Doctrine of the Church* strongly condemns the practice, noting that exploitive loans have a stranglehold on the lives of many people, including in developing countries.[8] The condemnation of usury is so serious that, if financial problems as a result of the loan lead to death, then the lender is guilty of "indirect homicide." Pope Leo XIII brings up usury early in *Rerum Novarum* as a key component of the misery of the working class, and lays it directly at the feet of "covetous and grasping men."[9] In *Caritas in Veritate*, Pope Benedict XVI highlights how a global system of finance uses usury to exploit the poor.[10]

In the United States, and the West more generally, we often consider these kinds of moral concerns strange, even archaic. Shouldn't the market determine how much it should cost a borrower to get a loan? If the borrower makes a poor decision, critics of the Church's teaching might respond by saying "buyer beware" and insist that consumers suffer the consequences of their poor choices. That's what makes market efficiency work, and our economy simply couldn't function without an efficient credit market. After all, as a result of this market, ordinary people can own cars and homes and attend very good colleges and universities, despite not having the cash on hand to purchase them outright. This is a very good thing, isn't it? It is a shame that a few people make bad decisions, but the only way to make the credit market efficient enough to bring about these very good things is to allow the market to function. That will hurt some people, yes, but overall it will be so much better for the majority.

And while it is true that credit markets produce much good, they also make room for great evil. From college student loan debt on the verge of crushing a generation,[11] to predatory payday loans taking advantage of desperate poor people,[12] many millions are hurt by these markets as well. Our practice of paying close attention to the means by which we accomplish a good goal, and the missing voices and vulnerable populations who may be hurt by this means, looms large.

But perhaps even more important is the failure to take into account long-term considerations. The well-off get lower interest rates, pay back their debt more quickly, and pay less interest, but the less-well-off get higher interest rates, take much longer to pay back their debt, and pay

---

8. Pontifical Council for Peace and Justice, *Compendium of the Social Doctrine of the Church* (June 29, 2004).

9. Leo XIII, Encyclical Letter *Rerum Novarum* (May 15, 1891), 3.

10. Benedict XVI, Encyclical Letter *Caritas in Veritate* (June 29, 2009).

11. Mark Kantrowitz, "Why the Student Loan Crisis is Even Worse than People Think," *Time*, January 11, 2016, http://time.com/money/4168510/why-student-loan-crisis-is-worse-than-people-think / (accessed November 30, 2016).

12. LastWeekTonight, "Predatory Lending: Last Week Tonight with John Oliver (HBO)," filmed August 2014, YouTube video, 16:31, posted August 10, 2014, https://www.youtube.com/watch?v=PDylgzybWAw.

more interest. Over time, this not only dramatically enriches financial institutions, it contributes to an inequality gap unlike anything we have seen since the Gilded Age.[13] Furthermore, a strong argument could be made that a usurious mentality led to the financial crisis of 2008. At its heart was the widespread practice of banks giving out home loans to vulnerable people they *knew* would be exploited by the terms of the loan. To add insult to injury, certain profiteers began using credit default swaps to bet on the fact that these vulnerable people would default on the loan, lose their home, and have their credit devastated. The covetous and grasping men who engaged in these practices set off a global chain reaction of events which would erase an astonishing $15 *trillion*.[14]

Those who facilitate and benefit from these lending practices—from the head of JP Morgan Chase to local bankers in small rural branches—might name their own sin of usury here and work to change the financial culture to one that benefits (rather than exploits) the most vulnerable.

Assisted Suicide

As various states continue to pass (and attempt to pass) laws permitting assisted suicide, this debate looms large in US public discourse. While many agree such laws require strict safeguards against abuse, they nevertheless find it difficult to imagine why anyone would think there should be an exceptionless rule against assisted suicide. California recently legalized the practice while riding the wave of energy coming from the story of Brittany Maynard, a young woman with a devastating and likely fatal brain tumor who moved from California to Oregon so physicians could help her end her life. Who can be unmoved by stories like this? Why would anyone deny her the right to end her life? Again, all agree a law which permitted her to do so should have safeguards so it isn't abused, but shouldn't assisted suicide be something we carefully undertake so that people like Brittany aren't put into such terrible positions?

But, again, if we are to resist our prideful natures, we must be hyper-aware of the voiceless and vulnerable populations who may be hurt by our actions—while also keeping in mind long-term consequences. Of course,

13. Alexander Eichler, "Income Inequality Reaches Gilded Age Levels, Congressional Report Finds," *Huffington Post*, October 26, 2011, http://www.huffingtonpost.com/2011/10/26/income-inequality _n_1032632.html (accessed November 30, 2016).

14. Al Yoon, "Total Global Losses from Financial Crisis: $15 Trillion," *Wall Street Journal*, October 1, 2012, http://blogs.wsj.com/economics/2012/10/01/total-global-losses-from-financial-crisis-15-trillion/ (accessed November 30, 2016). For more on how to name sins rooted in this covetousness and its structural dynamics, see Nichole Flores's chapter on greed in this volume.

any good-hearted person is moved by the possibility of dying a painful death, but it turns out that in Oregon (where assisted suicide has been legal for a generation) pain doesn't even make the top five reasons people request assisted suicide. In almost all circumstances, palliative care can control the pain, while in the exceptional cases palliative sedation can be a compassionate response which does not kill an innocent person.

According to Oregon's public health department, the top reasons given for assisted suicide are loss of autonomy (91.5%), decreased ability to engage in enjoyable activities (88.7%), loss of dignity (79.3%), loss of control of body (50.1%) and becoming a burden on others (40%). In the United States, we've created a culture that worships freedom, autonomy and productivity, and pushes the vulnerable people who don't fit that picture to the margins. Is it any wonder that the poor, blacks and Latinos, and disability rights groups are skeptical of assisted suicide?[15] Think in particular about the message we are sending disabled people; each time a state tries to legalize assisted suicide, the rhetoric used directly states that if you lose your autonomy and control of your body—and become a burden on others—then you lose your dignity and should consider killing yourself.[16]

Notice that it is virtually impossible to logically contain this reasoning within the safeguards mentioned above. Both Oregon and California have laws which mandate that one must be within six months of death in order to get help to commit suicide, but what is the basis for that limit? Places like Belgium and the Netherlands, for instance, started out with similar safeguards with their laws permitting the practice—but blew right past them. Now the Dutch can get assisted suicide simply because they are going blind[17] and Belgians can get it simply for having suicidal thoughts.[18]

True to this trend, Oregon recently attempted to expand the threshold from six months to twelve months, but failed due in part to strong opposition from groups *in favor* of assisted suicide overall. The president of Death with Dignity in Portland, for instance, said that such an expansion

15. "Opinion about Laws on Doctor-Assisted Suicide," *Pew Research Center*, November 21, 2013, http://www.pewforum.org/2013/11/21/chapter-1-opinion-about-laws-on-doctor-assisted-suicide / (accessed November 30, 2016).

16. Portions of what follows below comes from Charles C. Camosy, "California's Right-to-die Law Betrays the Stay's Progressive Principles," *Los Angeles Times*, October 7, 2015, http://www.latimes.com /opinion/op-ed/la-oe-camosy-the-wrong-right-to-die-decision-20151007-story.html (accessed November 30, 2016).

17. Simon Caldwell, "Doctors Administered Lethal Injection to Blind Dutch Woman," *Daily Mail*, October 7, 2013, http://www.dailymail.co.uk/news/article-2448611/Blind-Dutch-woman-euthanised -loss-sight.html (accessed November 30, 2016).

18. Melissa Chan, "Belgian Woman, 24, Granted Right to Die By Euthanasia Over Suicidal Thoughts," *New York Daily News*, June 30, 2015, http://www.nydailynews.com/news/world/belgium-woman -24-granted-euthanasia-death-depression-article-1.2276577 (accessed November 30, 2016).

would send the wrong message to lawmakers in other states. "You just run the risk of the slippery-slope argument big time," he said.[19] Pro-assisted suicide groups are artificially limiting the natural progression of the legislation until it passes in other states, but this won't last forever. The social forces which produced the disasters in the Netherlands and Belgium will eventually be unleashed on Oregon and California. And it won't be pretty. One Belgian legal expert warned that the right to die is "going to become a kind of obligation."[20] Once the euthanasia crack opened, he said, it has just kept getting wider.

Obviously, those who directly participate in assisted suicide practices and legislation should name their sin in this regard. But that doesn't let the rest of us off the hook. To the extent we contribute to a youth- and autonomy-worshiping culture which pushes the sick, elderly, and otherwise dependent to the margins, we are also blameworthy and should name our sin.

Connecting Sex and Procreation

Perhaps the exceptionless rule for which the Church gets the most flak is that sex and procreation must always be connected. Among other things, this general rule leads to the prohibition of artificial contraception and certain reproductive technologies. For almost everyone, including the overwhelming majority of Catholics, these two things are so obviously good that they don't even need an argument justifying them. Who could be against the good of protecting against sexually transmitted diseases and unplanned pregnancies (and, by extension, abortions)? Who could be against the good of giving infertile couples hope for having a biologically related child? The fact that the Church promotes exceptionless rules which stand firmly against these practices, for many people, is the best evidence that Catholic leaders live in a world where things are far too simple. Not least because they are celibate, but maybe because they are simply disconnected from a more complex sexual reality coming out of the lived experience of those who have had sex.

There is no denying the goods mentioned above, but in the long run do the means proposed actually help us achieve them? The use of artificial

19. Jeff Mapes, "Bill to Expand Oregon's Death with Dignity Act Runs into a Buzz Saw of Opposition," *The Oregonian/Oregon Live*, March 4, 2015, http://www.oregonlive.com/mapes/index.ssf/2015/03/bil l_to_expand_oregons_death_w.html.

20. Graeme Hamilton, "'Suicide with the Approval of Society:' Belgian Warns of Slippery Slope as Euthanasia Becomes 'Normal,'" *National Post*, November 24, 2013, http://news.nationalpost.com /news/canada/suicide-with-the-approval-of-society-belgian-activist-warns-of-slippery-slope-as -euthanasia -becomes-normal (accessed November 30, 2016).

contraception has increased in recent decades, but the rates of STI's has increased right along with it. In fact, in some places such infections are at record levels,[21] and there is some evidence to show that introducing contraception into a population actually increases the kind of risky sex that leads to STIs.[22] There is evidence contraception (when used correctly) leads to fewer unintended pregnancies, but according to Europe's leading medical journal in reproductive medicine natural family planning (also when used correctly) is just as effective.[23] And it turns out that countries and states with the highest use of contraception actually have higher rates of abortion.[24] We can't be totally sure of the reason, but one plausible theory is that widespread use of contraception leads to something called the "contraceptive" mentality—in which sex is so disconnected from procreation that abortion becomes the "fail safe" in keeping one's sexual practices from leading to responsibility for a child.

So, when it comes to sex, our prideful natures can blind us even with regard to whether we are *actually achieving* our stated goals. And what about *the means* we employ to achieve those goals? How might they affect the vulnerable? For starters, the burden of contraception generally falls upon women,[25] and the birth control pill in particular can wreak both short- and long-term havoc on women's bodies.[26] Widespread use of contraception, along with the (false) belief that it makes "safe sex" possible, has also led to normalizing the "hook up." In some of the most important areas of popular culture (including on-demand online porn), our culture is taught that the most desirable sex is literally the use of another for their body, no strings attached. Many of my students have literally no idea what it

21. Youssef Rddad, "STD Rates in Minnesota Reach a New Record," *Star Tribune*, April 11, 2016, http://www.startribune.com/std-rates-in-minnesota-reach-a-new-record/375282141/ (accessed November 30, 2016).

22. Edward C. Green, "Condoms, HIV-AIDS and Africa - The Pope was Right," *Washington Post*, March 29, 2009, http://www.washingtonpost.com/wp-dyn/content/article/2009/03/27/AR2009032702825. html (accessed November 30, 2016).

23. "Natural Family Planning Method as Effective as Contraception, New Research Finds," *Science Daily*, February 1, 2007, https://www.sciencedaily.com/releases/2007/02/070221065200.htm (accessed November 30, 2016).

24. Megan McArdle, "Free Contraception Can't End the Abortion Debate," *Bloomberg*, August 7, 2015, https://www.bloomberg.com/view/articles/2015-08-07/free-contraception-can-t-end-the-abortion -debate (accessed November 30, 2016).

25. Kay Steiger, "Why Are There So Few Birth Control Options for Men?" *Jezebel*, August 28, 2009, http://jezebel.com/5347882/why-are-there-so-few-birth-control-options-for-men (accessed November 30, 2016).

26. Lizzie Crocker, "Should You Quit the Pill?" *Daily Beast*, November 6, 2011, http://www .thedailybeast.com/articles/2011/11/06/new-study-highlights-birth-control-pill-s-negative-side -effects.html (accessed November 30, 2016).

means to date someone, but they know all about the games that are played in order to get a pornified "hook up." And the most disturbing aspect of the hook-up culture is how easily it leads to sexual violence. A cultural green light to use another person's body as a mere thing, combined with alcohol or other drugs (usually an essential part of the hook-up culture) has had tragically predictable consequences. Adelaide Mena and Caitlin Seery La Ruffa put it this way:

> But once we get used to heedlessly using one another's bodies, it is dangerously easy to see using another's body for our own gratification as unproblematic, even if the other person isn't doing the same to us. A hook-up culture based on mutual use and lack of consequence can't help but lead in the direction of unilateral use of another's body.[27]

Is it really any surprise that experience of sexual violence for first-year college women is at "epidemic" levels?[28]

But even if we were to concede that the Church might be onto something in claiming we have lost something intrinsic about sex when it is not connected to procreation, it still doesn't follow that all procreation needs to be connected to sex. Especially because of economic pressures unique to our current times, many people feel forced to delay childbearing and therefore disproportionately run into the pain of infertility. What possible reason could we have for denying these hurting people a chance to bear and raise a child?

But when we look hard at the means by which we accomplish this very good goal, we again find deep moral problems. Our current practices of creating embryos via *in vitro* fertilization end up absolutely terrible for all kinds of vulnerable populations. Most obvious in this scenario are the "excess" members of the species *Homo sapiens* who are created, but not implanted, and then simply thrown away. And in an era where we can use technology to do a "genetic diagnosis" of such embryos, they can be thrown away simply because they may have a disability or other undesirable trait. This is not only obviously horrific with regard to embryos who are discarded as so much trash, but also sends a horrific message to disabled-but-older members of the *Homo sapiens* family who have the very same genetic traits.

27. Adelaide Mena and Caitlin La Ruffa, "Sexual Assault: What Does the Hook-Up Culture Have to Do with It?" *Public Discourse*, July 16, 2014, http://www.thepublicdiscourse.com/2014/07/13505 / (accessed November 30, 2016).

28. Abby Ohlheiser, "Study Finds 'Epidemic' of Sexual Assault among First-Year Women at One U.S. College," *Washington Post*, May 20, 2015, https://www.washingtonpost.com/news/grade-point /wp/2015/05/20/study-finds-epidemic-of-sexual-assault-among-first-year-women-at-one-u-s-college / (accessed November 30, 2016).

Furthermore, depending on the infertility involved, many attempts to have a child with artificial reproductive technology involve the use of a surrogate mother. And when the logic of the market is applied, this becomes just a transaction in which a woman's womb is literally rented for money. Legal contracts designed to regulate the transaction are drawn up, some which mandate that the surrogate mother must have an abortion if the baby is found to have a disability like Down syndrome.[29] Abuse and exploitation can be even worse when a rich Western couple rents the womb of a poor woman from the developing world much more cheaply.[30] The problems of exploitation got so bad in Sweden that even that very secular country is on the verge of totally banning the practice.[31]

And by now we know that we also need to ask ourselves about the long-term consequences of these practices. If the practice of creating children apart from sex continues along its current trajectory, where is it likely to end up? It seems reasonable to assume that we will get even better at making sure our children have the traits we want and not the traits we don't want. Once artificial wombs are created (an artificial placenta may be only about ten years away[32]), the baby-making process could take place apart from any real human interaction. Indeed, given the dramatic rise of robots even in our own time, it is reasonable to assume that a generation from now robots will run the laboratories in which new, made-to-order humans would be created.

If current trends continue, the script will be flipped in terms of which method of reproduction would be normal and which abnormal. The 1997 movie *Gattaca*—which predicted a dystopian future in which technology completely controls our reproductive practices—suggested that the way we currently have children will eventually be undertaken only by religious fanatics who don't agree that we need total quality control over our offspring. I often watch this movie with my medical ethics students at the end of the semester and, given what they have learned about our culture's

29. Beth Greenfield, "California Couple Shares Surrogate Story in the Wake of Thailand Controversy," *Yahoo!*, October 17, 2014, https://www.yahoo.com/beauty/california-couple-shares-surrogate-story-in-wake-of-95207128652.html (accessed November 30, 2016).

30. Arthur Caplan, "Paid Surrogacy is Exploitative," *New York Times*, September 23, 2014, http://www.nytimes.com/roomfordebate/2014/09/22/hiring-a-woman-for-her-womb/paid-surrogacy-is-exploitative (accessed November 30, 2016).

31. Kajsa Ekis Ekman, "All Surrogacy is Exploitation—The World Should Follow Sweden's Ban," *Guardian*, February 25, 2016, http://www.theguardian.com/commentisfree/2016/feb/25/surrogacy-sweden-ban (accessed November 30, 2016).

32. Beata Mostafavi, "Artificial Placenta Holds Promise for Extremely Premature Infants," *University of Michigan Health Lab*, April 27, 2016, http://labblog.uofmhealth.org/health-tech/artificial-placenta-holds-promise-for-extremely-premature-infants (accessed November 30, 2016).

current reproductive trajectory, many find it difficult to see how we avoid this kind of future without holding firm to the idea that procreation must be connected with sex.

Now, the cases I've presented on each of the three topics aren't knock-down arguments that will convince any reasonable person. Making a full case would involve a book-length project for each topic. But, especially given what we've seen is involved in the vice of pride, what has been presented should at least give us pause. Should we really trust in our own ability to pick out the vulnerable people, nonhuman creatures, and even places, hurt by our practices? Even in the short-term we can be blinded by self-interest and self-deception, and our limited ability to anticipate how people may be hurt in the future is even more problematic. The exception-less rules the Church proposes are not naïve attempts to control others based on arbitrary, outdated principles. To the contrary, they come from a tradition of wisdom which itself comes from centuries of experience and God's inspired direction. If we seek to name our sins of pride, we should begin with posture of faith and openness to the wisdom of this tradition before substituting our own judgment.

Social Media

That social media is quickly replacing other forms of interaction is so obvious that it hardly needs to be mentioned. Whole lives are narrated on Facebook. Presidential campaigns are dominated by Twitter. Within some communities, if there isn't a picture of an event somewhere on social media, "it didn't happen."[33] Any serious attempt to resist the vice of pride, if it is to be relevant to our current age, must therefore name the sins appearing because of our culture's turn to social media.

The first step is to see the *full* dignity of the person. People are complex, unable to be captured by their Instagram account, Facebook wall, or Tweets over the past week. This full dignity must be put ahead of our typical social media practice, which often exacerbates our natural sinful tendency to put people into narrow and dismissible boxes:

"Oh, now I get it, they're a hypocritical limousine liberal."

"See, see! I told you the only people who believe this stuff are religious fanatics!"

"Ugh. More nonsense from a cis white male."

"Well, what would we expect from low-information voters?"

33. Jacob Silverman, "Pics or It Didn't Happen – The Mantra of the Instagram Era," *Guardian*, February 26, 2015, http://www.theguardian.com/news/2015/feb/26/pics-or-it-didnt-happen-mantra-instagram -era-facebook-twitter (accessed November 30, 2016).

"This stuff comes from the elites, so it must be designed to keep me down."

If we are committed to the view that we have something to learn from our perceived opponents, most often what is available to us about them via social media just isn't enough.

Furthermore, the tendency to put others in dismissible social media boxes leads directly to seeing them through an "us versus them" lens—one in which we get much of our identity from being against them. The kinds of challenges (and, indeed, insults) we are able to marshal on social media are almost invariably far too simplistic for the full reality of complex issues which divide us. Predictably, the response from our perceived opponents will also be limited by the simplistic medium, thus perpetuating the cycle of shallow social media violence.

And notice the violent discourse we find on social media is most often perpetuated by those who aren't aware of the hurt and pain they may be causing another person. We can be sitting on our laptops watching Netflix or on our smartphones walking to the gym, hit send, and watch all the likes and hearts pour in from "our side"—but often the very nature of the medium keeps us from understanding what we are doing to real-life people on the "other side." If we are truly committed to resisting the vice of pride, we should be hyper-aware of the limitations of our point of view and our capacity for self-deception, and take every reasonable opportunity to engage the full reality of the other person. Often, this will mean refusing to let social media be the primary way we interact with them. Personal, embodied relationships are the way to go if we are to be truly challenged by a genuine encounter with someone who thinks differently.

Recall also the commitment we should have to genuinely diverse political and theological communities. When it comes to social media, this means making conscious efforts to connect with people who do more than simply confirm our biases and join in on the hit parade against "the other side." We should resist the urge to unfollow, defriend, or mute people who make our blood boil, but instead embrace it as a chance to resist our pride and be genuinely challenged by a point of view we find distasteful.

Beyond this prideful tendency to dismiss others, the even more obvious place where the vice of pride intersects with social media is oversharing and raw self-promotion. At a very basic level, there is nothing wrong with using social media as a method of sharing your thoughts and experiences. We are made to be in relationships with others, and it would be strange if a flourishing person didn't want to share one's self with others via these new media. Done well, social media can simply provide a new and healthy way to do that.

But what does "doing it well" look like? Recall that pride is concerned with "inordinate and unjustified belief in yourself." If all you're doing on social media is promoting your own ideas and experiences, this is clearly "inordinate" and ought to be balanced by promoting the ideas and experiences of others. It also means taking a hard, in-depth, critical look at your goals in sharing your ideas and experiences. There is nothing wrong with promoting good things about yourself online, but here's a good test: is such sharing aimed at genuine relationship? Or might it be aimed at trying to create on online persona, one quite different from the person you actually are? This projection of yourself on social media is literally "unjustified" by the facts. Genuine relationships are based on truth, not misleading or even false personae made possible by thin media like Instagram, Facebook, and Twitter. I recently saw someone who claimed to be "much more interesting online than in person." Resisting the vice of pride means refusing to cave to the temptation to create a misleading or false self via social media, as wonderful as this person might be considered by one's friends and followers. Social media can be a wonderful tool for healthy sharing of who we are with others, but in order for it to be healthy, it must be authentic.

The Nation-State

Human beings have been created to become our best selves when in relationships with others, and that we find such relationships in our communities and associations is a very good thing. We simply can't be who we are without being a part of communities and associations. But, as discussed above, the vice of pride enters the picture when our attachment to such associations becomes inordinate and unjustified. Indeed, perhaps because of just how deeply necessary communities and associations are for human flourishing, our attachment to them poses a special risk for sins rooted in the vice of pride. We end up valuing these connections so much that they end up taking a much higher place in our lives than they should. A particular community or association can even become our source of ultimate concern, replacing our relationship with God. Even more nefariously, we can end up worshiping a false god who uncritically affirms our communities and associations. This is the very definition of idolatry.

We've seen above how this can happen with our political party and even our religious community. But perhaps the most widespread example is our connection to the nation-state. There is nothing wrong, of course with taking justified pride in the good things for which one's country stands. It would be foolish to deny the fact that United States has done great things for its citizens and for others around the world. The problem comes when we move from justified praise to elevating the good of our nation-state beyond its due limits. During my time as a high school teacher, for instance, the president of the school once claimed in a newsletter that the founding documents of the United States were "divinely inspired." President Ronald Reagan tried to lift American spirits in by encouraging us to think of our country as the Biblical "shining city on a hill," inspiring the rest of the world. Of course, God cares deeply about Americans, and has blessed us with many wonderful gifts, but idolatrous attachment to our nation-state can lead to a prideful insistence that God has made us special. That God is somehow on "our side" in ways that God is not on "their side."

This has dangerous implications, not least because of the idea that what is good for our nation-state is necessarily what God wills—and therefore what we ought to pursue. Consider our national debate about immigrants and refugees. What should our stance be toward these groups of fellow human beings? On the one hand, if one takes the "America First" stance of Donald Trump's stunning 2016 run to the White House, one can make a strong argument that what benefits the country most of all is having clear and strong border protection which keeps out foreigners who take our jobs, lower our wages, don't speak our language, don't share our values, and may be trying to use violence to destabilize our country. Think the final point is over the top? Groups like ISIS have already used refugee status to gain admittance to European countries they mean to destabilize through terrorism, and the problem has bubbled up occasionally even here in the United States.[34] Those who put "America First" are actually not wrong to advocate for strict measures about who can and cannot enter the country, even if these measures end up excluding the most vulnerable.

But Christian Americans, at least if they are not making an idol out of the good of their country, are called to "put first" some different values. Christ, and the tradition of His Church could not be more clear: we are commanded to welcome the stranger. Indeed, Christ tells us that it is as the vulnerable stranger—as one of the least among us—that He comes to be in our midst. When we contribute to exclusion of the vulnerable stranger, we contribute to the exclusion of Christ. This is obviously problematic for someone who claims to have their faith as their source of ultimate concern. Indeed, it is a sin we ought to name.

Might some American Christians—especially those espousing who favor building a wall and having mass deportation—respond rather harshly to this proposition? Wouldn't they claim that, without a wall, the

---

34. Catherine E. Shoichet, "Feds Arrest 2 Middle East Refugees on Terror-Related Charges," *CNN*, January 8, 2016, http://www.cnn.com/2016/01/07/us/terror-charges-refugees/ (accessed November 30, 2016).

borders between the United States and Mexico will simply continue to be porous and fuzzy? Won't we continue to have immigration that is beyond our control, and therefore a national boundary and cultural identity that is beyond our control? Won't we risk letting in terrorists who want to destabilize our country through terrorism? Doesn't this mean that, regrettably, we must exclude the vulnerable in the interests of national security and national identity?

The answers to all these questions is Yes, excepting the final one. God's command to welcome the stranger is not without risk, especially when it comes to the good of the nation-state, but Christians are called to put God's commands first. Yes, the community we have as Americans is a very good thing. But this otherwise good attachment risks becoming disordered by the vice of prideful idolatry when we put the flourishing the nation-state ahead of our very clear Christian commitments. The attachment we have to our national identity, at that point, has become inordinate and unjustified.

And once we commit to looking at the world through this particular pride-busting lens, we see that our problems go well beyond how we respond to immigrants and refugees. Much of the war-like violence we Americans support (or, perhaps even worse, turn a blind eye to) is also bound up with idolatrous, prideful attachment to the nation-state. And consider other questionable ways we rely on violence: from torture, to police actions, to the death penalty, to mass incarceration, Christians often get too comfortable with values and practices that are at odds with the nonviolence and concern for the vulnerable to which our Master and Teacher Jesus Christ calls us.

Conclusion: Resisting Pride is Rooted in Faith

Pope Francis' wonderful example of beginning with naming himself as a sinner is the "that without which" we cannot hope to resist the vice of pride. This vice is deeply embedded in fallen human nature, and can powerfully shape even a well-meaning, smart, otherwise good person into the kind of person who simply cannot see how their goals and actions exploit the most vulnerable. It is this basic insight—that we are all sinners—which lays the foundation for all else in this chapter. Perhaps this insight can lead us to look again at the example of Francis, someone who even as pope makes a very big and public deal of his regularly receiving the sacrament of Reconciliation. That such a practice is so out of favor in today's culture is itself yet another example of how strongly we find ourselves in grips of the vice of pride!

But let's conclude by making something explicit that thus far may have been only implicit: resisting pride and embracing humility is not a matter of cutting ourselves down or denying ourselves happiness. Indeed, it is rather our prideful choices and behavior which lead to distortion of the self, along with deep and powerful *unhappiness*. The exercise of humility that may look like weakness to others, especially those in a Western secular culture with the very different understanding of pride, is actually strength. In his second letter to the Corinthians, St. Paul holds up Jesus' faithful example of following the command of God to empty himself. For, Paul notes, we are like Jesus in that when we give ourselves over to God—making our own powers weak—it is then that we become strong.

Putting our faith in the Wisdom of God and God's Church may look to some as if we are weak-minded lemmings who are blindly following an authority figure down an irrational and harmful path. But, as we have seen above, it is the vice of pride which leads us to irrationally conclude that we can simply rely on our own individual, rational judgement. Our finite and sinful natures cannot bear the weight our pride puts on them. Self-deception and confirmation bias mean that most often we see what we expect to see, and what we expect to see is just as often determined by self-interest. Our faith in God and in God's Church, however, is a bulwark against the prideful part of ourselves which is so easily deceived. Humbly resisting this part of who we are, therefore, is not about hatred or loathing of the self. On the contrary, it is a necessary first step toward lifting up the best and most life-giving parts of who we are.

Chapter 9

Confessions of a Priest

The Unused Potential of the Rite of Penance

Fr. James Donohue, CR

O RDAINED IN 1983, I have presided and participated in the sacraments revised in accord with the directives of the Second Vatican Council. For the most part, my experience of the celebration of the sacraments has been a very positive one. I could provide clear personal testimony about how countless people (including myself) over the years have been enriched by the celebration of the sacraments. Whether it be a weekday or Sunday Eucharist, a baptism of a newborn infant or an adult who has journeyed through the Rite of Christian Initiation of Adults (RCIA), a confirmation at the Easter Vigil, a marriage with or without the Eucharist, or the anointing of the sick in an individual or communal setting, I have found that the sacraments have provided tangible moments for people to encounter Christ in ways that authentically touch their lives. By this, I mean that there seems to be a clear connection between the liturgy and the lives of people celebrating the liturgy. The real-life experiences of people are brought to the liturgy, potentially transforming these experiences so that people "return" to the world differently. Encountering Christ in the liturgy leads to the possibility that people will be more closely conformed to Christ, and it is these transformed people who return to life after the liturgy.

I have often wondered why my experience of the sacrament of reconciliation is not as transformative. The uneasiness cannot be pinned on the smaller number of people who, compared to previous decades, celebrate the sacrament. Indeed, while sacramental reconciliation has declined, liturgists and theologians are divided in their evaluation of whether this is a negative or positive sign. Some would argue, for instance, that two important reforms of the Eucharist have had an effect on the frequency of the use of the sacrament of penance. First, the Eucharistic reforms included the retrieval of some liturgical elements such as the sign of peace where people now are actively reflecting upon the need to forgive and be forgiven before approaching the Table of the Lord. Second, since the Eucharist is celebrated in the vernacular, it has become clearer that the Eucharist itself is for the forgiveness of sins, and that its forgiving and reconciling aspects—that is, the penitential rite, the Lord's Prayer, and the Lamb of God sequence before communion—became more obvious, helping people to realize that the forgiveness of sins can be sought in other sacraments besides the sacrament of penance.[1] These types of reforms of the Eucharist prompted people to ask why they had to seek mercy and forgiveness in the confessional box or the reconciliation room.

There are other theological changes that potentially led to the shift in the sacrament of penance. For example, as the introduction to this book notes, there was a huge shift in people's understanding of sin from what we might call a "rule-based ethic" to a "relationship-based ethic" as well as a changed understanding of what constitutes mortal sin and the frequency that people might commit mortal sin. In addition, as writings of Scripture and the Church Fathers became more accessible, people learned of the many "ordinary ways" that sin could be forgiven: works of charity in the form of prayer, fasting, and almsgiving—for their practice "covers a multitude of sins" (1 Pt 4:8).[2]

Certainly, the problems facing the celebration of the sacrament of penance are not so blatant as to hold that people do not encounter Christ in this sacrament. People who celebrate the sacrament do have an encounter with Christ in compassion and mercy, and this experience is a transformational one as they move from sacramental celebration to the living of life. Yet it seems that something lies deeper at the root of my discontent. I would maintain that people who celebrate the Rite of Penance, through sign and symbol, do not have the same opportunity to realize as fully the potential of being transformed in Christ as they do in other sacraments.

1. See United States Catholic Conference of Bishops, *The Rite of Penance* (Washington, DC: United States Catholic Conference, 1975), 2, which states: "In the sacrifice of the Mass the passion of Christ is again made present; his body given for us and his blood shed for the forgiveness of sins are offered to God again by the Church for the salvation of the world. For in the Eucharist Christ is present and is offered as 'the sacrifice which has made our peace with God' and in order that 'we may be brought together in unity' by his Holy Spirit."

2. In fact, the *Catechism of the Catholic Church* includes these ordinary ways to forgive sins (1433) as well as other various ways: "Conversion is accomplished in daily life by gestures of reconciliation, concern for the poor, the exercise and defense of justice and right, by the admission of faults to one's brethren, fraternal correction, revision of life, examination of conscience, spiritual direction, acceptance of suffering, endurance of persecution for the sake of righteousness. Taking up one's cross each day and following Jesus is the surest way of penance" (1435). And as I mentioned already, the Eucharist is a means for forgiveness: "Daily conversion and penance find their source and nourishment in the Eucharist, for in it is made present the sacrifice of Christ which has reconciled us with God" (1436).

What do I mean by this? Perhaps the challenge can be seen by recognizing how the meanings of baptism and Eucharist are meant to shape the experience of the Rite of Penance— but often enough do not do so clearly. Through baptism—especially when this is celebrated through immersion—we symbolically die to our old selves and come to new life in Christ. Early church baptismal fonts helped to shape people's imaginations in this way. They were often in the shape of a cross or an octagon (representing the day of the Resurrection on the "eighth day"). The font had steps that people walked down into the water, were submerged into it, and then walked up another set of steps to exit the font. These actions symbolized that the "old" self was "drowned" and the "new" self has been "raised to new life" in Christ. As St. Paul wrote:

> ...are you unaware that we who were baptized into Christ Jesus were baptized into his death? We were indeed buried with him through baptism into death, so that, just as Christ was raised from the dead by the glory of the Father, we too might live in newness of life. For if we have grown into union with him through a death like his, we shall also be united with him in the resurrection. (Rom 6:3–5)

Through baptism, Christians continue to recognize this pattern of living—suffering, death, and resurrection—and see this pattern as a way of imitating and conforming themselves to Christ in the actions of their daily lives.

Similarly, the Eucharist is the weekly (or, for some, the daily) manner that this action is repeated in the memorial of the Last Supper, where Jesus gives of himself in his suffering and death, trusting in God's faithfulness to raise Jesus to new life. The action of the Eucharist—breaking this bread and sharing this cup in memorial of Jesus whose body was broken and whose blood was poured out for all in service and sacrifice—reminds Christians that they are to imitate Jesus in their service and self-sacrifice for others, trusting that God will bring new life out of their suffering and dying to self in service to others. These repeated actions—and reflection upon these actions through the prism of the suffering, death, and resurrection of Jesus—makes the Christian, over time, more and more closely conformed to Christ. Ultimately, like St. Paul, they are able to exclaim, "I have been crucified with Christ; yet I live, no longer I, but Christ lives in me" (Gal 2:19–20).

These communal conformations to the self-giving patterns of Christ are supposed to be the context for entering into the sacrament of reconciliation. M. Francis Mannion, making note of the early reference to baptism and Eucharist in the Rite of Penance, states: "What is underscored in these quotations is the significance of sacramental initiation in effecting repentance, the forgiveness of sin, and reconciliation with God, and in bringing men and women into the community of the redeemed."[3] In baptism, a person is "plunged into the paschal mystery of Christ,"[4] receiving a share of new life, becoming a son or daughter of God and a member of the Church. It is through the Eucharist that Christians continue to meet and experience their ongoing incorporation into the reconciling Christ. Only after setting out this liturgical and ecclesial context of baptism and Eucharist does the introduction to the Rite of Penance begin to speak specifically about the sacrament of reconciliation.

In this context, sin is what separates us from Christ and his Body, the Church, which is wounded by our sins. But I think the tendency to celebrate the sacrament of reconciliation in its individual ritual form diminishes this social awareness of sin and of the celebration of the paschal mystery of dying and rising with Christ underscored in baptism and Eucharist because of a lack of a *liturgical* and *communal* experience that the other sacraments provide. I would point to the sacrament of the anointing of the sick as an example of what I am trying to express. I have anointed people in individual settings where it has seemed more perfunctory: the Rite of Anointing of the Sick is truncated, the person is alone and is the only recipient of the sacrament, the oil is present in a tiny container filled with a cotton ball, time is at a premium, and there has been little interaction between the minister and the sick person. But, I have also anointed people in communal settings every month where the Rite of Anointing of the Sick is celebrated fully with readings and intercessions, the community is present and many people are anointed, the oil is clearly observable in a glass bowl and is used more lavishly, and there is interaction before and after the sacrament, learning people's names and the struggles they are facing. I am not, of course, suggesting through this generalization that in one setting the sacrament is effective and in the other it is not. But, if God works through signs and symbols, the potential for God's healing and grace to become manifest is greater in one setting than in another. Hearing God's word of compassion and healing for the sick and marginalized, observing the touch of a husband on his wife's shoulder as she is anointed, praying not only for your own healing but the healing of the others who are present, and gathering as a community are tangible elements in the sacramental celebration that have a greater potential to assist the anointed person to encounter Christ fully through word, sacrament, and community.

---

3. M. Francis Mannion, "Penance and Reconciliation: A Systematic Analysis," *Worship* 60, no. 2 (March 1986): 101, citing *Sacrosantum Concilium*, no. 6.

4. Vatican Council II, *Sacrosantum Concilium* in *The Documents of Vatican II*, ed. Walter M. Abbott (New York: The America Press, 1966), 140.

In my view, in the Rite of Penance, we have a sacrament that was revised, but not adequately implemented as well as other reformed rituals. Kathleen Hughes summarizes this view when she writes that "as the last of the major rites to be revised, it found both clergy and community weary of change. It is understandable, human nature being what it is, that this ritual reform was downplayed, that the theological presuppositions were not developed, that the variety of ritual reforms was not exploited."[5] Thus, following on the insights above, I want to highlight the two key aspects of the sacrament of reconciliation that, if understood better, would enable people to recognize and name their sin at its deepest root and to experience the love, mercy, and forgiveness of God more easily and tangibly at that point so that healing remedies may be applied.[6] The first is that the sacrament seldom is *celebrated as a liturgy,* and the second is that we still need to go a long way to help people to see the *social dimension of sin* and the *communal nature of reconciliation* in the celebration of this sacrament.

The Rite of Penance is a Liturgy

I wonder how many penitents think of "going to confession" as the celebration of a liturgy. Indeed, it has the four usual parts—introductory rite, liturgy of the word, liturgy of the sacrament, and concluding rite—though some parts are short and, in most cases, some parts are not included in the celebration of the Rite of Penance by the penitent or presider. In a liturgy, the priest presider represents the community and acts as the community's host, as public minister, and presider of prayer. The rubrics for the Rite of Penance instruct that "when the penitent comes to confess his sins, the priest welcomes him warmly and greets him with kindness."[7] This opening gesture, though small, reminds the penitent at the outset that he or she is entering into a liturgy, in which Christ is present where two or more are gathered in his name. The kindly welcome and invitation to trust in God is an early attempt to create an environment where the penitent will be able to have an "enlightened heart," will accept help "to know [his/her] sins," and "trust in [God's] mercy."[8]

5. Kathleen Hughes, "Reconciliation: Disquieting Pastoral Reflections," in *Repentance and Reconciliation in the Church,* ed. Michael J. Henchal (Collegeville, MN: The Liturgical Press, 1987), 75.

6. Since the majority of people celebrate the sacrament using Rite A: Rite for Reconciliation of Individual Penitents, I will be referring to this rite most frequently, with occasional references to Rite B: Rite for Reconciliation for Several Penitents with Individual Confession and Absolution.

7. *The Rite of Penance* in the *Rites of the Catholic Church,* vol. I, trans. International Commission on English in the Liturgy (New York: Pueblo Press, 1983), 41.

8. *Rite of Penance,* 42.

In its own way, the word of God, although optional, provides an important impetus to move the penitent beyond an individual and private sense of sin, conversion and reconciliation.[9] The penitent's solidarity with others in sin and redemption is a pronounced feature of the suggested scripture texts.[10] The penitent is reminded that he or she does not stand alone in sin for "we like sheep have gone astray" (Is 53:6), and "we are sinners" (Rom 5:8). Further, the penitent, through the scriptures, remembers that he or she has been redeemed as a member of a people, for God indicated that "they shall be my people" (Ezek 11:19–20) and that they are "God's chosen ones" (Col 3:12).[11] Indeed, the Christian stands with others for "Christ loved us" (Eph 5:1–2) and "he has delivered us" (Col 1:13–14). The social nature of sin and the Christian life are highlighted in the texts that stress forgiveness of others (Mt 6:14–15), right conduct toward others (Luke 6:31–38), and the importance of fellowship with others (1 Jn 1:6–7, 9). Even the reaction of the community over the conversion of the sinner is symbolized through the image of rejoicing friends and neighbors (Luke 15:1–7). The effect of listening to God's word is for the penitent to see sin in a broader light, to understand that he or she is part of a community of people gathered by God, and to seek to remedy the effects of sin through both the knowledge of sin and trust in God's mercy. Many of these passages do not focus on a particular sin, such as theft or greed or adultery; rather, they are passages that challenge the hearer to reflect upon his or her journey in the Christian life, particularly in relationship with self, others, and God. Through these readings, we come to realize the good news that Jesus has come not for the healthy but for the sick, not for the righteous but for the sinner. Reflections upon these biblical passages provide an opportunity to look deeper into one's life and focus on the root cause of sinfulness that manifests itself in particular sinful acts. In addition, the inclusion of Sacred Scripture—an essential part of any liturgy—is crucial if the Rite of Penance is in any way to express clearly the corporate involvement in sin and reconciliation and to become a clear sign of the community's worship by expressing the rediscovered sense of liturgy as the activity of the Church gathered.[12]

9. My own experience is that few people come ready to share the Word of God. If I am able, after the penitent's initial "Bless me, Father, for I have sinned and it has been four weeks since my last confession," I try to insert something like this: "Indeed, I want to bless you. I want you to know and experience all the blessings of God who sent his Son, who reminded us that 'I have come not for the healthy but for the sick, not for the righteous, but for the sinner.'" This is usually met by a pause and "Gee, thanks!"

10. *Rite of Penance*, 72–83.

11. See also verses 8–10 and 13.

12. Richard Gula, "Confession and Communal Penance," *New Catholic World* 228 (November/December 1985): 267–71.

Part of any liturgy is its dialogical nature; the Rite of Penance presumes this in the prayers of the penitent and absolution. Only after the penitent expresses his or her sorrow does the priest pray the prayer of absolution. The absolution formula reminds the penitent that he or she is reconciled through the ministry of the Church, and the imposition of hands is a sign of the conferring of the Holy Spirit and of reconciliation with the Church.[13] Surprising to most, the Rite of Penance, like all liturgies, has a concluding rite. After absolution, the priest continues: "Give thanks to the Lord, for he is good." And the penitent responds: "His mercy endures forever." Similar to the formulary at the Eucharist, the priest sends forth the penitent with the words: "The Lord has freed you from your sins. Go in peace." There are two other dismissals that the priest may use, the first of which I believe would be very helpful:

> May the Passion of our Lord Jesus Christ,
> the intercession of the Blessed Virgin Mary,
> and of all the saints,
> whatever good you do and suffering you endure,
> heal your sins,
> help you to grow in holiness,
> and reward you with eternal life.
> Go in peace.[14]

The prayer's opening supplication calls attention to the passion (suffering and death) of Christ as the means of healing for us. This is not something that we do ourselves, for as sinners we need to be saved by God's grace in the action of Jesus. The graced moment of this encounter with Christ is that we have an opportunity to experience God's love and mercy at the exact point where we, as sinners, do not deserve it. But that is why it is called "grace." To the degree that we appreciate that we are loved and for-given precisely where we do not deserve it, we will be able to rejoice in what God has done within us through Christ's suffering, death, and res-urrection. Being transformed in this way, we are different—more Christ-like—and can now give freely to others what was bestowed freely upon us—Christ's compassion, forgiveness and mercy. In other words, through the passion of Christ, the forgiveness of sins unites us to Christ so that we can be Christ in the world. What is striking about this prayer is not only its roots in the paschal mystery—the experience of dying to sin and rising to

---

13. *Rite of Penance*, 46.
14. *Rite of Penance*, 47.

new life in Christ—but its reminder that the sins that often mark us need continual healing and that this healing can come through the good we do and the suffering we endure. For many of us, individual "sins" are not the problem; they are the symptom of something that lies deeper within. For instance, while one might confess gossiping three times about a friend, the real problem may be that a person feels insecure in relation to the friend. This prayer holds out hope that continued healing can happen as the person seeks to do good for his or her friend and might even encounter some suffering as he or she makes sacrifices to change certain thoughts, attitudes, and behavior in relation to the friend. This suggests that the sacrament is working as a deeper level where healing is needed. It is precisely at this point, in our need of healing that God's grace of mercy and forgiveness meet us so that we can grow in holiness. As St. Paul puts it: "I will rather boast most gladly of my weaknesses, in order that the power of Christ may dwell with me" (2 Cor 12:9). By pointing the penitent to the sacrifice of Christ, then, this closing prayer would, like the use of God's word, be a liturgical connection back to the central mysteries celebrated in baptism and Eucharist.

Reconciliation Involves a Corporate Understanding of Sin and Reconciliation

The penitent's experience of sin and reconciliation will be affected not only by his or her experience of the liturgical celebration of the sacrament but also by the experience of how sin and reconciliation is understood in relation to their social and communal dimensions. The introduction to the Rite of Penance clearly states that the whole Church is affected by the sin of one of its members. "In the sacrament of penance the faithful obtain from the mercy of God pardon for their sins against him; at the same time they are reconciled with the Church which they have wounded by their sins and which work for their conversion by charity, examples, and prayer."[15]

Further, sin has a social aspect in relation to the people of God. "By the hidden and loving mystery of God's design men are joined together in the bonds of supernatural solidarity, so much so that the sin of one harms the others just as the holiness of one benefits the others. Penance always entails reconciliation with our brothers and sisters who are always harmed by our sins."[16] The Introduction also notes that because sin "has divided and scattered" and "has brought weakness [and] death",[17] the priest should

---

15. *Rite of Penance*, 4.
16. *Rite of Penance*, 5.
17. *Rite of Penance*, 9.

advise the penitent to make appropriate restitution for any harm or scandal that he or she has caused.

When specifically discussing Rite A: Rite for Reconciliation of Individual Penitents, the Introduction notes that acts of penance "may suitably take the form of prayer, self-denial, and especially, service of one's neighbor and works of mercy" for "these will underline the fact that sin and its forgiveness have a social aspect."[18] Frequently, I will ask penitents if they can think of a penance that will help them move from vice to virtue, in other words, something that will heal not only themselves but also those they have harmed by their sins. In the case where someone has confessed speaking or acting badly toward another, I have found that the penitent will most often suggest that he or she pray for the wronged person. My usual response is to praise this idea, but to gently ask if the penitent could think of some act of charity or kindness that he or she could do as well. My experience is that people actually relish this opportunity to respond not only spiritually but also materially in charity and service to make some wrong right.

Another example of trying to help people move from vice to virtue comes from my experience of hearing confessions on a college campus. It is not uncommon for students to confess acts of nonmarital sex. I admire their courage to make such a confession and their trust in me as the Church's minister to confess this (most frequently) face-to-face. Coupled with remorse for engaging in the act itself, the penitent also feels guilt that he or she may have led the other person into sin, which motivates an intention to avoid this iniquity in the future. I have found it helpful to ask the penitent if he or she could, as penance, have a conversation with the other person, particularly about the feelings of guilt and remorse about the nonmarital sex, the fear that the act has resulted in harm for the other person, the fact that the penitent confessed this sin, and the desire to avoid this behavior in the future. I have seen faces light up as it dawns on the penitent that this is something of significance that can be discussed with the other and not carried as a burden alone. I have had young people who have really struggled in this manner come to me outside of the sacrament and tell me how this penance helped them in their relationship. One young man in particular told me that, after initiating this conversation, he and his girlfriend found it easier to avoid nonmarital sex because they had not previously thought through how this act was affecting both of them not only physically and emotionally, but also spiritually.

The communal celebrations of Rite B: Rite for Reconciliation of Several Penitents with Individual Confession and Absolution and Rite C: Rite of Reconciliation of Penitents with General Confession and Absolution more clearly show the social nature of sin. After the community has heard

18. *Rite of Penance*, 18.

the word of God, the homilist is encouraged to remind the faithful that "sin works against God, against the community and one's neighbors, and against the sinner himself."[19] The homilist is instructed to recall (among other things) "the social aspect of grace and sin, by which the actions of individuals in some degree affect the whole body of the Church"[20] and "the duty to make satisfaction for sin, which is effective because of Christ's work of reparation and requires especially, in addition to the works of penance, the exercise of true charity toward God and neighbor."[21] The examination of conscience that is provided in Appendix III also highlights the social nature of sin: "Have I genuine love for my neighbors? . . . Do I do my best to help the victims of oppression, misfortune, and poverty?"

Just as sin has its social and communal effects, so too does reconciliation. Through sin, the penitent has upset the relationships that he or she has with the community. Reconciliation means that the sinner is once more fully incorporated into the community, signified completely in his or her participation in the Eucharist. The Introduction to the Rite of Penance puts it this way:

> In the sacrament of penance the Father receives the repentant son who comes back to him, Christ places the lost sheep on his shoulders and brings it back to the sheepfold, and the Holy Spirit sanctifies this temple of God again or lives more fully within it. This is finally expressed in a renewed and more fervent sharing of the Lord's table, and there is great joy at the banquet of God's Church over the son who has returned from afar.[22]

The Introduction to the Rite of Penance describes two other elements that symbolize the penitent's reconciliation with the Church: the formula for absolution which reminds the penitent that pardon and peace comes "through the ministry of the Church," and the imposition of hands which long has been understood as a conferring of the Holy Spirit and as a sign of reconciliation with the Church.[23]

Reflections Going Forward

It is important that the Rite of Penance is celebrated as a liturgy and that the social and communal dimensions of sin and reconciliation are brought to the fore because these two aspects of the rite have a significant influence on how the penitent will understand sin and reconciliation, including her

19. *Rite of Penance*, 25.
20. *Rite of Penance*, 25c.
21. *Rite of Penance*, 25d.
22. *Rite of Penance*, 6d.
23. *Rite of Penance*, 19.

or his preparation for the confession of sins. As we have seen, the liturgical, ecclesial, and communal dimensions of this sacrament are emphasized in the Introduction's stress on baptism and the Eucharist. Christ's victory over sin "is first brought to light in baptism where our fallen nature is crucified with Christ so that the body of sin may be destroyed and we may no longer be slaves to sin, but rise with Christ and live for God."[24] This victory is completed in the Eucharist where "Christ is present and is offered as 'the sacrifice which has made our peace' with God [Eucharistic Prayer III] and in order that 'we may be brought together in unity' by his Holy Spirit" [Eucharistic Prayer II].[25] In the context of baptism and the Eucharist, sin is what separates us from Christ and his body, the Church. It is the refusal to conform oneself to Christ, rejecting the invitation to participate more fully in the paschal mystery by dying to our selfish tendencies, and refusing to trust that what seems like the path to diminishment—living selflessly for others—is really the path to the fullness of life.

Returning to my opening concerns, I fear that a list of sins confessed, accompanied by an automatic or rote penance, and the prayer of absolution in the isolation of the confessional will neither help the penitent to come to an understanding of the deeper wounds that these sins manifest nor, even more importantly, assist the penitent to make a clearer connection between this sacrament and life. By contrast, if the sacrament of reconciliation is enacted as a liturgy and the communal dimension of sin and reconciliation are highlighted, then a dimension opens up that otherwise remains concealed. My fear is that when these aspects of this sacrament are diminished or obscured, the focus is shifted to the penitent and the penitent's individual infractions. The rite starts to appear like a "work"—an exchange where the penitent does something and then gets something in return from the priest. What is lost is, as the *Catechism* wisely points out, that sacraments are the work of the Holy Trinity.[26] In this light, within the larger context of the person's initiation and formation into the paschal mystery celebrated in baptism and the Eucharist, the penitent will be more likely to see the importance of God's action: God the Father is blessing the penitent, Jesus Christ is making God's grace efficaciously present to the penitent, and the Holy Spirit is bringing the gift of faith to the penitent, transforming him or her into the mystery of Christ and uniting him or her to the Church community.[27]

24. *Rite of Penance*, 2.

25. *Rite of Penance*, 2.

26. See Section One: The Sacramental Economy in the *CCC*, which begins with a part entitled, "The Liturgy—Work of the Holy Trinity."

27. This insight is attributed to Kenan B. Osborne, *Sacramental Theology: 50 Years after Vatican II* (Hobe Sound, FL: Lectio, 2014), whose work I reviewed in *Horizons* 43 (June 2016): 204–05. In his

To be more specific, I would like to illustrate scenarios in how the sacrament is celebrated and some possible outcomes in each case. In one instance, a person enters the confessional, makes the sign of the cross, asks the priest for a blessing (with no time given to receive one), notes that it has been three weeks since the last confession, and confesses that he or she has lied three times, taken the Lord's name in vain six times, was impatient with friends and family ten times, was distracted in prayer several times, and has been jealous of spiritual or material gifts in others. The priest responds with some words of compassion and encouragement and provides a penance of saying three times each the Hail Mary and the Our Father. Leaving aside the differences between confessing face-to-face or behind a screen, there is much to say here. Certainly, the penitent demonstrated contrition by his or her very presence, confessed his or her sins, received absolution, and resolved to complete the penance. The sacrament was celebrated validly. But could we imagine that the sacrament might also be celebrated more fruitfully?

In a second instance, the person enters the confessional and makes the sign of the cross and then says, "Bless me, Father, for I have sinned. It has been three weeks since my last confession." As the penitent takes his or her next breath, the priest says, "Oh, I am so happy that you asked me to bless you because that is what God the Father is doing in our lives right now in this sacrament. God the Father is blessing us with the presence of Jesus in our midst right now and with the presence of the Holy Spirit who has been at work within you, leading you here this moment. Of course, God is blessing you because he loves you so much that he sent his Son to be among us and to remind us that though we are sinners, we are loved. That is exactly what Jesus meant when he said, 'I have come not for the healthy but for the sick, not for the righteous, but for the sinner.' What is it that you want to confess so that you will come to a deeper sense of God's love and forgiveness in your life?" In response to the same sins listed in the first scenario, the priest might say the following: "You have made a good confession and a wonderful effort of remembering and confessing these different sins. Have you ever wondered what might be the cause or what lies beneath these sins?"

This is a crucial insight of the essays in this book: the need for the confession of sin to move beyond a list of rules broken toward a naming of the manifestations of deeper patterns of sin in one's life.[28] In my own

---

work, Osborne points out that entire discussion of sacraments changes if we take God's action on us as the starting point. Indeed, his analysis shows how Part Two, Section One of the CCC, "The Sacramental Economy," is devoted to this truth, beginning with article 1, "The Liturgy—Work of the Holy Trinity."

28. At the heart of this distinction is how people think about sin as rules broken or relationships lived. I ask my students what they would think if I confessed the following: "I have a good friend about whom I talked badly to others three times, with whom I lost my temper twice, and of whom I

experience, I have found it amazing how quickly people will respond with simple, yet insightful comments such as "I have been too self-centered lately" or "I am feeling like the world is crashing in on me right now" or "I have been taking people for granted in my life." Once the penitent is able to articulate some such thought, the penance flows naturally and can be better addressed to bring healing to the root and peace and reconciliation to people and elements of life that have been the subject of confession. At the end of every confession, I always remind penitents that through their confession, they have conformed themselves more closely to Christ, dying to sinfulness so that they can rise to new life with Christ, and that this means that they are called to be Christ as they go forth: having received God's love and forgiveness freely and undeservedly, the penitent now tries to be more loving and forgiving in their own lives.

If, indeed, a more meaningful liturgical celebration of penance will help the penitent to connect the experience of sin and forgiveness within the context of his or her entire sacramental life—which celebrates the action of the Trinity upon him or her—a deeper understanding of the social and communal dimensions of sin and reconciliation will aid the penitent in making connections with his or her larger life. Here, not only is sin seen in the context of wounding the body of Christ but reconciliation is seen within the greater context of the whole Church, who as a priestly people, acts in different ways in the work of reconciliation which has been entrusted to it by the Lord.[29]

---

was jealous once. Besides this, everything is okay with us." Most students start to laugh because they understand that in a real friendship—especially in a good friendship—we do not focus only on acts of commission, but also on the things that we could and should have done to enhance the friendship—acts of omission. In this light, what I might confess sounds quite different: "I did a few acts that I am embarrassed about in relation with my good friend: I talked badly about her to others three times, I lost my temper with her twice, and I was jealous of her once. But, just as importantly, I missed a number of opportunities to encourage her this week because I know that she was really overwhelmed. I also could have spent more time with her and helped her with a project that I know was overwhelming her."

29. *Rite of Penance*, 8.

Chapter 10

Reflections from a Priest

Reconciliation as Ruptured Relationships Restored

FR. SATISH JOSEPH

"Are You Saved?"

IT IS NOT OFTEN THAT YOU get to your car after grocery shopping and salvation stares you in the face from your windshield. As I would often do, I had just bought my weekly groceries from a small Asian grocery store located at a strip mall in Centerville, Ohio. A small Christian church occupied one of the spaces on the strip. A night club also rented space in the same strip. Perhaps the location of the church was strategic. I am convinced that the best location for any church is where there is the most foot traffic and where its presence is pastorally relevant. After all, Jesus hung out among the most unlikely people and in the most unlikely places. Putting those thoughts aside, I turned my attention to the tract that a concerned church member had placed on my windshield. (See the next page, pg. 182, for what it read.)

Instead of the grocery store, I might as well have emerged out of the night club after a night of wild frolicking. Yet at that very moment, sitting in the comfort and privacy of my car, I was told that all my sins could be forgiven and I could be saved. The Catholic in me was amused at the ease with which I was being promised forgiveness, and indeed, salvation. While in a way, this tract took sin very seriously, the fact that it was placed on my windshield like an ad for a fast-food chain left me uneasy. The tract promised fast-food-style repentance and salvation! It reminded me of Dietrich Bonhoeffer's concept of "cheap grace."[1] Cheap grace is grace that comes all too easily. Cheap grace is grace that does not make a demand of the recipient. I felt that the tract cheapened Christ's suffering and the price he paid for our redemption. Moreover, as a Catholic, I thought that if we learn to name and identify sin well, then likewise, our participation in

---

1. See Dietrich Bonhoeffer, *The Cost of Discipleship*, revised edition (New York: Collier Books, 1959), 45–60.

"DO YOU KNOW FOR <u>SURE</u> IF YOU DIED <u>TODAY</u> THAT YOU WOULD GO TO <u>HEAVEN</u>???"

You Can be Saved and you <u>Know</u> It

All have sinned (Rom 3: 10; Rom 3: 23)

The penalty of sin is death and hell (Rom 6:23; Luke 16: 23)

Jesus died for our sins (Rom 5: 8)

Jesus rose from the dead (Rom 10: 9; Rom 6:23)

Jesus invites you to be saved <u>today</u>

<u>SIMPLY PRAY THIS PRAYER FROM YOUR HEART:</u>

Dear Jesus, I confess that I am a sinner and I need to be saved. I believe that you shed your blood on the cross to pay my sin debt and arose from the dead to give me everlasting life. I ask you, Jesus, to come in to my heart and save my soul.

reconciliation involves a deeper communal process than the simple prayer outlined in the tract.

Catholics are not simply invited to name sin well. We do so as part of a larger invitation to live a new life. For example, in contrast to the tract, consider the following hypothetical situation. Imagine your child has come home from a school with a note from the principal. The note mentions that your child has been bullying another student. It also says that unless your child makes amends he or she is suspended from the school. You speak to your child, and your child is remorseful. Yet your child refuses to apologize to the victim, saying that he or she has already sought God's forgiveness and hence does not need to make further amends. If we follow the instruction that the tract on my windshield suggested, then this child is justified and forgiven. However, any reasonable parent knows that the child must seek not only God's forgiveness but the forgiveness of the bullied student and indeed the school community. The school community is represented by the school principal. The principal has the authority to reconcile the student to the school community. In fact, the principal's action represents the entire community. Once the principal has restored the student to the community, no person has the authority to treat the student any differently than what the principal has determined. The Catholic understanding of sin and reconciliation is something like this illustration. It involves the wider process and the broader community. The argument here is not that God does not forgive sins that we privately confess to God, but that genuine reconciliation involves more than a simple prayer.

This book has invited us to consider how to name our sins in preparation for receiving the sacrament of reconciliation. The authors of these chapters have invited us to think in new ways about sin and its effects and hold on our lives.

In this chapter, I invite readers back to a direct consideration of the sacrament of reconciliation. In the first chapter, we saw that prior to the Second Vatican Council, people often described reciting a laundry list of sins as part of their experience of the sacrament. It was perhaps just as limited (though in a different way) as the tract I saw on my windshield. Yet in my experience of the sacrament as a priest, I find that the sacrament of reconciliation is so much more than the tract or the laundry list.

First, I will discuss the difference between the Catholic understanding of sin and reconciliation and those traditions that represent the tract. As I look at Scripture and Sacred Tradition, I see that sin and reconciliation are about a person's striving to be the most loving Christian that he or she can be in relation to God, others, oneself, and creation. As David Cloutier and Jana Bennett described in the first chapter, sin must be understood as more than a private act of an individual. Naming sin involves examining our lives in and for our communities. Similarly, the sacrament of reconciliation must be seen as a community event.

Second, I will describe the rite of the sacrament of reconciliation, especially emphasizing how certain contentious points can be best understood from this perspective of the event as a communal one. For example, I will discuss the role of the priest in the sacrament. The introductory chapter suggested that the role of the priest has shifted since Vatican II; people used to understand the priest's role as a stern, angry father standing in for God the Father. Since the Second Vatican Council, our catechetical emphasis has been to use the Parable of the Loving Father. Those images affect how people think about the sacrament. Here, I offer another way to understand the role of the priest. I also provide practical ways to conduct an examination of conscience. My suggestions complement the discussion of virtue and vice in this book since virtue is about living Christian life fully in relationship with each other.

Finally, I will explain more holistically the role of a "penance"—an often-misunderstood concept. Yet as I hinted above about the child bully, responding to God and to the community through penance is an important part of the sacrament.

Sin is a Community Affair

The Catholic understanding of sin and salvation is radically different from the view of sin and salvation that the tract outlined. Sin, repentance, and salvation are communal events rather than personal experiences. Such an understanding has strong biblical foundations. In the Bible, sin and salvation are inherently communal experiences. In fact, sin, by nature, is a social act even if it is committed by a single individual. In the Bible, even the most private sin has social implications.

The story of the very first sin (Gn 3:1–34), Adam and Eve's temptation to eat from the tree of the knowledge of good and evil in Eden, helps us to understand sin's relational nature. The story of the fall of Adam and Eve is told from the perspective of relationships. For this reason, I choose to define sin as a "rupture in relationships." In fact, the way Genesis portrays the story of the fall, one sinful act simultaneously destroys four relationships: with God, with others, with the self, and with nature. Sin is the destruction of love.

First, sin ruptures the relationship between God and the human person. This is made amply clear in the way Adam and Eve acted after their original disobedience. The very first thing they did was to hide. They hid because of fear. Adam's reply when God came looking for them was, "I heard you in the garden; but I was afraid, because I was naked, so I hid" (Gn 3:10). His reply reminds me of my childhood misbehavior. If I had a bad day at school and if it was because I had done something wrong, I avoided my parents all evening. I would hide in my room. Strangely, I did not have to say anything. My parents knew something was wrong if I was not prancing all over the house. My 'hiding' said it all. This is also true of us as adults. When we are in sin, we find it difficult to come into prayer and worship. Sin makes us uncomfortable in God's presence. It is easier to hide.

Strangely, the initial rupture in Adam and Eve's relationship with God had a ripple effect on their relationship with each other. Love was lost. Somehow, they became distrusting of each other. The Genesis story captures this phenomenon in the need they felt to cover their nakedness. Until the initial act of disobedience, they were at ease with each other. However, after their disobedience, they began to hide from each other just as they had initially hidden from God. They sewed leaves to cover this newfound discomfort, and their initial distrust with each other led to a deeper cycle of distrust. Note that in their post-disobedience conversation with God, Adam blamed Eve, who in turn blamed the serpent for the sin. This cycle continued to affect even the children of the first parents. The same distrust led Cain to murder Abel. This point is significant since this means that the original act of disobedience affected successive generations. Our first parents would have never imagined this to be the consequence of their sin. Catholic Tradition calls this phenomenon, "original sin." In fact, original sin affects every person born into the world, even to this day. It is original sin that necessitated the need of a Savior. This is the Bible's way of saying that sin is a terrible thing; that fear is a terrible thing. Sin creates intense distrust. It makes us avoid taking responsibility and blame others for our actions. Sin creates a cycle of sins. But most importantly, individual sin affects the entire community.

The above discussion has implications for us today. It means that what might begin for individual persons as a private act of disobedience leads to unforeseen effects. In fact, we can never calculate the effects of our individual sins. The implication is also immense for the Christian community. In baptism, each baptized person enters into a common bond with every other baptized Christian. In fact, our baptism makes us part of the Church or the Christian family. The primary call of the Church is holiness. In the same way that the first sin affected the first family's call to holiness, our individual sins affect our Christian family and its call to holiness. In this sense, even our most private sin is not a private act, or our sins against one another are in some way directed against other private individuals. Thus, our sins end up affecting the Christian family, even when we do not intend to do so. Our most private sin diminishes the holiness of the Church, which is the Body of Christ. The Church can only be as sinful or sanctified as her members. In this sense, we are responsible for one another.

To these sins of "commission" (sins in our actions), we must also add the sins of "omission" (sins caused by our neglect of duty). For example, stealing from someone is a sin against the fifth commandment. This is a sin of commission caused by the lack of love for another. However, if I notice someone stealing and deliberately fail to notify the rightful authority, that is also sinful. This is sin by omission of a loving act. Either way, the point to be noted here is that both sins of commission and omission affect the community at large, especially the Church.

There is a third relationship which is affected by the first sin—the relationship of a person with his or her own self. Originally, made in the image and likeness of God (Gn 1:27), man and woman were placed among God's creation (Gn 1:31). Yet, by the end of the story, man and his wife found themselves outside the garden of Eden (Gn 3:23). They had compromised the image in which they were created. Sin had damaged the original image in which they were created. Man and woman became who they were not created to be. It is Christ who would ultimately restore all humanity to this original image by his redemptive death. However, the return to our original image is a process. Christ's redemptive death is the beginning of this process. Beyond Christ's redeeming action, every human person is invited to be transformed in the image of Christ, which is mankind's original image. By the time of our death, we must look as much like Christ as possible. Unfortunately, sin stands in the way. But we are not helpless. The sacrament of reconciliation aids us in this process.

In these days of ecological consciousness, we also become aware of a fourth relationship that sin ruptures—human relationship with nature. As a result of the first sin, the serpent and the ground were cursed. Nature bore the brunt of human sin and continues to do so. Pope Francis's *Laudato Si'* captures this point beautifully:

> This sister [the earth] now cries out to us because of the harm we have inflicted on her by our irresponsible use and abuse of the goods with which God has endowed her. We have come to see ourselves as her lords and masters, entitled to plunder her at will. The violence present in our hearts, wounded by sin, is also reflected in the symptoms of sickness evident in the soil, in the water, in the air and in all forms of life. This is why the earth herself, burdened and laid waste, is among the most abandoned and maltreated of our poor; she "groans in travail"

(Rom 8:22). We have forgotten that we ourselves are dust of the earth (cf. Gn 2:7); our very bodies are made up of her elements, we breathe her air and we receive life and refreshment from her waters.[2]

In light of the existing ecological crisis, ancient Israel's sensitivity to nature and the natural balance, depicted in the commandments, should be greatly appreciated and cherished. The Sabbath Year, observed every seventh year, and the Jubilee year, observed every fiftieth year of the Hebrew calendar, tell us about the awareness of our foreparents that nature was flawed by human sin. St. Paul, in the New Testament, captures creation's need for redemption when he says, "For creation awaits with eager expectation the revelation of the children of God; for creation was made subject to futility, not of its own accord but because of the one who subjected it, in hope that creation itself would be set free from slavery to corruption and share in the glorious freedom of the children of God" (Rom 8:19–21).

This communal account of sin and reconciliation is reflected in the Hebrew liturgical practices depicted in Scripture. In ancient Judaism, when families made their annual pilgrimage to Jerusalem, they made sin offerings in proportion to the grievousness of their offenses. Their sin offerings were celebrated not as a personal event but rather as a communal celebration of a person's admission of sins and attempts to be reconciled and restored to the community. Many of the psalms that express sorrow for sin were written to accompany the sin offering of the penitents in the temple. A classic example is Psalm 51, attributed to David in repentance for his sin against Uriah (2 Sm 11:5–27). He prays, "Have mercy on me, God, in accord with your merciful love; in your abundant compassion blot out my transgressions./ Thoroughly wash away my guilt; and from my sin cleanse me" (Ps 51:3–4). One can imagine numerous penitent sinners entering the temple along with other worshippers reciting these very words. The Jewish purification rituals further emphasize the communal nature of sin. The celebration of the Day of Atonement, for example, underscores this point. Notice the communal nature of atonement in the following passage from Leviticus 16:20–22: "When he has finished purging the inner sanctuary, the tent of meeting and the altar, Aaron shall bring forward the live goat. Laying both hands on its head, he shall confess over it all the iniquities of the Israelites and their trespasses, including all their sins, and so put them on the goat's head. He shall then have it led into the wilderness by an attendant. The goat will carry off all their iniquities to an isolated region." The Day of Atonement is, as it were, a national day of repentance.

2. Francis, Encyclical Letter *Laudato Si'* (May 24, 2015), 2.

This very brief survey of a few Old Testament passages suggests that sin and reconciliation are hardly personal, private, and exclusive affairs. It suggests the need to think more deeply about naming sins with respect to these relationships. The authors in this book have provided discussions and offered examples that invite us to reflect deeply on our relationships with God, our community, ourselves, and God's creation. Such an understanding of sin calls for a deeper and wider process of reconciliation—certainly more elaborate than the simple prayer the tract invited me to pray. This is the process we find in the Catholic sacrament of reconciliation.

The Sacrament of Reconciliation: A Community Affair

As described above, if sin ruptures four relationships, then what might restore these four relationships? The Catholic tradition proposes that the sacrament of reconciliation is that process that restores the four relationships destroyed by sin. Since the Church's understanding of sin is communal, the process of reconciliation is also communal.

The biblical foundation for the Catholic understanding of the sacrament of reconciliation is based on numerous New Testament texts. Matthew 16:19 and John 20:19–23 are the two most prominent texts. Jesus's post-resurrection appearance in the latter passage offers a particularly unique insight into the sacrament of reconciliation. It connects us directly to the Genesis story. First, for different reasons but similar to the first man and woman, the disciples too were in fear and in hiding. Second, similar to God who came looking for the man and woman, Jesus came to the disciples and stood in their midst. Because Christ's ministry was a reconciling one, he offers them peace. Twice, during this appearance, Jesus says to his disciples, "Peace be with you." Third, just like God breathed the breath of life on the clay images in Genesis, Jesus breathes the same Spirit on the disciples. This is John's way of proclaiming that with the resurrection, a new creation is replacing the old. Christ's words following his action raises his ministry of reconciliation to a sacrament in the Christian community. "Receive the Holy Spirit," he said. "Whose sins you forgive are forgiven, and whose sins you retain are retained" (John 20:22–23). These words of Christ revolutionized the ministry of reconciliation. Until now, God and only God had the authority to forgive and retain sins. For the first time, the authority to forgive and retain sins is shared with human beings. Eleven apostles were commissioned that day with these words, "As the Father has sent me, so I send you." Christ's ministry of reconciliation was in this way commissioned for the entire world.

The Johannine resurrection appearance helps explain the sacramental nature of reconciliation in the Catholic tradition. It is true! God and only God has the authority to forgive and retain sins. Yet, Christ makes the "outward sign of an inward grace," a reality when he gave the power to forgive and retain sins to his first apostles. In other words, Christ made it possible for us to experience in a concrete and tangible way what was otherwise an intangible reality.

I was struck by the absence of this sacramental aspect of reconciliation that day as I sat in the car and read the tract. At the end of it all, I missed the concrete assurance that my sins were indeed forgiven and that I was saved. Compare having a piece of paper and confessing sins in your head to actually walking into a confessional, speaking to a priest, verbally acknowledging sins in someone's hearing, receiving a penance, uttering words of contrition, feeling gentle hands over one's head, and hearing the words of absolution.

I remember when at a retreat many years ago in India, a young lady who had never been to the sacrament, finally came to me to tell it all. It took almost an hour and a half for her to share her story. After I had pronounced the words of absolution, I looked straight into her eyes and said, "Your sins are forgiven. Go in peace!" There was stunned silence. And then she said to me, "I have asked God forgiveness many times before, but this is the first time someone actually told me that my sins are forgiven." For this young woman, my action of laying my hands on her head and the accompanying prayer became a concrete experience. It was not something that she had to convince herself of. Moreover, the words of absolution, "Your sins are forgiven," actually assured her of God's action within her. It is in this sense we say that Christ instituted the sacraments. He gave us the words and the actions to perform rites that make tangible otherwise intangible spiritual realities.

While the recent history of the sacrament of reconciliation was outlined in the introductory chapter, it is important to know that the practice of reconciliation stretches back to the development of the practice of public penance in the early Church. For much of the Church's practice, sin and reconciliation were understood as communal realities. Even when the more private, individual confession of sins developed, the idea of sin as a communal act did not diminish. Indeed, if it had, the entire practice of the sacrament of reconciliation would have disappeared. The fact that sin still needed to be brought to sacramental confession and absolution emphasizes the point that the communal nature of sin was never compromised with the development of private confession.

The Priest: A Minister of God and the Community and Not an Intruder

This brings us to one of the most contentious aspects of the sacrament of reconciliation— mediated forgiveness or the need of a priest for the forgiveness of sins. Why name sins to a human being? From the Catholic perspective, the presence of the priest in the confessional is necessitated by the communal nature of sin and reconciliation. But one of the most prominent objections in non-Catholic circles about the sacrament of reconciliation is the role of the priest. What makes the place of a mediator necessary in the sacrament? If the Johannine passage describes Jesus appointing his apostles to his ministry of reconciliation, how does it translate into the priest's presence in the confessional?

In order to understand this, we must examine the concept of apostolic succession. Some early New Testament authors believed in the imminent coming of Christ. Many of them believed that Christ would come before the end of their own lifetime. It was a gradual realization in the community that Christ's coming was delayed beyond expectation. This gave rise, already witnessed in the New Testament, to the most reasonable tradition of apostolic succession, meaning that the apostles handed over to their successors, by the laying on of hands, the ministries entrusted to them by Jesus. For example, in Acts 6:6, the apostolic succession by laying on of hands is warranted by a pastoral need, describing the process. As the early Church grew in numbers, the apostles found themselves overwhelmed by the demands of ministry. The ministry of the word suffered because of their serving at the table. The dissatisfaction expressed by some of the people, led the apostles to a very novel solution. They chose seven reputable men to share their task. When these men were ready, the apostles laid hands on them and passed on to them the authority to perform tasks that otherwise was their prerogative. This practice continues even today. The bishops are the apostolic successors. They are ordained bishops by the laying on of hands and they in turn ordain priests by the same practice. The bishops delegate to the priests the very authority that Christ gave to his first apostles. For our purposes, this also applies to the authority to either forgive or retain sins. The bishops and priests, thus, perform a dual role. On the one hand, they represent Christ. On the other hand, they represent the community. They are present before the sinner in the confessional representing God and the community. Through one act, they have the authority to reconcile the penitent to both God and the community.

Seeking Forgiveness from God and Many Others

The social nature or the communal dimension of sin is further emphasized in Catholic liturgy. Every celebration of the Eucharist is a communal celebration. One of the first actions of the gathered community is the recognition and confession of sin. First, the priest invites the community to call to mind its sins and failures. Even though each person calls their individual sins to mind, the fact that the community engages in the same act together bears witness to the community's common consciousness of sin. However, it is in the praying of the *Confiteor* that the communal nature of sin truly becomes prominent.[3] Twice in the Confiteor, the penitents call upon those present to pray for them. The first time, the penitents acknowledge to the gathered believers that they have sinned. The penitents say, "I confess to almighty God and to you, my brothers and sisters, that I have greatly sinned…" This is based on James's instruction to the Christian community, "Therefore, confess your sins to one another and pray for one another, that you may be healed" (Jas 5:16). The second time, the penitents seek the prayers of the blessed Mary ever-Virgin, all the angels and saints, and "you my brothers and sisters, to pray for me to the Lord our God." In response, the celebrant pronounces the absolution in the words, "May almighty God have mercy on us, forgive us our sins and bring us to everlasting life." The entire worshipping community responds with a resounding, "Amen." Even though this process of confession and reconciliation excludes private confession of sin and individual reconciliation, it still is very different from the process the tract on my windshield invited me to. Sin is always communal, confession of it is always communal, and reconciliation is always communal.[4]

Does this mean that even our most private sins are social in nature? The Catholic answer is clearly yes. Let me give an example. Recently, some of the parish staff and I were returning to the office after lunch. We saw a shabbily dressed woman heading toward the rectory. No one said a word. However, I had made my own judgments about this person based on her looks and clothing. Very soon, the doorbell to the rectory rang. I opened the door and standing at the door was this very woman. I was so sure

3. The prayer sometimes said during the opening minutes of the Mass, which begins, "I confess to almighty God and to you my brothers and sisters that I have greatly sinned…"

4. I must add a caveat here. My emphasis on the communal nature of sin and reconciliation does not mean that God's mercy is limited by communal rituals. Mercy, compassion, and forgiveness are God's prerogatives, and God may exercise God's authority in any way God chooses. A person may individually repent for his or her sins and experience God's healing touch. The point being made here is that the biblical data seems to indicate that sin and reconciliation are communal realities and even when one is truly sorry for his or her sins, holistic confession and reconciliation demands a communal awareness.

that she would ask for money—I even had all my defenses worked out. The woman sought to speak to the pastor. When I introduced myself, she simply asked me if I would pray over her. I was sure that this was only a means to get to the real reason she was here. After I prayed over her, she thanked me profusely and walked out the door. I stood there stunned. I was ashamed of my prejudice.

My prejudice and judgement about this person seemed to be a very private act about my own unspoken thoughts about this woman. But was it? As many of the previous chapters have noted, naming our sins requires us to recognize the deeper distortion of relationships that is rooted in our desires. Even in this very private act, my desires and feelings were very apparent! I broke four relationships in this very private act. First, I ruptured my relationship with God by approaching another person contrary to the image in which God created her. Second, I sinned against the person I judged. By acting sinfully, I also deprived the Church of her holiness. That day, the Church experienced sinfulness because of me. Third, by denying another person her dignity, I compromised my own God-given dignity. When we deny other people their human dignity, we deny that everything that God created was good. Scripture tells us that God saw all that God created and saw that it was good. When we deny others their human dignity, we deny that God created this person just as God created us. Consequently, to deny others their dignity is to deny ourselves our own dignity. When the person left the rectory, I felt shame. I experienced guilt because I had acted in a way that God did not create me to act. I found myself at odds with my own self. My relationship with myself was ruptured. Fourth, by acting in a prejudicial and judgmental way, I had further damaged the balance of God's creation. If we revisit the Genesis account of the first sin, human distrust of each other resulted in the ground being cursed. In the final analysis, it led to Abel's brutal death. Even though I did not physically take anyone's life, denying another person his or her dignity is a form of bringing death to that person. Denying another person his or her dignity is a kind of death sentence, an undermining of God's creation and, in this way, hurting all of God's creation.

The Sacrament of Reconciliation: One Act that Reconciles Four Relationships

The "sacrament of reconciliation" has only recently been called by this name. Reconciliation, meaning the restoration of friendly relationship, better describes what is accomplished by the sacrament than its previous name—"confession." We have not completely abandoned this archaic vocabulary since we still employ the term "confessional." Hence, many well-meaning Catholics still frequent the confessional with the idea of "confessing sins" in terms of rule violations. Their focus is on some sinful act and the number of times they may have committed it.

With such a focus, the communal character of both sin and the sacrament can disappear. Perhaps an illustration will help. For many Catholics, sexual morality occupies a central place in the examination of conscience. Often, sin means the violation of the sixth and the ninth commandments. In this digital age, pornography is a new avatar of these two commandments. Truly remorseful addicts often come confessing the sin and the number of times they may have engaged in it. Pornography is a serious moral depravity in itself, yet it is rarely confessed as a relational sin. As Jason King's chapter on lust emphasized, St. Thomas Aquinas's understanding of this sin is about how our lustful feelings narrow our focus, screening out the proper consideration of others. Yet ninety-nine out of a hundred times, there is hardly any consideration of the fact that another person is being either exploited or objectified for the pleasure of the viewing public. When I suggest to the penitent to consider how he or she might contribute or be part of the exploitation or objectification of another person, a light-bulb goes off in their head. I often hear the penitent reply, "I never thought about it like that, Father." Equally important is the penitent's neglect of the relationships at home, especially a spouse and/or children. The mind does not often consider the implications of pornography on the rest of the family members. In the spiritual direction that I offer to such penitents, I also associate pornography with the stripping of Jesus before he was crucified. I tell the penitents that Jesus was paying the price for every illegitimate, indecent, and forced stripping of individuals. I further tell them that when we engage in illicit, disrespectful, or manipulative stripping through pornography, we indirectly participate in the stripping of Jesus. Because most penitents are also people who love God immensely, casting pornography in the context of the relationship with Christ becomes a strong motivation against it. For this very reason, they also begin to look at other individuals, their own families, and their own selves differently. In contrast to the act-oriented approach, the real purpose of the sacrament of reconciliation is far deeper. It's a place where relationships are reconciled. It is the place where lives are restored. It is the place where one act reconciles four relationships.

The Examination of Conscience: A Way to Examine Relationships

It is customary for Catholics to examine their consciences before they frequent the sacrament of reconciliation. Since I have defined sin as a rupture in four relationships, I also recommend an examination of conscience based on four relationships, which could be connected to all the vices discussed in this book. I recommend that penitents examine their relationships with God, others (including family members, coworkers, neighbors, and the poor), self, and nature. For example, penitents, in examining the quality of their relationship with God, may examine their prayer life, the quality and frequency of community worship, the influence faith has on daily life decisions, and other aspects of their relationship with God. With regards to their relationship with others, penitents may examine the various relationships that may be strained due to sinful thoughts, words and actions. This is also the place to examine acts of omission. As earlier mentioned, sin is not only about what we may have done but also what we have omitted to do as Christian disciples. Speaking uncharitably to a family member is as serious as omitting to help a poor brother or sister in need. Sins against the self are harder to examine. However, honesty; sincerity; diligence with family, work, and social responsibilities; purity of heart, mind, and body; justice; and the desire for peace are all areas where we constantly need conversion. In our times, sins against nature have taken on a new relevancy. As mentioned earlier, Pope Francis's *Laudato Si'* had drawn the world's attention to the notion that the earth is crying out to us in pain. A Christian's examination of conscience must include an examination of his or her relationship with the earth. To the extent that we damage God's creation, we must seek to restore it to the Creator's original intention.

This book is "about" the seven deadly sins. Yet if we see the seven sins simply as a list of sins to check off and recite little different from a list of the Ten Commandments, we misunderstand what this book is trying to do and we shortchange ourselves! Reflection on the seven deadly sins exposes our problems with relationships. As William Mattison says in his earlier chapter on anger, "Something is sinful when it impedes true human flourishing... a person's individual and communal flourishing." [5] Conversely, good actions are those that ultimately promote the flourishing of the individual and the human community to which he or she belongs This means that sin and virtue are about a person's relationship with the rest of humanity.

Let me outline an examination of conscience with regard to sloth. Conducting this examination as a priest, I would consider the ways in which my sloth may be affecting my relationship with God, others, self and nature. As Julie Hanlon Rubio's chapter noted, sloth includes a lack of hard work, but also a busyness that represents a deeper avoidance of the challenges of the relationships for which God made us. In regard to my relationship

5. Ch. 6, pg. 109.

with God, I would examine if I am diligent in my prayer and reflection on God's word; but I would also examine the sincerity of my heart as I preside at Eucharistic celebrations and ask if I indeed employ my body, mind, and soul to make the worship a genuine experience of the divine. I would examine if I work hard to reflect deeply on God's word and take the time to prepare a meaningful and practical homily. With regard to sloth and my relationship with others, I would examine my availability to my parishioners, my diligence at parish activities, the effort I put into sacramental formation, the time I invest in my family, the time and resources I spend on the poor, the effort I take to create a just world, and other similar social concerns. With regard to my relationship with myself, I would examine the time and effort I spend on study, exercise, and rest and relaxation. I would examine if my sloth was affecting staff members or people in my life. With regard to my relationship with nature, I would examine if I were diligent in caring for the environment, in keeping my surrounding clean, in recycling, and if I was making an impact of reducing my carbon footprint on the earth. I would also examine if I was doing my part in making sure that another person does not get displaced in the world because of my lifestyle. This method of "relationship-centered" examination of conscience rather than an "act-centered" examination can make the sacrament a life-transforming experience.

The Absolution: Four Restored Relationships

After a sincere examination of conscience, the penitent reaches face-to-face with the priest. No other element of the sacrament of reconciliation captures the four relationships being restored than the prayer of absolution the minister pronounces over the penitent. This prayer is replete with meaning and depth. After the penitent has brought his or her sins before God, the minister, with a hand raised, says, "God the Father of mercies, through the death and resurrection of his Son has reconciled the world to himself and sent the Holy Spirit among us for the forgiveness of sins [do not miss the reference to John 20:19–22]; through the ministry of the Church may God grant you pardon and peace, and I absolve you from all your sins. In the name of the Father, and of the Son, and of the Holy Spirit."[6] The prayer of absolution highlights two restored relationships. The ordained minister, standing between God/community and the penitent pronounces "pardon and peace" on behalf of God, and "absolution"

---

6. United States Catholic Conference of Bishops, *The Rite of Penance* (Washington, DC: United States Catholic Conference, 1975), 46.

on behalf of the community. In one act, two relationships are restored. The practice of seeking to do penance by the penitent restores the third relationship—with the self.

The Penance: An Act of Love

Rightly understood, the penance offered within the sacrament of reconciliation, is far more than a few quick prayers. The stereotypical "three Our Fathers" and "three Hail Marys" hardly captures the true intention of the practice of penance. In theological language, this penance is called satisfaction and is defined as an act of reparation for the injury done to the honor of God through sin. A penance is also a preventive remedy in that it is meant to hinder further sin. I think of penance as an act of love. Again, an illustration may help. Imagine that an otherwise loving and faithful husband forgets his wedding anniversary. As a result of his oversight, he chooses to cook his wife's favorite meal, arranges for babysitters for their children, and surprises her with a gift. Imagine again that he does so not as an act of punishment, reparation, or preventive remedy, but out of genuine love and sorrow that he missed an opportunity to strengthen his relationship with his wife on their anniversary. Penance, rightly understood, is an act of love. It strengthens, cements, and furthers a penitent's love for God and for the community which has been weakened by sin.

As mentioned before, penance becomes a means through which a third relationship ruptured by sin is restored. Penance is an effort through which the penitent strives to return to the image of God in which he or she is created. Through penance, we restore our relationship with ourselves by striving to become more like the persons that God intends us to be.

The above three relationships restored lead to what Scripture calls a "new creation." In Romans 8:22, Paul refers to creation "groaning in labor pains even until now." This groaning is the result of human sin. When humanity is reconciled to God, we can hope that its effect on creation will be as dramatic as it was after the first sin—only, now it will be in the right direction. Apart from this eschatological hope, human turning away from sin in the sacrament of reconciliation also leads us to act humanely toward creation. After all, environmental degradation is a result of human selfishness. Reconciliation with God, others, and self must and will lead us to reconciliation with nature as well. Conversion has ecological impact.

Often, when I conclude the celebration of the sacrament, I remind the penitents that the person who came into the confessional is not the same person who is returning back to the world. This is because the penitent has been reconciled, cleansed, healed, and given grace. In reality, the world has become a better place because one more person has been reconciled. The sacrament of reconciliation makes God's creation a better place because more and more people within it are reconciled and restored. As opposed to the Genesis story where relationships fail and even the very earth and its creatures are diminished because of sin, in the sacrament of reconciliation, communities rejoice and all creation is blessed.

Conclusion

I began this chapter in the privacy of my car, reading a tract that invited me to salvation. I am ending this chapter by inviting the readers to think of salvation as a broader process than the movement of an individual soul from sin to forgiveness. If we really think about it, God could have saved by the click of a finger. Instead, God chose to come among us as a human person, help us become children of God, love each other as God loved us, restore humanity to the original image in which God had created us, and, in the process, save not just humanity, but all creation. All these things are about relationships. Salvation is about relationships. If we must be saved, we must be in harmonious relationships—with God, others, self, and nature. In the final analysis, it is about love.

Perhaps, the best way to end this chapter is with a parable. It is a parable of a young girl who had lost her way in life. She was so desperate, hopeless, and alone that one day she decided to end it all. She went to the edge of cliff that faced the ocean and was ready to jump into it headlong. As she stood there, she began to tremble. She was overcome with fear. Her fear only frustrated her further. She said, "I am a coward. I cannot even run away from myself." Just as she was thinking these thoughts, a huge wave hit the cliff. She was thrown back and she landed on the hard rock. Sea water washed over her trembling body. Now she was enraged with herself. As she lay on her back on the hard rock, she heard a voice. The voice asked her to get up. Puzzled, she slowly stood up and looked skyward. The voice then asked her to look at the tip of her tiny finger. She lifted her trembling palms and noticed a tiny drop of water barely clinging to the finger. The voice then said to her, "Those are your sins." She looked and she saw that the tiny drop of water was real. Her sins were real. Her sins stared her in the face. The voice spoke once again. This time it asked her to cast a glance over the ocean. The girl lifted her eyes and looked at the ocean. It was vast, endless, and deep. Then the voice said to her, "The tiny drop of water on your little finger, those were your sins. This ocean, my child, that's my love for you." The voice then asked the girl to let the tiny drop of water fall into the ocean. She did. She saw her sin disappear into the vast ocean of God's love. She had found her way back to hope.

The sacrament of reconciliation is a vast ocean of love. Often understood as a place to confess sins, the sacrament is a place where love is restored in the form of relationships. God is love and God created us for love. To sin is to walk away from love. Salvation is to walk back into love—not alone, but with the rest of humanity and creation.

Bibliography

Abbey, Antonia. "Alcohol-Related Sexual Assault: A Common Problem among College Students." *Journal of Studies on Alcohol, Supplement* 14 (2002): 118–28.

Ahern, Kevin. *Structures of Grace: Catholic Organizations Serving the Global Common Good.* Maryknoll, NY: Orbis Books, 2015.

Andolsen, Barbara Hilkert. "Whose Sexuality? Whose Tradition? Women, Experience, and Roman Catholic Sexual Ethics." In *Readings in Moral Theology No. 9: Feminist Ethics and the Catholic Moral Tradition*, edited by Charles Curran, Margaret Farley, and Richard McCormick, SJ, 207–39. Mahwah, NJ: Paulist Press, 1996.

Annas, Julia. *The Morality of Happiness.* New York: Oxford University Press, 1993.

Aristotle. *Nicomachean Ethics.* In *The Basic Works of Aristotle*, translated by W.D. Ross and edited by Richard McKeon, 927–1112. New York: Random House, 1941.

Armstrong, Elizabeth, Paula England, and Alison Fogarty. "Accounting for Women's Orgasm and Sexual Enjoyment in College Hookups and Relationships." *American Sociological Review* 77, no. 3 (2012): 435–62.

Augustine. *Confessions.* Translated by Henry Chadwick. New York: Oxford University Press, 2008.

Bales, Kevin, and Ron Soodalter. *The Slave Next Door.* Berkeley, CA: University of California Press, 2009.

Baumeister, Roy, Kathleen Catanese, and Kathleen Vohs. "Is There a Gender Difference in Strength of Sex Drive? Theoretical Views, Conceptual Distinctions, and a Review of Relevant Evidence." *Personality and Social Psychology Review* 5, no. 3 (2001): 242–73.

Bay-Cheng, Laina Y., and Rebecca K. Eliseo-Arras. "The Making of Unwanted Sex: Gendered and Neoliberal Norms in College Women's Unwanted Sexual Experiences." *Journal of Sex Research* 45, no. 4 (2008): 386–97.

Benedict XVI. *Caritas in Veritate.* Encyclical letter. June 29, 2009.

Bennett, Jana M. *Aquinas on the Web? Doing Theology in an Internet Age.* New York: Continuum, 2012.

Blow, Adrian, and Kelly Harnett. "Infidelity in Committed Relationships II: A Substantive Review." *Journal of Marital & Family Therapy* 31, no. 2 (2005): 217–33.

Bonhoeffer, Dietrich. *The Cost of Discipleship*. Revised edition. New York: Collier Books, 1959.

Brackley, Dean, SJ. *The Call to Discernment in Troubled Times: New Perspectives on the Transformative Wisdom of Ignatius of Loyola*. New York: Crossroad, 2004.

Bridges, A. J. R., et al. "Aggression and Sexual Behavior in Best Selling Pornography Videos: A Content Analysis Update." *Violence Against Women* 16, no. 10 (2010): 1065–85.

Bridges, Sara, and Sharon Horne. "Sexual Satisfaction and Desire Discrepancy in Same Sex Women's Relationships." *Journal of Sex & Marriage Therapy* 33, no. 1 (2007): 41–53.

Brumberg, Joan Jacob. *Fasting Girls: The History of Anorexia Nervosa*. Cambridge, MA: Harvard University Press, 2000.

Buchwald, Emilie, Pamela Fletch, and Martha Roth, editors. *Transforming a Rape Culture*. Minneapolis: Milkweed Editions, 1993.

Byers, E. Sandra. "Relationship Satisfaction and Sexual Satisfaction: A Longitudinal Study of Individuals in Long-Term Relationship." *The Journal of Sex Research* 42, no. 2 (2005): 113–18.

Cafaro, Phillip. "Gluttony, Arrogance, Greed, and Apathy: An Exploration of an Environmental Vice." In *Environmental Virtue Ethics*, edited by Ronald Sandler and Philip Cafaro, 135–58. Lanham, MD: Rowman & Littlefield, 2005.

Catechism of the Catholic Church. 2nd. ed. Vatican City and Washington, DC: Libreria Editrice Vaticana and United States Catholic Conference, 2000.

Cates, Diana Fritz. *Aquinas on the Emotions: A Religious-Ethical Inquiry*. Washington, DC: Georgetown University Press, 2009.

Cavadini, John. "Feeling Right: Augustine on the Passions and Sexual Desire." *Augustinian Studies* 36, no. 1 (2005): 195–217.

———. "Spousal Vision: A Study of Text and History in the Theology of St. Augustine." *Augustinian Studies* 43, no. 1 (2012): 127–38.

Cavanaugh, William T. *Being Consumed: Economics and Christian Desire*. Grand Rapids, MI: William B. Eerdmans, 2008.

Clark, Meghan J. *The Vision of Catholic Social Thought: The Virtue of Solidarity and the Praxis of Human Rights*. Minneapolis: Fortress Press, 2014.

Cloutier, David, and William Mattison III. "Bodies Poured Out in Christ: Marriage Beyond the Theology of the Body." In *Leaving and*

Coming Home: New Wineskins for Catholic Sexual Ethics, edited by David Cloutier, 206–55. Eugene, OR: Cascade Books, 2010.

Cloutier, David. *The Vice of Luxury: Economic Excess in a Consumer Age.* Washington, DC: Georgetown University Press, 2015.

Coffey, David. *The Sacrament of Reconciliation.* Collegeville, MN: Liturgical Press, 2001.

Collingwood, R.G. *The Idea of Nature.* London: Oxford University Press, 1978.

Cooper, M. Lynne, and Cheryl M. Shapiro. "Motivations for Sex and Risky Sexual Behavior Among Adolescents and Young Adults: A Functional Perspective." *Journal of Personality and Social Psychology* 73, no. 6 (1998): 1528–58.

Copeland, M. Shawn. *Enfleshing Freedom: Body, Race, and Being.* Minneapolis: Fortress Press, 2010.

Daly, Daniel J. "Structures of Virtue and Vice," *New Blackfriars* 92, no. 1039 (2010): 341–57.

Daly, Robert W. "Before Depression: The Medieval Vice of Acedia." *Psychiatry: Interpersonal & Biological Processes* 70, no. 1 (2007): 30–51.

Damasio, Antonio. *Descartes' Error: Emotion, Reason, and the Human Brain.* New York: Putnam, 1994.

Dante Alighieri. *Purgatorio.* Translated by Jean Hollander and Robert Hollander. New York: Anchor Books, 2003.

———. *Paradiso.* Translated by Jean Hollander and Robert Hollander. New York: Anchor Books, 2007.

Davis, Henry, SJ. *Human Acts, Law, Sin, Virtue.* Volume one of *Moral and Pastoral Theology.* Fourth revised edition. London: Sheed and Ward, 1945.

DeLamater, John, and Morgan Sill. "Sexual Desire in Later Life." *The Journal of Sex Research* 42, no. 2 (2005): 138–49.

DeYoung, Rebecca Konyndyk. *Glittering Vices.* Grand Rapids, MI: Brazos Press, 2009.

———. "Sloth: Some Historical Reflections on Laziness, Effort, and Resistance to the Demands of Love." In *Virtues and Their Vices*, edited by Kevin Timple and Craig A. Boyd, 177–98. New York: Oxford University Press, 2014.

Dolan, Jay. *The American Catholic Experience.* Notre Dame, IN: University of Notre Dame Press, 1993.

Donohue, James, CR. "Review of Kenan B. Osborne, *Sacramental Theology: 50 Years after Vatican II* (Hobe Sound, FL: Lectio, 2014)." *Horizons* 43 (June 2016): 204–05.

Douglas, Mark, and Elizabeth Hinson-Hasty. "Revisiting Valerie Saiving's Challenge to Reinhold Niebuhr." *Journal of Feminist Studies in Religion* 28, no. 1 (2012): 75–114.

Edwards, Sarah R., and David L. Vogel. "Young Men's Likelihood Ratings to Be Sexually Aggressive as a Function of Norms and Perceived Sexual Interest." *Psychology of Men and Masculinity* 16, no. 1 (2015): 88–96.

Emmons, Robert. *Thanks!: How Practicing Gratitude Can Make You Happier.* Boston: Houghton Mifflin Co., 2007. Reprinted New York: Mariner Book, 2008.

Epstein, Marina, J. P. Calzo, Andrew Smiler, and L. Monique Ward. "'Anything from Making Out to Having Sex': Men's Negotiations of Hooking Up and Friends with Benefits Scripts." *Journal of Sex Research* 46, no. 5 (2009): 414–24.

Epstein, Joseph. *Envy.* New York: Oxford University Press, 2003.

Farley, Margaret. *Just Love: A Framework for Christian Sexual Ethics.* New York: Continuum International Publishing Group, 2006.

Fisher, Regina Marie. "First Reconciliation: Renewal of our Baptism." *Catechist* 32 (January 1999): 40–41.

Fisher, Helen. "Lust, Attraction, Attachment: Biology and Evolution of the Three Primary Emotion Systems for Mating, Reproduction, and Parenting." *Journal of Sex Education and Therapy* 25, no. 1 (2000): 96–104.

Foley, Jonathan, et al. "Solutions for a Cultivated Planet." *Nature* 478 (October 20, 2011): 337–42.

Francis. *Amoris Laetitia.* Apostolic Exhortation. March 19, 2016.

———. *General Audience.* February 19, 2014.

———. *Laudato Si'.* Encyclical Letter. May 24, 2015.

———. *Lumen Fidei.* Encyclical Letter. June 29, 2013.

———. *The Name of God is Mercy: A Conversation with Andrea Tornielli.* Translated by Oonagh Stransky. New York: Random House, 2016.

———. *Those Who Take Away the Keys.* Daily Meditation. October 15, 2015.

Frankfurt, Harry. *On B---s---.* Princeton, NJ: Princeton University Press, 2005.

Freitas, Donna. *The End of Sex: How Hookup Culture is Leaving a Generation Unhappy, Sexually Unfulfilled and Confused About Intimacy.* New York: Basic Books, 2013.

Frohlich, Penny, and Cindy Meston. "Sexual Functioning and Self-Reported Depressive Symptoms Among College Women." *The Journal of Sex Research* 39, no. 4 (2002): 321–25.

Gaillardetz, Richard A. *Daring Promise: A Spirituality for Christian Marriage.* Revised edition. Liguori, MO: Liguori Press, 2007.

Gallagher, David. "Thomas Aquinas on Self-Love as the Basis for Love of Others." *Acta Philosophica* 8, no. 1 (1999): 23–44.

Garcia, Justin, Chris Reiber, Sean G. Massey, and Ann M. Merriwether, "Sexual HookUp Culture: A Review." *Review of General Psychology* 16, no. 2 (2012): 161–76.

Grimes, Katie. "Breaking the Body of Christ: The Sacraments of Initiation in the Habitat of White Supremacy." *Political Theology* 18, no. 1 (2017): 22–43.

Gudorf, Christine E. *Body, Sex, and Pleasure: Reconstructing Christian Sexual Ethics*. Cleveland, OH: The Pilgrim Press, 1994.

———. "Parenting, Mutual Love, and Sacrifice." In *Women's Consciousness and Women's Conscience: A Reader in Feminist Ethics,* edited by Barbara Hilkert Andolsen, Christine E. Gudorf and Mary Pellauer, 175–91. New York: Harper and Row, 1985.

Gula, Richard. "Confession and Communal Penance." *New Catholic World* 228 (November/December 1985): 267–71.

Harrison, Beverly Wildung. "The Power of Anger in the Work of Love." In *Making the Connections: Essays in Feminist Social Ethics,* edited by Carol S. Robb and Beverly Wildung Harrison, 3–21. Boston: Beacon, 1986.

Heise, Lori, and Claudia Garcia-Moreno. "Violence by Intimate Partners." In *World Report on Violence and Health,* edited by Etienne Krug, et al., 87–121. Geneva, Switzerland: World Health Organization, 2002.

Heldman, Caroline, and Lisa Wade. "Hook-Up Culture: Setting a New Research Agenda." *Sexual Research and Social Policy* 7, no. 4 (2010): 323–33.

Heyer, Kristin E. *Kinship Across Borders: A Christian Ethic of Immigration.* Washington, DC: Georgetown University Press, 2012.

Hill, Susan E. *Eating to Excess: The Meaning of Gluttony and the Fat Body in the Ancient World.* Santa Barbara, CA: Praeger, 2011.

Hoffman, W. et. al. "Everyday Temptations: An Experience Sampling Study of Desire, Conflict, and Self Control." *Journal of Personality and Social Psychology* 102, no. 6 (2012): 1318–35.

Hogben, Matthew Donn Byrne, Merle E. Hamburger, and Julie Osland. "Legitimized Aggression and Sexual Coercion: Individual Differences in Cultural Spillover." *Aggressive Behavior* 27, no. 1 (2001): 26–43.

Hollenbach, David, SJ. *The Common Good and Christian Ethics.* Cambridge, UK: Cambridge University Press, 2002.

Holmberg, Diane, and Karen Blair. "Sexual Desire, Communication, Satisfaction, and Preferences of Men and Women in Same-Sex Versus Mixed-Sex Relationships." *Journal of Sex Research* 46, no. 1 (2009): 57–66.

Howard, Judith, Philip Blumstein, and Pepper Schwartz. "Sex, Power, and Influence Tactics in Intimate Relationships." *Journal of Personality and Social Psychology* 51, no. 1 (1986): 102–09.

Huang, Alison, Leslee Subak, David Thom, Stephen Van Den Eeden, Arona Ragins, Miriam Kuppermann, Hui Shen, and Jeanette Brown. "Sexual Function and Again in Racially and Ethnically Diverse Women," *Journal of the American Geriatrics Society* 57, no. 8 (2009): 1362–68.

Hughes, Kathleen. "Reconciliation: Disquieting Pastoral Reflections." In *Repentance and Reconciliation in the Church*, edited by Michael J. Henchal, 57–77. Collegeville, MN: The Liturgical Press, 1987.

International Theological Commission. *In Search of a Universal Ethic: A New Look at Natural Law.* 2009.

Jennings, Willie. *The Christian Imagination: Theology and the Origins of Race.* New Haven, CT: Yale University Press, 2010.

John Cassian. *Conferences.* Translated by Colm Luibheid. Mahwah, NJ: Paulist Press, 1985.

———. *Institutes.* Translated by Boniface Ramsey. Mahwah, NJ: The Newman Press, 2000.

John of the Cross. *Dark Night of the Soul.* Translated by E. Allison Peers. Westminster, MD: Newman Press, 1953.

John Paul II. *Centesimus Annus.* Encyclical letter. May 1, 1991.

———. *Ecclesia in America.* Apostolic Exhortation. January 22, 1999.

———. *Familiaris Consortio.* Apostolic Exhortation. November 22, 1981.

———. *Holy Mass at Yankee Stadium.* Homily. October 2, 1979.

———. *Sollicitudo Rei Socialis.* Encyclical letter. December 30, 1987.

Jone, Heribert, OFM. *Moral Theology.* Translated by Urban Adelman. Westminster, MD: Newman, 1945.

Jones, Serene. *Feminist Theory and Christian Theology: Cartographies of Grace.* Minneapolis: Fortress Press, 2000.

Jung, Shannon. *Sharing Food: Christian Practices for Enjoyment.* Minneapolis: Fortress Press, 2006.

Kahn, Arnold S. "What College Women Do and Do Not Experience as Rape." *Psychology of Women Quarterly* 28, no. 1 (2004): 9–15.

Keenan, James, SJ. *Moral Wisdom: Lessons and Texts from the Catholic Tradition.* Lanham, MD: Rowman & Littlefield, 2004.

Kessler, David. *The End of Overeating: Taking Control of Insatiable American Appetite.* New York: Rodale, 2009.

King, Jason. *Faith with Benefits: Hookup Culture on Catholic Campuses.* New York: Oxford University Press, 2017.

Kinghorn, Warren. "'Hope That Is Seen Is No Hope at All:' Theological Constructions of Hope in Psychotherapy." *Bulletin of The Menninger Clinic* 77, no. 4 (2013): 369–94.

Kliman, Todd. "The Perfect Chef." In *Cornbread Nation 7: The Best of Southern Food Writing*, edited by Francis Lam, 55–70. Athens, GA: University of Georgia Press, 2014.

Kochuthara, Shaji George. *The Concept of Sexual Pleasure in the Catholic Moral Tradition*. Rome: Gregorian and Biblical Press, 2007.

Lake, Amelia, and Tim Townsend. "Obesogenic Environments: Exploring the Built and Food Environments." *The Journal for the Royal Society for the Promotion of Health* 126, no. 6 (2006): 262–67.

Leach, William. *Land of Desire: Merchants, Power, and the Rise of a New American Culture*. New York: Random House, 1993.

Lebacqz, Karen. "Love Your Enemy: Sex, Power, and Christian Ethics," *Annual of the Society of Christian Ethics* 10, no. 1 (1990): 3–23. Reprinted in *Feminist Theological Ethics: A Reader*, ed. Lois K. Daly, 244–61. Louisville: Westminster, 1994.

Leo XIII. *Rerum Novarum*. Encyclical Letter. May 15, 1891.

Lelwica, Michelle M. *The Religion of Thinness: Satisfying the Spiritual Hungers Behind Women's Obsession with Food and Weight*. Carlsbad, CA: Gurze Books, 2010.

Levinovitz, Alan. *The Gluten Lie: And Other Myths About What You Eat*. New York: Regan Arts, 2015.

Lewis, C.S. *Mere Christianity*. New York: HarperCollins, 2001.

———. *The Screwtape Letters*. New York: HarperCollins, 1942.

Luscombe, Belinda. "Porn and the Threat to Virility." *Time* (April 11, 2016): 41–47.

Lysaught, M. Therese. "Love Your Enemies: Toward a Christoform Bioethic." In *Gathered for the Journey: Moral Theology in Catholic Perspective*, edited by David Matzko McCarthy and M. Therese Lysaught, 307–28. Grand Rapids, MI: Eerdmans, 2007.

Mann, Ruth, and Clive Hollin. "Sexual Offenders' Explanation for Their Offending." *Journal of Sexual Aggression* 13, no. 1 (2007): 3–9.

Mannion, M. Francis. "Penance and Reconciliation: A Systematic Analysis." *Worship* 60, no. 2 (March 1986): 98–118.

Maritain, Jacques. *The Person and the Common Good*. Notre Dame, IN: University of Notre Dame Press, 1946.

Mark, Kristen. "The Impact of Daily Sexual Desire and Daily Sexual Desire Discrepancy on the Quality of the Sexual Experience in Couples." *Canadian Journal of Human Sexuality* 23, no. 1 (2014): 27–33.

Mark, Kristen, Justin Garcia, and Helen Fisher. "Perceived Emotional and Sexual Satisfaction Across Sexual Relationship Contexts: Gender and Sexual Orientation Differences and Similarities." *The Canadian Journal of Human Sexuality* 24, no. 2 (2015): 120–30.

Marx, Karl. "Estranged Labor." In *The Marx-Engels Reader*, second edition, edited by Robert C. Tucker. New York: W.W. Norton & Company, 1978.

McCabe, Marita, and Denisa Goldhammer. "Demographic and Psychological Factors Related to Sexual Desire Among Heterosexual Women in Relationship." *Journal of Sex Research* 49, no. 1 (2012): 78–81.

McCarthy, David Matzko. *Sex and Love in the Home: A Theology of the Household.* London: SCM Press, 2001.

Meston, Cindy, and David Buss. "Why Humans Have Sex." *Archives of Sexual Behavior* 36, no. 4 (2007): 477–507.

Milhaven, John. "Thomas Aquinas on Sexual Pleasure." *Journal of Religious Ethics* 5, no. 2 (1977): 157–81.

Miller, Vincent J. *Consuming Religion: Christian Faith and Practice in a Consumer Religion.* London: Continuum, 2005.

Mitchell, Kristin, Kaye Wellings, and Cynthia Graham. "How Do Men and Women Define Sexual Desire and Sexual Arousal?" *Journal of Sex & Marital Therapy* 40, no. 1 (2014): 17–32.

Morioka, Mashahiro. "A Phenomenological Study of 'Herbivore Men.'" *The Review of Life Studies* 4 (September 2013): 1–20.

Morrow, Maria. *Sin in the Sixties: Catholics and Confession, 1955–1975.* Washington, DC: The Catholic University of America Press, 2016.

Mowat, Barbara, Paul Werstine, Michael Poston, Rebecca Niles, eds. *The Tragedy of Othello, the Moor of Venice.* Washington, DC: Folger Shakespeare Library, n.d.

Murdoch, Iris. *The Sovereignty of Good.* New York: Routledge Classics, 1971.

Murray, Sarah, Olga Sutherland, and Robin Milhausen. "Young Women's Descriptions of Sexual Desire in Long-Term Relationships." *Sexual and Relationship Therapy* 27, no. 1 (2012): 3–16.

The New Catholic Encyclopedia, 2nd ed. Detroit: Thomson/Gale; Washington, DC: Catholic University of America Press, 2002.

O'Donovan, Oliver. "A Summons to Reality." In *Considering Veritatis Splendor*, edited John Wilkins, 41–45. Cleveland, OH: The Pilgrim Press, 1994.

Okholm, Dennis L. "Gluttony: Thought for Food." *American Benedictine Review* 49, no. 1 (March 1998): 43–59.

Osborne, Kenan B. *Sacramental Theology: 50 Years after Vatican II.* Hobe Sound, FL: Lectio, 2014.

Ozer, Emily J., M. Margaret Dolcini, and Gary W. Harper. "Adolescents' Reasons for Having Sex: Gender Differences." *Journal of Adolescent Health* 33, no. 5 (2003): 317–19.

Paul, Pamela. *Pornified: How Pornography is Damaging Our Lives, Our Relationships, and Our Families.* New York: Times Books, 2005.

Pinches, Charles. *Theology and Action: After Theory in Christian Ethics.* Grand Rapids, MI: Eerdmans, 2002.

Pinckaers, Servais, OP. *Morality: A Catholic View.* South Bend, IN: St. Augustine's Press, 2001.

Pineda-Madrid, Nancy. "Sex Trafficking and Feminicide Along the Border: Re-Membering Our Daughters." In *Living With(out) Borders: Catholic Theological Ethics on the Migration of Peoples*, edited by Agnes M. Brazal and María Teresa Dávila, 81–90. Maryknoll, NY: Orbis Books, 2016.

Pontifical Council for Justice and Peace. *Compendium of the Social Doctrine of the Church.* 2006.

Porter, Jean. *Nature as Reason: A Thomistic Theory of the Natural Law.* Grand Rapids, MI: Eerdmans, 2005.

Prose, Francine. *Gluttony.* New York: Oxford University Press, 2003.

Rahner, Karl. *Foundations of Christian Faith.* Translated by William V. Dych. New York: Crossroad, 1978.

Richardson, Elaine. "Developing Critical Hip Hop Feminist Literacies: Centrality and Subversion of Sexuality in the Lives of Black Girls." *Equity and Excellence in Education* 46, no. 3 (2013): 327–41.

Ridgely, Susan B. "Decentering Sin: First Reconciliation and the Nurturing of Post-Vatican II Catholics." *Journal of Religion* 86, no. 4 (2006): 606–34.

Ridley, Carl, Rodney Cate, Dawn Collins, Amy Reesing, Ana Lecero, Michael Gilson, and David Alemedia. "The Ebb and Flow of Marital Lust: A Relational Approach," *The Journal of Sex Research* 43, no. 2 (2006): 144–53.

Ridley, Carl, Brian Ogolsky, Pamela Payne, Casey Totenhagen, and Rodney Cate. "Sexual Expression: Its Emotional Context in Heterosexual, Gay, and Lesbian Couples." *Journal of Sex Research* 45, no. 3 (2008): 305–14.

Rose, Darya. *Foodist: Using Real Food and Real Science to Lose Weight Without Dieting.* New York: HarperCollins, 2013.

Rubio, Julie Hanlon. *A Christian Theology of Marriage and Family.* New York: Paulist Press, 2003.

———. *Hope for Common Ground: Mediating the Personal and the Political in a Divided Church.* Washington, DC: Georgetown University Press, 2016.

————. "The Practice of Sex in Christian Marriage." In *Leaving and Coming Home: New Wineskins for Catholic Sexual Ethics*, edited by David Cloutier, 226–49. Eugene, OR: Cascade Books, 2010.

Saiving. Valerie. "The Human Situation: A Feminine View." *The Journal of Religion*, 40, no. 2 (1960): 100–12.

Sales, Nancy Jo. *American Girls: Social Media and the Secret Lives of Teenagers*. New York: Knopf, 2016.

Sandel, Michael J. *What Money Can't Buy: The Moral Limits of Markets*. New York: Farrar, Straus and Giroux, 2012.

Schweiker, William. *Theological Ethics and Global Dynamics: In the Time of Many Worlds* Oxford, UK: Blackwell Publishing, 2004.

Skafte, Ina, and Margrethe Silberschmidt. "Female Gratification, Sexual Power and Safer Sex: Female Sexuality as Empowering Research among Women in Rwanda." *Culture, Health, and Sexuality* 16, no. 1 (2014): 1–13.

Slater, Thomas, SJ. *A Manual of Moral Theology for English-Speaking Countries*, vol. 1, sixth revised edition. London: Burns, Oates, & Washbourne, 1928.

Smil, V. "Worldwide Transformation of Diets, Burdens of Meat Productions, and Opportunities for Novel Food Proteins." *Enzyme and Microbial Technology* 30 (2002): 305–11.

Spadaro, Antonio, SJ. "A Big Heart Open to God." *America* 209, no. 8 (September 30, 2015).

Steingarten, Jeffrey. *It Must Have Been Something I Ate: The Return of the Man Who Ate Everything*. New York: Vintage Books, 2002.

Stone, Lawrence. "Passionate Attachments in the West in Historical Perspective." In *Perspectives on Marriage: A Reader*, edited by Kieran Scott and Michael Warren, 176–85. New York: Oxford University Press, 2007.

Taylor, Charles. "What is Human Agency?" In *Human Agency and Language: Philosophical Papers I*, 15–44. New York: Cambridge University Press, 1985.

Thomas Aquinas. *Summa Theologica*, Complete English Edition in Five Volumes. Translated by the Fathers of the English Dominican Province. Allen, TX: Christian Classics, 1948.

————. *On Evil*. Translated by John and Jean Oesterle. Notre Dame, IN: University of Notre Dame Press, 1995.

Thompson, Paul B. *From Field to Fork: Food Ethics for Everyone*. New York: Oxford University Press, 2015.

United States Conference of Catholic Bishops. "Economic Justice for All." Pastoral Letter. November 1986.

———. *The Rite of Penance*. Washington, DC: United States Catholic Conference, 1975.

Vatican Council II. *Sacrosanctum Concilium*. Dogmatic Constitution. December 4, 1963. In *The Documents of Vatican II*, edited by Walter M. Abbott. New York: The America Press, 1966.

Wansink, Brian. *Mindless Eating: Why We Eat More Than We Think*. New York: Bantam, 2006.

Wasserstein, Wendy. *Sloth: The Seven Deadly Sins*. New York, Oxford University Press, 2005.

Weekes, Debbie. "Get Your Freak On: How Black Girls Sexualize Identity." *Sex Education* 2, no. 3 (2002): 251–62.

Willimon, William H. *Sinning Like a Christian: A New Look at the Seven Deadly Sins*. Nashville: Abingdon Press, 2005.

Wilson, Gary. *Your Brain on Porn: Internet Pornography and the Emerging Science of Addiction*. N.P.: Commonwealth Publishing, 2014.

Zurbriggen, Eileen, and Megan Yost. "Power, Desire, and Pleasure in Sexual Fantasies." *The Journal of Sex Research* 41, no. 3 (2004): 288–300.

Contributors

Jana M. Bennett is professor of theological ethics at the University of Dayton. Jana Bennett has a BA from Colorado College, an MDiv from Garrett-Evangelical Theological Seminary and a PhD from Duke University. Her interests include theological reflection on disability technologies in relation to health care, as well as family and community relationships, including single states of life. Among her books are *Singleness and the Church: A New Theology of the Single Life* and *Water is Thicker than Blood: An Augustinian Theology of Marriage and Singleness*, both from Oxford University Press.

Charles C. Camosy is associate professor of theological and social ethics at Fordham University, where he has taught since finishing his PhD in theology at Notre Dame in 2008. His published articles have appeared in, among other places, the *American Journal of Bioethics*, the *Journal of Medicine and Philosophy*, the *Journal of the Catholic Health Association*, the *San Francisco Chronicle*, the *Washington Post*, the *Los Angeles Times*, the *New York Daily News* and *America: The Jesuit Review of Faith and Culture*. He is the author of several books, including *Beyond the Abortion Wars: A Way Forward for a New Generation* (Eerdmans).

David Cloutier is associate professor of theology at The Catholic University of America in Washington, DC. He formerly held the Knott Professorship in Catholic Theology at Mount St. Mary's University (Maryland), where he also directed a year-long seminar on the Catholic Intellectual Tradition for faculty across the university. He received his PhD from Duke University and is the author of several books, including *The Vice of Luxury: Economic Excess in a Consumer Age* (Georgetown University Press) and *Walking God's Earth: The Environment and Catholic Faith* (Liturgical Press).

Dana L. Dillon is an associate professor at Providence College, where she holds a joint appointment in theology and public and community service studies. Most of her teaching centers around Catholic social ethics, community service and engagement, and racial justice. Her latest writing projects involve Catholic approaches to diversity, inclusion, and social change. She received her PhD from Duke University, after earning her BA and MDiv from the University of Notre Dame.

Fr. James Donohue, CR, is Knott Professor of Catholic Theology at Mount St. Mary's University (Maryland), where he has taught since 1996. He earned his PhD in systematic theology from The Catholic University of America, and teaches a wide range of courses, including Christology, sacraments, moral theology, and pastoral courses. Fr. Jim's professional work is primarily in sacramental and liturgical studies, focusing especially upon the liturgical rites for the sick, the dying, and the deceased, and is a popular speaker at both the parish and diocesan levels.

Nichole M. Flores is assistant professor of religious studies at the University of Virginia. She speaks, writes, and teaches about the significance of Catholic and Latinx theology and ethics in plural social, political, and ecclesial contexts. She has published articles in the *Journal of Religious Ethics*, the *Journal of the Society of Christian Ethics*, and the *Journal of Religion & Society*. She earned her PhD in theological ethics from Boston College and is a contributing author at *America: The Jesuit Review of Faith and Culture*.

Beth Haile has her PhD in moral theology from Boston College, writing on the concept of intellectual habits and "connatural knowledge" to the problem of eating and body image disorders. Her interests include St. Thomas Aquinas, natural law, virtue ethics, health care, and bioethics. She has taught at Carroll College and currently lives in Iowa and stays at home with her four children.

Fr. Satish Joseph is the senior pastor at Our Lady of the Immaculate Conception and St. Helen parishes in Dayton, Ohio. He is also the founder of Ite Missa Est ministries. He has a PhD in theology from the University of Dayton and is the author of *Globalization and Militant Hindu Nationalism: The New Context for Theology in India* (Lambert Academic Publishing).

Jason King is professor of theology at Saint Vincent College in Latrobe, Pennsylvania. He is also editor of the *Journal of Moral Theology*. He completed his PhD at The Catholic University of America. He is the author of, among other books, *Faith with Benefits: Hookup Culture on Catholic Campuses* (Oxford University Press).

William C. Mattison III is associate professor of theology at the University of Notre Dame, where he received his PhD and where he currently serves as the Senior Advisor: Theological Formation for the Alliance for Catholic Education. His teaching and research focus on fundamental moral theology, especially virtue ethics and the thought of St. Thomas Aquinas. He also works in the areas of Scripture and ethics, and marriage and family. His single-author books are *The Sermon on the Mount and Moral Theology: A Virtue Perspective* (Cambridge University Press) and *Introducing Moral Theology: True Happiness and the Virtues* (Brazos Press).

Julie Hanlon Rubio is professor of theology at the Jesuit School of Theology in Berkeley, California, after many years as professor of Christian ethics at Saint Louis University. She earned her PhD in religious ethics from the University of Southern California. She is the author of, among other books, *Hope for Common Ground: Mediating the Personal and the Political in a Divided Church* (Georgetown University Press) and *A Christian Theology of Marriage and Family* (Paulist Press) as well as coeditor of *Readings in Moral Theology No. 15: Marriage.*

Index

Abortion, 3, 7, 158–159; of disabled fetus, 161

Abuse, 84; Church scandals, 7, 150; in romantic or family relationships, 102. *See also* women

Acedia, 89, 91–94

Affections, 74. *See also* emotions

Anger, 15–16, 97, 106–25, 135, 194; emotion of, 108–09, 114–21; lack of, 114; not sinful; 25, 101, 107, 113–22, 124; restoration of relationships and, 111–20, 122–23, 128

Apostolic succession, 190

Appetite, 35, 38, 39, 47, 49–51, 78, 112; concupiscible, 35–36; natural, 35–36, 38; rational, 27; sensitive, 35–36, 119, 132

Aquinas, Thomas, 15–16, 23, 193; on anger; 107–15, 119–22; on envy, 129–36; on gluttony, 33–37, 47–48; on greed, 74–81; on lust, 53–55; on pride, 147; on sloth; 93–96, 100, 103, 105

Aristotle, 34, 38–39, 115, 119

Augustine, 15n29, 56, 148

Avarice. *See* greed

Baptism, 5n11, 9, 168, 170–71, 175, 178, 185

Benedict XVI, 103, 155

Bisexuality, 57

Bonhoeffer, Dietrich, 181

Catechism: *of the Catholic Church*, 2, 15, 25n46, 109, 127, 128, 169n2, 178, 179n27; 1941 edition of *Baltimore*, 4

Catholic social teaching, 24, 80, 83, 103

Catholic social thought, 82, 103, 135

Cavadini, John, 56–57

Cavanaugh, William, 76, 87

Centesimus Annus. See John Paul II

Charity, 97, 103, 127–30, 134–45, 169, 175–77

Children, 4–5, 18, 49, 55, 66, 68–70, 71, 81, 94, 99, 100n41, 104–05, 112–113, 118, 122, 124, 149, 152, 161, 183–184, 193, 196; of God, 4, 124, 187, 197

Choice, 14–15, 17–19, 30–32, 45, 71, 90, 101, 118, 130, 148, 154, 167; consumer, 38–39, 83–85, 155; lack of, 32, 60, 130

Coffey, David, 5, 6

College: debt, 155; grades: 21; students: 58, 60, 63, 64n65, 104–105, 160, 176

Compassion, 4, 12, 53, 55, 55, 103, 138, 140, 157, 169, 171, 174, 179, 187, 191

Concupiscence. *See* appetite; passions

Confession, 2–13, 80, 85, 126, 143, 172–73, 176–80, 189–92. *See also* Reconciliation, sacrament of

Confessional, 1–6, 11, 20, 27, 94, 178–79, 189, 190–91, 193, 196; face-to-face, 2, 176, 179, 195

Consumerism, 24, 45, 50, 73–77, 82–88

Contraception, 7, 158–59

Copeland, M. Shawn, 103–105

Dante, 52–53, 137–39

Descriptions (of sins, actions, experiences, etc.), 21–24, 26, 36, 41, 59, 82n28, 84, 96n23, 99, 133

Desire, 46, 53, 63, 73, 78, 86, 104, 119, 127, 176; appetites and, 36, 51; bodily, 27, 29, 31, 47; consumerist, 74–77, 85; dissipation of, 61–66; distorting, 80; domination and, 56–57; for justice, 194; humans' for God, 86, 93, 137; God's for humans, 96–97; inordinate, 26, 35, 78–79, 85; irrational, 53, 55; pleasures and, 37, 39, 49, 55; relationships and, 54–55, 59, 62, 63–66, 70, 71, 114, 138–39, 192; sexual, 53–72, 116, 146; to rectify perceived injustices, 107–10, 111, 117–18, 121; truncation of, 66–70. See also anger; lust

DeYoung, Rebecca Konyndyk, 76n9, 90, 92, 93, 96–99, 100, 127

Disciples/discipleship, 15, 53, 69–70, 72, 105, 194; Jesus', 14, 137, 142, 188

Dissipating lust. See lust

Dominating lust. See lust

Eating disorders, 30, 41

Ecology. See environment

Ecclesia in America. See John Paul II

Emotions, 68, 74, 106–107; anger as, 108–10, 114–120; biological

nature of, 62; relationships and, 63, 123; rightly ordered, 56, 121, 125

Enjoy/enjoyment, 58–59, 61, 64, 74, 75, 95, 157

Environment, 40, 44–54, 94, 152, 187, 195, 196; social, 32, 39, 60, 119, 172

Envy, 27, 126–45; causes of envy, 134–36; opposed to charity, 128, 129–30; solidarity as antidote, 140–145

Eucharist, 9, 103, 137, 144, 168–71, 174–75, 177–78, 191, 195

Euthanasia, 157–158

Faith, 5, 85, 88, 100, 105, 140, 162, 165, 167, 178, 194; theological virtue of, 14, 152–53

Familiaris Consortio. See John Paul II

Farley, Margaret, 53–54

Feminist theology, 7, 98–102, 104

Forgiveness, 2, 8–9, 140, 169, 181; Christ's, 11, 174; community and, 176; God's, 11, 125, 172, 175, 179–80, 183, 189; mediated through priest, 190; other people and, 102, 113, 123, 137, 173. See also mercy

Francis, 2, 3, 11–12, 19, 50, 142, 151, 166; Laudato Si', 26, 50, 84, 88, 149n4, 186, 194; Lumen Fidei, 85

Freedom, 16, 59–60, 68, 153, 157, 187

Freitas, Donna, 60, 63

Friendship, 2, 103, 123, 138, 179n28

Gaillardetz, Richard, 97–98

Gattaca, 161

Gender concerns. See bisexuality; homosexuality; women; men

Gluttony, 27, 52–72, 78, 147; of
    consumption, 36, 47–49; of
    delicacy, 36, 41–46; of excess, 36,
    37–41
Grace, 2, 7, 26, 78, 101, 125, 137,
    142, 174–75; "cheap", 182; sacra-
    ment as means of, 43, 171, 178,
    189; table, 51; social structures
    of, 88, 177
Greed, 14, 26, 27, 33, 73–88, 106,
    127, 173; individual nature of,
    74, 76, 77n12, 78, 86–87; "is
    good," 76, 146; social nature of,
    74–76, 77, 80–83, 87–88
Gudorf, Christine, 66n71, 100n41
Guilt: feeling of, 7, 20, 24, 25, 25,
    26, 30, 42, 51, 90, 176, 176, 192;
    objective, 51, 83, 155, 187

Habit/habituation, 31, 32n4,
    39–40, 44n35, 48, 86–87, 118,
    125, 126, 131, 140, 143; liturgi-
    cal and sacramental life as, 2, 4,
    95; in virtues and vices, 14, 15,
    35, 45, 74, 77, 97, 110, 116, 131,
    133, 147
Happiness, 16n31, 19–20,
Hatred, 92, 112, 130, 131, 150, 167
Hauerwas, Stanley, 98n30
Holy Spirit, 97, 141, 152, 169n1,
    174, 177, 178, 179, 188, 195
Hollenbach, David, 80–81
Homosexuality, 57, 147, 150
Hookup culture, 60, 62–65,
    159–60
Humility, 8, 147, 148, 152, 167
Hütter, Reinhard, 59
Hypocrisy, 162

Idolatry, 164–166
Intellect, 27, 35, 54, 130

Jealousy. See envy
Jesus, 11, 19, 33, 71, 95, 101, 141,
    148, 166, 169n2, 174, 178, 182,
    193; baptized into the life, death,
    and resurrection of, 170; com-
    mandments of, 25, 86, 122, 167;
    food laws and, 14; friend, 125,
    173, 179, 181; Mary of Beth-
    any and, 94; post-resurrection
    appearances, 188; Sermon on the
    Mount, 115, 122, 138; tax collec-
    tors and, 142, 151; way, truth, and
    life, 128; Wedding at Cana, 137
John Cassian, 33, 43
John of the Cross, 50–51
John Paul II, 19, 50, 70, 103, 141;
    Centesimus Annus, 92; Ecclesia
    in America, 101; Familiaris Con-
    sortio, 68; Sollicitudo Rei Socialis,
    140; Theology of the Body, 67
John XXIII, 103
Joy, 66, 72, 95, 97, 103, 119, 130,
    131, 138, 177
Justice, 59, 70, 72, 74, 80, 88, 113–
    22, 123, 127, 134, 148, 152, 169,
    194; anger in relation to, 101,
    107–08, 110–14, 117–18, 121–22,
    124–25, 150; Aquinas on, 78–80,
    107–25, 133, 135n26; racial, 20,
    124; social, 3, 83, 102; as virtue,
    14–78–79, 108

Keenan, James, 21

Laudato Si'. See Francis
Lazarus, 50
Laziness, 19, 89–93, 98, 101–02. See
    also sloth
Lent, 45, 89, 94
Lewis, C. S., 41–42, 147–48
LGBTQ. See homosexuality

Libido dominandi. See Lust

Love, 21, 53, 56–57, 71, 131; in
    anger, 101, 113, 123; of enemies,
    102, 122, 137–38, 141, 151; of
    God and neighbor, 3, 25, 67,
    69–70, 72, 88, 93, 96–98, 100,
    103, 105, 109, 127–29, 131–32,
    136, 141, 177, 184–86, 193, 197;
    God's for us, 68, 95, 97, 125, 172–
    74, 179–80, 187, 197–98; marital,
    67–69, 111; of money, 75–78,
    84; of political groups, 150; in
    romantic relationships, 62, 65,
    72, 133, 149; in the sacrament of
    Reconciliation, 11, 172–80, 196;
    of self, 65, 102, 104; of siblings,
    127, 143; of sports teams, 146;
    as virtue, 14, 128–29. *See also*
    Charity

Lumen Fidei. See Francis

Lust, 23, 27, 43, 52–72, 78, 106, 116,
    126, 146, 193; in Aquinas, 54–55;
    in Augustine, 56; in Dante, 55;
    dissipating, 61–66; dominating,
    56–61; truncating, 66–71

Luxury, 32, 44, 74n3, 77, 81, 86

Meaning of life, 16–17, 19, 23–27,
    93, 97,

Men, 57–59, 63–65, 99, 102, 106,
    153, 162; Japanese, 61–62

Mercy, 3, 10–13, 15, 20–21, 78, 125,
    137, 140, 142, 144, 169, 172–176,
    187, 191, 195

Moderation, 34–35, 50, 78, 85

Mortal sin, 4, 34, 55, 79, 130–32,
    148, 169

Natural appetite. *See* appetite
Natural inclinations, 17–19, 134

O'Donovan, Oliver, 22
Othello, 132–33
Overconsumption. *See* gluttony

Passion(s), 54–55, 56n22, 114, 116,
    119, 132–34, 136; concupiscent,
    130–31; of Christ, 174

Paul VI, 7, 103

Penance, 2, 10, 51, 94, 184, 189, 196;
    Rite of, 168–80

Pickiness. *See* gluttony

Pinches, Charles, 17n32, 22–23

Pinckaers, Servais, 18

Politics, 9, 24, 56, 66, 68, 81–82, 101,
    104, 113, 146, 149–52, 163–64;
    Office, 90

Pope. *See* Apostolic succession.
    Benedict XVI, Francis, John
    Paul II, Paul VI

Pornography, 56, 58–59, 61, 64, 71,
    193; food as, 30

Portlandia, 30

Pride, 22, 26–27, 27, 99, 123,
    146–67; in Aquinas, 148; in
    Augustine, 148

Procreation, 71, 153, 158–62

Prudence, 14

Psychology, 7–8, 32n3, 64n66, 65,

Race, 104, 151

Racism, 3, 9–10, 104, 153

Rational appetite. *See* appetite

Reconciliation, sacrament of, 1–12,
    14, 26, 94, 105, 144, 166, 168–78,
    180, 182–84, 187–193, 195–6.
    See also Penance, rite of

Rectification, 107–08, 110–14, 116,
    118, 120–22, 124–25

Relationships. *See* anger; emotions;
    desire; love

Sacrament, 1–14, 26–27, 87, 94, 103, 125, 144, 166, 168–72, 175–80, 183–84, 186, 188–90, 192–193, 195–98

Sacrifice, 98, 100n41, 101–02, 104, 170, 175, 178; Paschal: 140–41, 169n1, 169n2, 175; for the sake of gluttony, 45; for the sake of greed, 73–74, 88

Saiving, Valerie, 99–100

Second Vatican Council. *See* Vatican II

Sensitive appetite. *See* appetite

Sex, 3–4, 6–7, 24, 27, 31, 52–72, 84, 102, 104, 107, 116, 118, 126, 146, 149–51, 153–54, 158–62, 176, 193

Sins. *See* anger; envy; gluttony; greed; lust; mortal sin; pride; sloth; venial sin; Sloppiness. *See* gluttony

Sloth, 27, 78, 89–105, 194–95

Shame, 10, 192

Smarm, 8

Social media, 40, 50, 59, 90–91, 105, 147, 162–64

Social structures, 51, 88, 100–01, 150; of sin, 9, 25–26, 74, 81–83, 85

Solidarity, 80, 83, 85–86, 88, 90, 92, 102–05, 139–40, 144, 151; in sin, 173–75; sin as injuring, 25, 109

Sollicitudo Rei Socialis. See John Paul II

Sorrow, 93, 95–96, 98, 105, 108, 128–33, 135–36, 139–40, 144, 174, 187, 196

Suicide: assisted, 154, 156–158; "social," 60, 63. *See also* euthanasia

Surrender, 89–90, 93, 96–100, 102, 123

Ten Commandments, 13, 34, 96, 126, 187, 193–94

Torture, 153, 166

Trafficking, human, 74, 83–85, 88

Truncating lust. *See* lust

Usury, 154–156

Vatican II, 1–7, 13, 94, 168, 171n4, 183–84

Venial sin, 4, 34, 130

Violence, 20, 56, 62, 113, 165–166, 186; media, 163. *See also* women

Vindicatio, 107, 110, 112, 120–21, 123–24

Voting, 104. *See also* politics

Virtue, 14, 17, 20, 23–25, 35, 38, 40n21, 41, 74, 78–83, 89–92, 96, 99–100, 102–05, 114, 117–18, 125, 127–31, 134, 137, 140–41, 146–47, 152–53, 176, 184, 194

Wrath, 106, 108. *See also* anger

Women, 30–31, 41, 63–65, 80, 98–100, 149, 152, 159; sex trafficking and, 84; violence against, 55, 57–60, 102, 104, 160